The Age of Trade

EXPLORING WORLD HISTORY
Series Editors:
John McNeill, Georgetown University
Kenneth Pomeranz, University of Chicago

As the world grows ever more closely linked, students and general readers alike are appreciating the need to become internationally aware. World history offers the crucial connection to understanding past global links and how they influence the present. The series will expand that awareness by offering clear, concise supplemental texts for the undergraduate classroom as well as trade books that advance world history scholarship.

The series will be open to books taking a thematic approach—exploring commodities such as sugar, cotton, and petroleum; technologies; diseases and the like; or regional—for example, Islam in Southeast Asia or east Africa, the Indian Ocean, or the Ottoman Empire. The series sees regions not simply as fixed geographical entities but as evolving spatial frameworks that have reflected and shaped the movement of people, ideas, goods, capital, institutions, and information. Thus, regional books would move beyond traditional borders to consider the flows that have characterized the global system.

Edited by two of the leading historians in the field, this series will work to synthesize world history for students, engage general readers, and expand the boundaries for scholars.

The Age of Trade

The Manila Galleons and the
Dawn of the Global Economy

Arturo Giraldez

ROWMAN & LITTLEFIELD
Lanham • Boulder • New York • London

Published by Rowman & Littlefield
A wholly owned subsidary of The Rowman & Littlefield Publishing Group, Inc.
4501 Forbes Boulevard, Suite 200, Lanham, Maryland 20706
www.rowman.com

Unit A, Whitacre Mews, 26-34 Stannary Street, London SE11 4AB

British Library Cataloguing in Publication Information Available

Library of Congress Cataloging-in-Publication Data Available

ISBN 978-0-7425-5663-8 (cloth : alk. paper)
ISBN 978-1-4422-4352-1 (electronic)

∞™ The paper used in this publication meets the minimum requirements of
American National Standard for Information Sciences—Permanence of Paper
for Printed Library Materials, ANSI/NISO Z39.48-1992.

Printed in the United States of America

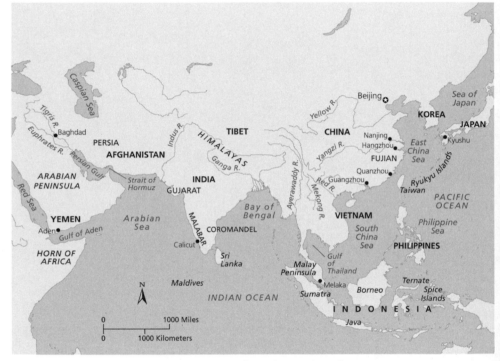

The countries bordering the Indian and Pacific Oceans

Contents

~

Acknowledgments

This book would have been impossible without the labors of the historians quoted in the bibliography. I really wrote on the shoulders of giants. Excellent examples among those scholars are Shirley Fish, Pablo E. Pérez-Mallaína, and William Lytle Schurz, who have done indispensable work on the galleons. For a number of years my colleague D. O. Flynn and I discussed the economic history of the Modern Era and coauthored publications; these pages are an offshoot of our work together. I am extremely thankful for his friendship and intellectual collaboration. Prof. Luis Alonso Alvarez from Universidade da Coruña (Spain) and Prof. Antonio García-Abásolo, Dr. Ana María Prieto Lucena, Dr. Inmaculada Alva Rodríguez from Universidad de Córdoba (Spain), Dra. Ma. Dolores Elizalde from Consejo Superior de Investigaciones Científicas (Spain), and Dr. Patricio Hidalgo Nuchera, Universidad Autónoma Madrid (Spain) have shared their publications with me and kindly have answered my queries. I take this opportunity to warmly thank them for their generosity. Colleagues at the University of the Pacific Library have been uniformly helpful with questions and requests. I would like to particularly mention the interlibrary loan service that has always fulfilled petitions promptly and without fail. I owe these colleagues a large debt of gratitude. I completed this work during a sabbatical leave granted by the office of the provost at the University of the Pacific, for which I am grateful. Susan McEachen at Rowman & Littlefield has shown a considerable amount

of encouragement and advice throughout the process; my editor Lea Popie-
linski has made the manuscript much better; they and anonymous readers
have made helpful suggestions that greatly improved the original text. Any
remaining shortcomings or errors are mine.

I dedicate this work to Prof. Dr. Leo Noordegraaf from the University of
Amsterdam.

~

Introduction

Maynila, the "Place of the Water Lilies," was a thriving marketplace in 1570. On the western shore of today's Manila Bay, Maynila was ruled by Rajah Ladyang Matanda and his heir and nephew, Rajah Suleyman, who were related by marriage to the Sultanate of Brunei in Borneo. Chinese and Bruneian merchants regularly arrived to exchange gold, beeswax, and forest products for silks, porcelain, gongs, and guns. A palisade encircled the chiefs' residence, the public storage buildings, and an artillery foundry in which a Portuguese smith busied himself making cannons. There was a plaza and quarters for Chinese and Japanese merchants. This enclave was located on the routes connecting Ming China, Japan, and the Spice Islands—the Molucca and Banda archipelagos, the only locations in the world in which the coveted clove and nutmeg grew. Since the fifteenth century, trade was on an upward trend in the Old World, and Maynila was integrated into these networks of exchange. There, large Chinese junks brought their goods, and smaller boats manned by Muslim seamen distributed them among numerous islands. This Filipino merchant class spread to Malacca, the crucial entrepôt between the Indian Ocean and the China Sea where merchants from Luzon became rich businessmen. In addition, each year two or three vessels sailed from Maynila to Malacca carrying gold, forest products, and foodstuffs. Maynila followed the same commercial patterns of numerous Southeast Asian entrepôts during the fifteenth and sixteenth centuries.

Across the Pacific, in Mexico, the Augustinian friar Andrés de Urdaneta recommended to Viceroy Luis de Velasco that a fellow Basque, Miguel López

1

de Legázpi, be appointed leader of the future expedition to the Philippines; in Legázpi's favor was his considerable experience as a public official in Spain and Mexico. Urdaneta's advice carried great weight because he had been an accountant on a previous expedition to the Moluccas, spoke Malay after years living on those islands, and had extensive knowledge of navigation. Conquests of new lands were usually a partnership between public and private interests, with the crown providing institutional support. Legázpi had sold all of his property in Mexico to finance the voyage. He received the title of "*Adelantado*" (an honorific title given to conquistadors), as well as the governorship of the yet-to-be-discovered lands.

The encounter between the Rajahs and the Spaniards transformed the islands' autonomous societies into a unified administrative dependency of a faraway viceroyalty in Mexico and the inhabitants into subjects of a distant king. New plants and animals arrived, altering the archipelago's ecology and economy. Missionaries were to transform local beliefs and rituals, imposing the Catholic religion, whose higher authority was far removed in Rome. Filipinos were required to pay tribute, work for the government, and provide foodstuffs and other supplies. These contributions were the main source of monetary support for the colonial establishment; the natives were financing their own colonization.

During the nineteenth century, the nation-state was the dominant political model, and Filipinos fought for an independent Philippine nation. The Spaniards left in 1898, but nationalist aspirations went unfulfilled as Spanish imperial strategy was followed by an American project of Pacific expansion. Only in 1946 did the Philippine Islands recover the autonomy that the archipelago's communities lost when Legázpi founded the city of Manila.

In contrast to the natives' perceptions, the Philippines in New Spain were enthusiastically received as a place of staggering opportunities for business. Sebastian Biscaino wrote to his father in glowing terms in 1590, "I can certify one thing that 200 ducats in Spanish commodities, and some Flemish wares which I carried with me thither, I made worth 1,400 ducats there in the country. So I make account that with those silks and other commodities which I brought with me from thence to Mexico, I got 2,500 ducats by the voyage."[1]

From a global perspective, Manila's founding implied that for the first time in the history of humanity the planet's landmasses were joined by uninterrupted interactions. To the exchanges of the Atlantic, the Indian Ocean, and the South China Sea, the Manila galleons added an incipient connection across the Pacific Ocean that—after the technological transformation initiated in Britain—gave birth to the world we inhabit. Just as the airports and aircraft of today began at Kitty Hawk with Wright Flyer I, the supertankers that cross the Pacific carrying thousands of tons of merchandise can be traced back to Manila's founding in 1571. Kirti N. Chaudhuri links our contemporary economy to the global trade that emerged in the sixteenth century: "When the Industrial Revolution changed the technological balance in favor of the Western countries during the nineteenth century, the existence of a global nexus of trade greatly facilitated the attempt by these countries to maximize economic gain through increased specialization."[2]

First we must adjust our contemporary perceptions. Before the nineteenth century, world trade was much smaller because world population was much smaller, compared to the 6 billion of the year 2000: about 545 million in 1600, 610 million in 1700, and 900 million in 1800. Trade was highly speculative in the sense that price instability and large price differentials between markets gave merchants prospects for large profits. Communications were slow, and transportation was frequently disrupted by weather, pirates, and warfare, all of which caused price volatility and high transportation costs. A single ship was capable of making a difference in the value of goods or altering the price of bullion in a particular market. In the seventeenth and eighteenth centuries, commercial cities were organized along the same lines in Europe, India, the Middle East, China, and America, and northern Europeans had no institutional economic advantage when compared with businesspeople elsewhere in the world. The Manila galleons shared the same commercial characteristics as English or Dutch Indiamen (as the ships were called), except that direct access to silver allowed for substantial profits, given the price discrepancies between American and Asian markets; likewise, cheap Chinese silks were highly marketable in the viceroyalties even if demand was smaller than it is today. In the seventeenth century the population of the American viceroyalties was estimated to be a little over 10 million and, in the final years of the eighteenth century, about 16 million; in such small societies, the galleons' impact was great.

An examination of the galleon line's operations from the sixteenth century until its end shows how relevant the ship was to the Spanish Empire in America and to Asian countries. China's role is especially central, both for its capacity to satisfy the global market's demand for inexpensive manufactured products and for its determining power on global finances. Until the nineteenth century the global economy's monetary regime was dependent upon China's demand for American silver. The Spanish Empire would have been impossible to operate without China. In this modern trade network, the only place for businessmen to have direct access to Asian markets was the route connecting Acapulco and Manila. Merchants in the Viceroyalties of Peru and New Spain had an alternative outlet for highly profitable investments in addition to the marketing of goods brought by the Atlantic fleet.

Their privileged position allowed them to generously support the American defense against hostile nations and to send substantial contributions, *donativos*, to the king's treasury in Spain. Without these elites' support, the empire in America would have crumbled; profits generated by the commercial exchanges across the Atlantic and Pacific sustained their loyalties.

Landmasses are all divided into separate scholarly specialties; consequently, American viceroyalties and Philippine history belong to distant academic compartments while the vicissitudes of the Spanish Empire are narrated from a European perspective at quite an intellectual distance from the Americas and Asia. Nevertheless, due to the lower cost of water transportation compared to land routes, the oceans were the essential links connecting distant territories in the Spanish Empire's single enterprise, as they were for the English, Dutch, French, Portuguese, and so on. From this maritime perspective, the decks of the Manila galleons were a privileged place from which to watch the history of the world unfold. The peoples in the Philippines and in America, Africa, Europe, China, and India, along with their manifold interactions, were linked to a greater or lesser extent by the vessels plying the Pacific. A different theory of imperialism in general and of the Spanish Empire in particular is required if one is to understand the significance of the Manila galleons. Henry Kamen observes, "No empire has, at any time, been viewed in retrospect as a success. It is this acute consciousness of failure, unfortunately, that helps to launch the endless mythologies associated with the history of Spain's world dominion."[3] The Portuguese applied the first European colonial system, imitated by the Dutch, English, and French; the Spaniards did likewise but over larger territories than any other nation had until the nineteenth century. Financed by American silver, Spain's prominence was fueled by its capacity to gather together the resources of diverse peoples and to gain the willing partnership of local elites. Italy supplied fleets in the Mediterranean, the Flemish fought against the Dutch in the Atlantic, Germans provided technology, Genoese and Portuguese bankers contributed financial expertise, Armenian and Sephardic diasporas were active on the imperial networks of exchange, and native authorities collected tributes and organized labor forces; all these nations and ethnic populations constituted the multinational enterprise known as the empire. During the modern centuries, imperial territories' tax accounting documents prove Kamen's assertion: "The real secret of the empire, as in the case of any good multinational, was the successful integration of regional business and an effective 'autonomy of cost,' paying for each enterprise on the spot rather than the center."[4]

Like any other empire in history, the Spanish one was established and maintained through the exercise of violence; it was a government-sponsored

conglomerate, a transnational organization, providing protection and trying to increase the flow of resources, rationalize costs, and regulate disputed
property rights and conflicts of a diverse nature. The profits accrued to its
stakeholders kept the empire in existence. Mexican merchants during the
eighteenth century are a good example: when the Spanish central government changed its mercantile policies to squeeze out their guild from control
of the textile market, the colonial agreement was broken, and in a few decades Mexico was independent.

The Manila galleons' line constituted one of several routes connecting the
world in the modern era. Merchants from diverse national and ethnic origins
participated in its exchanges when it was profitable; when revenues in the
last decades of the eighteenth century disappeared, they stopped investing,
and the line folded, as had the Dutch and English East India Companies.

Some examples indicate the nature of the Manila galleons' exchanges
and their effects. Japan had a "Christian Century," in which friars from the
Philippines played a fundamental role. The theater of Sor Juana Inés de
la Cruz (1651–1695)—a nun writing in Mexico City—was represented in
Manila; Africans and Filipinos belonged to religious brotherhoods in Manila
and Mexico City. In 1697, Italian observer Gemelli Careri wrote that in an
Easter procession in the capital of New Spain, the Franciscan assemblage
was called "the Procession of the Chinese" because all participants were
from the Philippines—in Mexico, all Asians were called "Chinos." Filipinos
taught native Mexicans how to manufacture wine from palm trees. Some
years before, in 1635, Spanish barbers complained to the municipal council
about foreign competition. It appeared that two hundred Chinese hair and
beard trimmers, as well as low-ranking medical providers, had established
their shops in the Plaza Mayor and were treating people with a combination
of Eastern and Western medicine that included cauterization, acupuncture,
bloodletting, and Chinese herbal medicine. They were particularly skilled
in treating periodontal disease. Puebla pottery copied the decorations of
Ming dynasty porcelain. Africans arriving on the galleons lived and worked
in Acapulco. Religious vestments for California missions were made with
Chinese silks, and a revolving tabernacle, brought in 1701 by the *San Carlos*
from Manila, can still be seen today in Mission Dolores in San Francisco, an
indication of the relationship between Spanish colonization of California
and the galleon's line. In the pages that follow, the galleons are placed in a
worldwide historical context to show how diverse disciplines—geology, climate history, ecology, economics, religion, and technology—and the study of
people's everyday lives are fundamentally interconnected with these vessels
that sailed the Pacific.

CHAPTER ONE

∼

The Philippines before the Spaniards

Monsoons, Islands, and the "Rim of Fire"

The 7,100 islands of the Philippine archipelago are spread over a 500,000-square-mile arc that extends from Taiwan and southern China in the north to Borneo in the south. Across the South China Sea from the islands, Vietnam stretches downward, and to the south, the Celebes Sea separates the archipelago from Indonesia. The Philippines are located in what today is considered Southeast Asia and in what the Chinese called the *Nanyang* (the "Southern Ocean"). Indian Ocean merchants placed the islands among "the lands below the winds."

Luzon and Mindanao are the largest islands of the archipelago, representing 95 percent of the 115,600 square miles that make up the Philippines of today. Between Luzon and Mindanao are a group of islands called the Visayas, and the Calamianes constitute the islands between Mindoro and Palawan. Valleys and chains of mountains span the territories of Luzon and Mindanao, while rivers and lakes provide irrigation and habitable land on their shores. Mountains, narrow valleys, and thousands of minor islands have shaped settlement patterns consisting of relatively small communities fringing bodies of water and sea coasts.

Monsoons regulate the Philippines's tropical climate. During winter, cold temperatures over the continent create high pressure systems that produce cold and dry winds; during summer, low pressure systems above the landmass attract moisture from the ocean, resulting in torrential rains. Monsoon winds follow a north–south pattern, twisted from east to west by Earth's revolu-

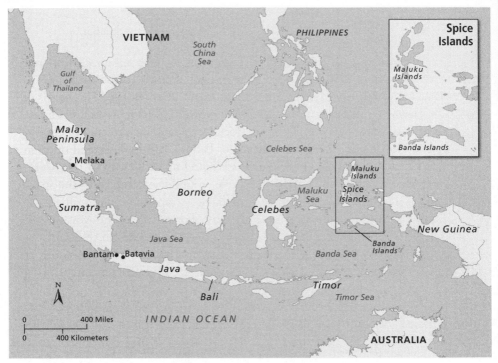

The Spice Islands in Southeast Asia

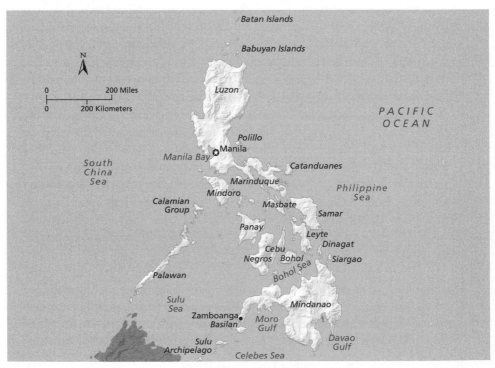

The Philippine Archipelago

tions. The archipelago has two main seasons: the wet season corresponds with the southern and southwestern monsoons, known to the Spaniards as *vendavales*, which blow from June through part of September. The winds of the northeastern monsoon, the dry *brisas*, begin in November or December. Tropical cyclones, called typhoons or, locally, *baguios*, are prevalent between July and November. The Jesuit chronicler Pedro Chirino described them in 1604: "They are furious winds which, springing up ordinarily in the north, veer toward the west and south, and move around the compass in the space of twenty hours or more."[1] These formidable storms have determined the location of Filipino communities in the past. For instance, the Muslim sultanates of Sulu and Mindanao were below the typhoon belt. In the northern islands, which sit directly in the baguios's destructive path, a river mouth or a coastal site on the western slope of mountains could provide shelter for a settlement, as is the case with Manila.

Each year, these tropical storms move west from the Caroline and Mariana Islands to the Philippines. The Manila galleon's track coincided with the typhoon belt: "This made the trade route reaching out from China through Manila to Mexico one of the most difficult passages to navigate in the world."[2] In addition to the threats posed by the baguios and adverse winds, the archipelago's irregular shoreline and its many reefs, coral shoals, and other submerged hazards were constant dangers to heavy sailing vessels.

Winds, currents, and the rugged topography of the numerous islands affected interactions among populations and shaped their social, linguistic, and cultural differences. Geographical fragmentation explains the intricate economic landscape that they shared with other groups of islands in Southeast Asia. Ecological diversity favored trade of resources among the islands and between mountains, hills, and coastal areas. As a French traveler of the seventeenth century reported, "These people are constrained to keep up constant intercourse with one another, the one supplying what the other needs."[3] At the time of Spanish arrival, this rough-hewn geography contributed to the Philippines's diverse polities, which encompassed Muslim sultanates, chiefdoms of varied size and complexity, upland tribal groups, and small bands of hunters and gatherers.[4]

As part of the Pacific's "rim" or "ring of fire," the Philippines is home to a number of active volcanoes. The Pacific's 63.8 million square miles make up about 46 percent of the Earth's water cover and one-third of its total surface, making it larger than all of the globe's landmasses together. It is the only one of the Earth's oceans encircled by subduction zones, which are regions where one tectonic plate slides under another and sinks into the earth's mantle. Sitting above the various subduction zones are several hundred active volcanoes, which justify the "ring of fire" nickname for the Pacific's shores. Tectonic displacement causes earthquakes, tsunamis, and volcanic activity. Eruptions and seismic commotions tragically punctuate Filipino history. In 1641, two volcanoes exploded simultaneously on January 4 in the Sulu Islands with such force that the eruptions were heard throughout the whole archipelago and as far away as Vietnam. Several days later an Augustinian friar, Fray Lucas de Aguilar, received a visiting group of mountain people, called Igorots, who brought startling news. On the same day of the eruption, there was "a sudden typhoon of such an intensity not house or tree was left standing, followed by an earthquake which threw boulders sixty feet into the air and an avalanche which released a torrent of subterranean water that swept away three whole villages." The natives attributed their misfortunes to their reluctance to follow the advice of a "beautiful lady of gentle demeanor" who had "rebuked them for not having received baptism."[5] In 1754, for six and a half months, the Taal Volcano ejected ashes and slag in such quantities that a layer of pumice stones covered the waters of Taal Lake. When Guillaume Le Gentil, a French astronomer, happened to be in Manila observing the transit of Venus, his celestial surveillance stopped on October 23, 1766, when "at 2 a.m. the Mayon volcano started to vomit out more water than it was possible to calculate. . . . Between Libog and Albay various rivers 30 yards wide were formed, rushing into the sea, considerably swollen and with great violence."[6]

The earthquake of 1645 forever transformed the architecture of colonial Manila. Prior to the tremor, houses typically had two stories above the ground floor, with a flat roof or *azotea* and a balcony on the first floor overhanging the sidewalk, to protect passersby from sun and rain. A contemporary eyewitness left a vivid description: "Stone walls swayed and swung as though they were paper or vellum shaken by the wind; towers trembled and bent like trees. . . . Heaps of stones from wrecked houses fell across the streets."[7] Six hundred people perished, and the quake destroyed several buildings, including the governor's palace and the hall of the *Audiencia*—the high court of the islands—in addition to houses, convents, churches, and schools. Only two chapels of Manila's cathedral remained standing. Stone buildings outside Manila suffered damage as well. In contrast, the earthquakes in 1654 and 1658 did little harm due to changes in construction: single-story houses, with thick walls supported by buttresses, had replaced tall mansions. On November 29, 1677, Pedro Cubero Sebastián, a Spanish priest, witnessed another tremor that "lasted from one o'clock at night until almost noontime of the following day." In Manila, the horrifying event appeared to signal the end of the world, "all the religious and the priests performing harsh and different modes of penance: some with chains, others with iron weights, others with crucifixes on the shoulders; still others wearing sacks with ashes on their heads . . . such was the confusion that it seemed like the Last Judgment." Despite the fear the earthquake engendered, only a few houses collapsed, and nobody perished.[8]

Generally, tropical areas have infertile soils. In contrast, the Philippines's land ranks among the more fertile in the tropics.[9] High year-round temperatures and abundant precipitation contribute to a rain forest filled with natural resources where areas of permanent cultivation occupy small patches in the middle of the jungle.[10] Tree densities necessitate slash-and-burn agriculture while providing wood, bamboo, and palm leaves to build dwellings; moreover, the forests teem with animals and plants that can be collected and commercialized.

Native Peoples on the Shores

Historically, demographics in the Philippines followed Southeast Asia's prevailing trends. Until the late eighteenth century, there was little population growth, and low population densities remained constant.[11] Scholars estimate that, at the time of the Spanish arrival, the total population of the Philippine archipelago was between 1.25 and 1.57 million people, an average of fewer than ten persons per square kilometer.[12] A large proportion of the islanders were concentrated in trading centers or areas of intensive wet rice cultivation, with population densities reaching more than twenty persons per square kilometer in Ilocos, Pampanga, and Manila.

Low birth rates resulted from extended breastfeeding, contraceptive herbs, abortion, and fertility-reducing diseases like malaria. Female swidden cultivators had a high workload that did not allow spending a large amount of time rearing children. Upper-class women interrupted their pregnancies to limit their lineage and preserve their heritage, while less affluent women did the same due to poverty. Christian Europeans wrote with surprise about the social acceptance of such practices. Governor Gómez Pérez Dasmariñas (1593–1596) observed in 1590, "After having one or two, the next time they get pregnant, when they are already three or four months, they kill the creature in the body and abort. There are women for this calling and by massaging the stomach and placing certain herbs . . . the pregnant woman aborts."[13] Writing in 1668, the Jesuit Francisco Ignacio Alzina attributed low population density to the infanticide of deformed or handicapped newborns and to the use of plants to induce abortion.[14]

Natives experienced periodic famines, typhoons, floods, volcanic eruptions, and limited agricultural productivity in addition to an array of diseases like malaria, dengue, leprosy, schistosomiasis, and tuberculosis, all of which thrived in the tropical climate.[15] Severe infections came from China or islands nearby, but they did not become endemic.[16] Even with these calamities Southeast Asians, in part due to lower child mortality rates, lived longer lives in comparison to sixteenth-century Europeans; in addition, owing to their diet and hygiene, natives enjoyed better overall health than their European contemporaries.[17] Regarding hygiene, Chirino remarked: "From the time when they are born, these islanders are brought up in the water. Consequently both men and women swim like fishes, even from childhood, and have no need of bridges to pass over rivers," and added, "even the woman after childbirth does not refrain from the bath, and children just born are bathed in the rivers and springs of cold water." They kept a basin "full of water before the door of every house; every person, whether belonging to the house or not, who enters it takes water from the jar with which to wash his feet before entering."[18] Antonio de Morga, a member of the Audiencia, in his well-known *Sucesos de las Islas Filipinas* of 1609, remarked about Filipinos' everyday bathing: "Both young and old quite commonly bathe their whole bodies in rivers and streams without reflecting that it could at any time be harmful to them." He added that the natives considered it "one of the greatest medicinal practices known to them and as soon as a child is born they immediately bathe it."[19] Alzina attributed female diseases to their frequent water immersions.[20] The rationale behind such statements aligned with contemporary Spanish medical theory, which maintained that bathing opened the skin's pores to harmful things, with dangerous results.[21] In general, Europeans considered frequent bathing voluptuous or unhealthy, with Cambridge University in England forbidding river bathing in 1571.[22]

The natives' staple diet consisted of rice, complemented by fish, root crops, fowl, swine, and palm wine. Francesca Bray considers East and Southeast Asia to form a macroregion unified by its reliance on rice, "with its technical logic of development."[23] A historian of the Philippines concurs with Bray's assertion: "Rice is the basic food of the people and ranks first among their crops."[24] Compared to other cereals, rice has many advantages: it is a high-yielding grain of high nutritious value that can be boiled without disintegrating. In naturally occurring paddies, nitrogen-fixing organisms enabled peasants to grow two or three crops a year in the same field.[25]

Filipinos practiced three types of rice cultivation, each with its own advantages and drawbacks. In the Visayas, Mindanao, and a large part of Luzon, one type of shifting cultivation involved clearing and burning a patch of forest in sloping areas; in these newly cleared fields, natives with sticks poked holes and dropped some grains into the earth. This system was the least demanding in terms of labor and supplied the needs of a family, but it did not produce surpluses for sale. A second, more productive method was to spread seed on a floodplain just before inundation. The water deposited nutrients that delivered large yields with minimal labor input. Before colonial times, *tubigan* (inundated rice) grew near Manila in the region of Laguna de Bay and near rivers in places like Lingayen, Cebu, and Butuan in Mindanao, as well as Jolo in the Sulu archipelago. The rice-watered land was the most valuable, and families who owned these parcels could inherit, purchase, barter, or pledge the property as collateral for debts. The third method of cultivation was the transplanting of seedlings into a bounded and plowed field in which cultivators managed the water level. This method generated maximum yields, though with lower returns in relation to the labor invested. An additional harvest of rice in the year was possible, as Dasmariñas observed in the Cagayan valley of Luzon: "Two crops of rice are gathered, one being irrigated, and the other allowed to grow by itself."[26] Compared to the two other methods, the wet-rice method was best for areas with greater population density, allowing improved harvesting and commercialization of surplus.[27]

In the most fertile terrain of Luzon and Panay, rice from the harvest provided enough food until the next crop, but a Spaniard observed in 1573 that "during the greater part of the year," the people on the majority of the islands "[lived] on millet, *borona*—corn bread—roasted bananas, certain roots resembling sweet potatoes called *oropisa*, as well as yams."[28] Corn, as well, had arrived from Mexico.[29] For three or four months of the year, instead of rice, the poor people of Mindanao had to eat flour produced from the fibrous pith of palm trees (sago). While rice was preferred, it could only be produced in sufficient quantities in a few places, making root crops more common.[30] Tubers were the primary staple at times of rice shortages or before the harvest, preventing mass starvation.[31]

Filipinos engaged in subsistence agriculture and did not produce surpluses. Nevertheless, left to themselves, in general people in the islands in the sixteenth and seventeenth centuries never suffered anything comparable to the devastating famines of Europe or China, even during periods of food scarcity. Reid affirms: "For the great majority of Southeast Asians serious hunger or malnutrition was never a danger."[32]

Wheeled vehicles or draft animals were absent in the Philippines, as was the case in other Southeast Asian regions. To provide the means of transportation to which they were accustomed, the Spaniards brought horses and other draft animals from Mexico, China, and Japan. According to Morga, natives communicated with each other by traveling among islands by boat; the most common were "*barangays* and *vireyes* which carry smaller crews and fewer people."

He was surprised by how the outriggers facilitated speed: "They skim over the water but do not interfere with the rowing and act as a counter-balance so that the ship cannot overturn or capsize, however rough the water may be, or however strong the wind may be in the sails." The most imposing crafts in the eyes of the Europeans were the *karakoas*, with numerous rowers on each side and soldiers stationed above the rowers on a platform.[33] The inhabitants of Catanduanes—an island near Luzon—were great carpenters who sold boats of differing sizes, transporting one craft inside another, with the largest ships carrying ten or twelve smaller hulls. These native boats were adapted for sailing in coastal waters full of reefs and rocks. Navigation required an intimate familiarity with the water's depth, shoals, and sandbanks, as well as knowledge of interisland passages and the Pacific's strong currents.[34]

Water transportation was faster and more economical than hauling goods by land. As a Chinese mandarin noted in a memorandum regarding shipping in the Ming Empire, "Transport by inland waterways is 30 to 40 percent cheaper than transport by land. Sea transport is 70 to 80 percent cheaper than transport by land."[35] Southeast Asia shared similar economic advantages. Despite the Philippines's rugged coast and currents and the seasonal whims of the baguios, other factors "made the Mediterranean of Southeast Asia more hospitable and inviting a meeting place and thoroughfare than that deeper and stormier Mediterranean in the West,"[36] including predictable winds, uniform water temperatures, and abundant timber for boats.

Demographic factors and an abundance of natural resources interacted with a political system that was based on controlling labor instead of territory. This political organization emphasized alliance-building activities such as giving gifts, creating extensive family ties, and ritualized feasting, all aimed at sustaining social cohesion in the Philippines's complex network of societies.[37] Before Spain's era of colonization, the majority of the archipelago's inhabitants—identified as Tagalog, a word meaning "people living along the river"—resided in small, kinship-based, autonomous communities called *barangays*, a word derived from the boats that brought the Malay immigrants to the Philippine Islands.[38] These groups were located on riverbanks or coastal areas that provided seafood and easy communication. Natives lived in abodes set above ground, supported by posts under the houses; women pounded rice and tended to animals in a fenced area. Each dwelling had a single room, which was built and roofed with timber and bamboo and covered with palm leaves. Chiefs' houses had more rooms and were larger, more comfortable, and occasionally furnished.

A chief, or *datu*, ruled each Tagalog settlement. In the Muslim sultanates of the south, the sultan had power over his datus, but the datus, in turn, ruled their own communities.[39] The Franciscan friar Juan de Plasencia (1589) described the relationship between the barangay and datus: "These chiefs ruled over but few people; sometimes as many as a hundred houses, sometimes even less than thirty. . . . They were not, however, subject to one another, except in friendship and relationship. The chiefs, in their various wars, helped one another with their respective barangays."[40] Datus were a hereditary aristocracy along patrilineal lines. They acted as political and judicial authorities and the leaders of maritime raids and trading expeditions. Each datu collected tributes and required labor from all the families under his authority, with the exception of the nobility. Political power and social prestige were shown in the amount of agricultural surplus, slaves, and luxury goods—porcelain, gold, silks, metal weaponry—owned by the chief and displayed at ritual feasts. Elites exchanged these goods for alliance building and to facilitate trade in ordinary merchandise. Political power and status were displayed and reinforced by feasts, through which datus competed against each other to show the wealth and power of their barangays. Captured slaves augmented the agricultural labor force, allowed local artisans to concentrate on making goods for exchange, and freed people to engage in trade. Datus and their nobles kept the best captives and sold the rest.[41] On occasion, captives were sacrificed, such as when their masters died.[42] Raiding rival settlements resulted in the seizure of a conquered community's accumulated export commodities, including foodstuffs and labor force, to eliminate unwanted competition. As a consequence, foreign merchants redirected their voyages to other, better-supplied ports of call, increasing their datus' riches. When the Spaniards arrived in the sixteenth century, all Filipino groups engaged in raiding for captives.[43]

Barangays and the Age of Commerce after 1405

After the "Black Death" of 1346–1348 there was a surge in the demand for exotic products in the northern hemisphere coinciding with two centuries of growth in wealth and population in Ming China, along with a revitalization of the spice trade to Europe. Cargoes from Alexandria and Beirut reached Venice, Genoa, and Barcelona. Reid considers 1405—the year of the first trade mission under the Chinese Admiral Zheng He—to signal the beginning of Southeast Asia's "age of commerce."[44]

In the Philippines this upsurge of economic activities resulted in an intensified collection of forest and sea products for sale. The expansion of trade led to an increase in raiding and the consolidation of chiefdoms into larger, more cohesive political entities. Barangays built fortifications and acquired guns for their forts and vessels, and a class of professional warriors emerged. When the Spaniards conquered Manila, they encountered an artillery foundry and cannons defending the palisade. Burial sites show evidence of violent deaths marking the increase in hostilities during this period. Among the Tagalog, before the conquest, head taking, human sacrifice, and the use of enemy body parts as trophies were common in feasts and death-related rituals. Plasencia wrote, "When some chief dies, to avenge his death, they had to cut off many heads, with which they would make many feasts and dances."[45] Some years later Morga observed, "In pursuit of an enemy they clutch his hair with one hand, while with the other, in a single blow of the *bararao*, they strike off his head and carry it away with them. Afterwards they keep such heads hung up in their houses on show."[46]

Datus were treated with great respect, evident in the way people addressed them and in the commoners' subservient demeanor in their presence. Chiefs and other nobles adorned themselves with jewelry of silver and gold, silk, high-quality cotton clothing, and intricate tattoos. Below the datus in the barangay hierarchy were the nobility, who were typically relatives of the datu. It was possible for others with fictive kin relations, specialized skills, or ambition to rise to the category of personal vassals,[47] who received a share of booty and captives, as well as the chief's protection. These elites also attended datus' feasts and acted as wine tasters, assisted in marriage negotiations, and played a role in death rites.[48] Occupying a third rank were commoners whose duties were to support the datu with tributes and services or as artisans. They went to battle with him and participated in his feasts. The chief provided protection and shared some of his wealth with them. What John L. Phelan conceptualizes as the lowest rank of society was a "servile dependent class whom the Spaniards misleadingly called slaves."[49] Among this dependent population there was a diverse degree of autonomy, property rights, and required labor contributions. Servitude was widespread: free men pledged themselves for dowries, and serfs themselves could hold debt peons and other dependents.[50] Melchor Dávalos, a member of the Philippines's Audiencia, described the institution in a letter to the king:

> Some are slaves because their fathers and grandfathers were such; others sold themselves . . . either to make use of the money or to pay their debts; others were captured in war; others became slaves because, being orphans, they were held in that condition for food and expenses; others were sold in times of famine by their fathers, mothers or brothers; others bear that name because of loans, for interest multiplies rapidly among the *Indios* and the *Moros*, and thus

a poor man becomes a slave. There are men who become slaves on account of crimes, and failure to pay fines and penalties.[51]

The pervasive nature of this dependent class corresponded to communities where low agricultural productivity required loans of food among natives in which the only available collateral was the borrower's person. With the exception of serfs living in their masters' houses, most of them supported themselves, providing labor time only according to their debt; some were actually only half-slave or quarter-slave. Morga observed, "These slaves constitute the main capital and wealth of the natives of these islands, since they are both very useful and necessary for the working of their farms. Thus they are sold, exchanged and traded, just like any other article of merchandise."[52]

Pre-conquest Filipinos lived in a subsistence economy dedicated primarily to agriculture and fishing, complemented by food gathering and hunting. There was some division of labor into specific professions, including metal workers, potters, midwives, traders, and so on, but everybody shared agricultural activities. Many tasks, like land preparation, planting, harvesting, and house building, were a collaborative effort among households. The family receiving help hosted a feast and drinking party.

Exchanges among barangays included foodstuffs, pottery, mats, utensils, and fish. When Miguel López de Legázpi was in Cebu in 1565, he saw several Luzon merchants trading with the Cebuans.[53] Filipino traders frequently sailed the seas of the archipelago in search of gold and slaves.[54] Morga observed, "Sometimes, when a cash price was paid, this was made in gold, as agreed upon, or else in metal gongs brought from China,"[55] adding that land, houses, fields, slaves, fishing grounds, and palm trees were among the articles exchanged.

Gold dust was used as a currency for transactions throughout the islands, and "gold-cast pellets stamped with Tagalog characters" of 0.09 to 2.00 grams had been utilized as currency since the tenth century.[56] In the Visayas, salt was used as small change before the colonial era.[57] Mountain people and lowland Filipinos carried with them a pair of scales to weigh out gold dust for all kinds of purchases. The basic weight was the *saga*, a little red seed (*Abrus precatorius*). Similar scales were common in China for silver payments. In 1609 Chirino observed that Filipinos, after much drinking, "if they have occasion to buy or sell anything, they not only make no mistake in the bargaining" despite their state of apparent intoxication, but "if it be necessary to weigh the gold or silver for the price," they used the customary scales "with such accuracy that the hand never trembles, nor is there any error in the weight."[58] Such procedures indicate a highly commercialized society in which exchanges were an everyday activity.

Commonalities existed among the principal tongues of the islands; nonetheless, there were enough disparities among them to distinguish between the languages of Zambals, Ilocanos, Pampangos, and Tagalog.[59] Regarding native script, Morga observed that "throughout the islands the natives write very well, using certain characters, almost like Greek or Arabic, fifteen in number, three of them being vowels equivalent of our five. . . The manner of writing, once on bamboo, is now on paper."[60] The Spaniards observed that females wrote and read more fluently than males.[61]

The Mountain Peoples

Quite different from the lowland Tagalogs were the native groups in the highlands of the islands, who presented many challenges to the colonizers. Their social and economic lives were quite diverse; they ranged from small bands of hunter-gatherers to tribes of swidden cultivators and groups with intensive agriculture ruled by emerging hierarchies.[62] The upland peoples received names like Tinguians, Zambals, Igorots, and Ifugaos in colonial sources. In fact, "Igorot" and "Ifugao" were native words meaning the inhabitants of the highlands. Other groups received the Spanish epithet *Negritos*—a Spanish priest wrote that the name was a sign of disrespect[63]—and were called *Aetas* by the Filipinos, meaning "mountain people." The Spaniards feared them. The author of a "Description of the Philippinas Islands" of 1618 stated, "They are so restless, so warlike, and so averse to trade and communication with other people that up to this time it has not been possible to subdue them effectively. Although on different occasions they have been severely chastised, there is still no security from them." He continued, "They are still so brutal and so averse to civilization that they scarcely deserve more than the name of men; for they often cut off the heads of their own fathers and brothers as a pastime, for no other reason than their natural cruelty and brutality." They had no fixed abode or settled agriculture, and their survival depended upon sweet potatoes, roots, and hunting game. The description concluded in a reiteration of their violent practices: "They hardly ever come to the plains or coasts except to make assaults and to cut off heads. The one who has cut off the greatest number of these is most feared and respected among them."[64] Since pre-Hispanic times the lowland Tagalog and these societies actively participated in trade networks that spanned beyond the islands. For instance, the Chinese required gold and forest goods in exchange for luxurious fabrics, gongs, and porcelain.

Consequently, coastal populations acted as intermediaries between the junk merchants and the Igorots, Aetas, and Tinguians.

The Igorots, who were located in gold mining regions, are particularly relevant. Before the conquest, Agoo in the Ilocos region—known to the Spaniards as *Puerto del Japón* (Japan's Port)—was a trading colony in which Chinese and Japanese merchants bartered for gold. About six months after Legázpi was established in Manila, his grandson Juan de Salcedo organized an exploration to northern Luzon, following rumors about the rich gold mines of Paracale. The young captain died, probably of dysentery, on his way there. Reports from expeditions are the first descriptions of the Igorots, whose numbers were estimated between eighteen and twenty thousand people. They practiced slash-and-burn agriculture, and their basic diet consisted of root crops such as taro, *camotes*, or yams. Rice was cultivated without plows or draft animals on the Ifugao terraces of the Cordillera, the stone walls of which extend for more than twenty thousand kilometers.[65]

Despite their proximity to gold mining regions, the Igorots did not accumulate bullion. The exception was personal jewelry, like the plates with which women decorated their teeth or the bits of gold attached to the burial blankets of prominent men. Men and women wore earrings, bracelets, and beads of seeds, shells, glass, or cornelians, which in the seventeenth century the Jesuit Francisco Colín said cost one piece of eight each when brought from Borneo or India. These semiprecious gems were widely used in the Visayas and in Luzon until the Spanish arrival.[66]

Eighteenth-century Spanish sources mention Igorot metallurgical activities and an increase in local specializations like the selling of foodstuffs and the use of slaves for work on mining fields. Iron bought in the lowlands was forged, with the assistance of bellows made of tree trunks, to produce knives, hoes, and spearheads. Axes, *bolos* (machetes), pots of copper, and forest products were exchanged by the Igorots for dogs, salt, wine, mats, blankets, dried fish, loincloths, porcelain plates and jars, wire to make bracelets, beads, precious stones, and iron pots. In Ilocos, however, until the establishment of the tobacco monopoly in 1780, Igorot tobacco was not an item of trade. When bees were absent due to deforestation, the mountain people purchased honey, though generally the Cordillera was a source of beeswax. Chinese junks trading with the islands exported beeswax and gold, as did the Manila galleons, which, since the beginning of the line, carried significant loads of this product to manufacture candles used in Mexico.[67]

With the exception of the chiefs, the Igorots wore bark cloth instead of cotton and covered themselves with Ilocano blankets. Their houses, built at ground level, were made of timber and thatching. Many of their differences from other Filipinos, like adherence to the tradition of head hunting, a tradition that the Tagalog population had abandoned, were the result of lowlanders' acculturation under Islamic or Spanish influence. In contrast, the Igorots continued to cut off heads and capture slaves.

They collected gold by mining and panning. Captain García de Aldana's expedition in 1620 observed hundreds of Igorots working in a mine with a drainage system. Other reports mentioned mining tunnels illuminated by pine torches. In the eighteenth century, sources indicated that these mines passed from father to son and that the mine owners extracted gold with forced labor.[68] The lords of the mine "don't let anybody enter but their own servants and slaves, who are pagans bought farther inland, and they punish them with whips, sticks, lashes and death if they steal, run away or don't obey their masters who have given them food."[69] People without mines panned for the yellow metal in rivers and streams. In the words of Morga, "With the gold still unrefined or purified, they go down to trade with the Ilocanos at certain places where they give them the gold in exchange for rice, pigs, carabaos and other things they lack, and the Ilocanos finish its refining and purify it perfectly and it passes through the whole land through their hands."[70]

To the Igorot, the Spaniards were an unwelcome presence. They arrived at the Cordillera with military expeditions, drove lowland people fleeing from the colonizers, and caused conflicts with neighbors who accompanied the Spanish forces as auxiliaries. Church authorities encouraged, and colonial administrators repeatedly attempted, the subjugation of these mountain peoples and exploitation of their mines. Among the suggested schemes was to build Spanish and Chinese settlements in the mining territories, or to send Mexican miners. Morga described these plans as if they were an El Dorado–type dream: "If the industry and energy of the Spaniards were devoted to extracting this gold, as much would be got from one of these islands, as from the most productive province anywhere in the world."[71] This exaggerated claim appeared in print in 1609. Nine years later, at the onset of the Thirty Years' War, Philip III became amenable to such suggestions because the treasury needed to collect all available bullion, and the gold of the Philippines appeared to be a welcome addition to the contributions coming from the Americas. As a result, Governor Alonso Fajardo (1618–1624) received the order to conquer and exploit the Igorot mines; nothing happened. The next king, Philip IV, was always in need of resources and encouraged the governor to take decisive steps. Finally, in 1620, an expedition was able to build two forts in mining territory. Peace rituals between the Igorots and the Spanish took place; the natives waited during the typhoon season for the Spaniards to exhaust their provisions, and when the heavy November rains rendered the matchlocks on Spanish guns useless, the natives attacked. The Japanese had had the foresight to add waterproof lacquer covers to their harquebus to protect the burning match during rainstorms and to hide the glowing wick at night,[72] but no such innovation or any equivalent had ever crossed the minds of European gun makers. The forts were no more. Four years later, on February 14, 1624, a military expedition entered Igorot territory with two Japanese miners; eleven black slaves; forty-seven Chinese carpenters, smiths, and sawyers; plus Spanish soldiers, some of them also miners, and a large number of Filipino forces. Like the two previous attempts, the enterprise was fruitless. An exasperated official from the Royal Treasury reported that after three expeditions, profits were nonexistent, costs were high, and—because many lowlanders accompanied the Spaniards—rice and cotton were in short supply. The Spanish never exploited the mines.

The Igorots were opposed to receiving missionaries because that implied the acceptance of a colonial regime that entailed tributes, personal services, and abuses by soldiers and local authorities, while Christian lowlanders did not encourage their neighbors to join the Christian faith, fearing a disruption of their monopoly on mountain wax. In 1695, Governor Fausto Cruzat (1690–1701) observed that lowland Filipinos obstructed the conversion of the Igorots based on "the profit which the said Christian natives have in the gold and wax they acquired from the said pagans." To hasten the Igorots' conversion and subjugation to the Crown, Cruzat forbade "all dealings, communications and commerce with the pagans, apostates, fugitives, Blacks and Zambals,"[73] but the ordinance had no consequences. An Augustinian provincial witnessed the presence of pagan traders in the Ilocos markets and the continuing exchanges between the plains and the mountains.

Ecclesiastical sources from the eighteenth century indicated that, in addition to herds of cattle, the Igorots accumulated silver coins. Le Gentil calculated in 1766 that the Igorots received 200,000 pesos in silver annually in exchange for their gold.[74] In 1789, the Dominican Francisco Antolín estimated that at least an eighth of the 200,000 pesos' worth of gold leaving the Philippines each year came from the Igorots. He noted that the Igorots measured their gold—"whose weight and value [they] know very well—with their little scales."[75]

The Spaniards failed to conquer the mountains of northwestern Luzon. Under Governor Manuel de Leon (1669–1677), there was an attempt to stabilize the frontier by creating a buffer zone between the Christianized populations and the mountain people. Protected by soldiers, missionaries occupied a series of outposts called *misiones vivas*; there were some minor

Spanish advances, but the Igorots maintained their independence until the last decades of the nineteenth century.

In addition to the Igorots of Luzon, there were independent populations, called *tinguianes*, living in the hills south and east of Manila. They maintained a profitable relationship with lowland Filipinos by providing them with forest products. On other islands, for the most part, the Aetas inhabiting the mountains were able to prevent Spanish penetration. Hostile acts by Muslims and mountain peoples paradoxically fortified the colonial system in the Philippines's lowlands because Spanish forces became the only protection those provinces had against their hostile neighbors' raids.[76]

The Gold of the Visayas and the Harvest of Cowries

Igorots' mines in northern Luzon were not the only sources of bullion in the Philippines; in fact, the most productive gold mines were in the Visayas. Jose Pacheco Maldonado, writing in 1575, informed Philip II about Japan, "whence is brought great quantities of silver. . . . Every year Japanese ships come to these islands laden with merchandise. Their principal trade is the exchange of gold for silver."[77] When the Spaniards arrived at Masbate Island, the natives had abandoned all mining activities and had left their tools behind them.[78] Morga observed among the Filipinos an abundance of gold jewelry on both men and women: "Round their necks are gold necklaces like spun wax, and with links, as in the European fashion, some larger than others. On their arms they wear wrought gold bracelets, called *colombigas*, which are very large and made in different patterns."[79] Regarding the neglect of gold mines, he wrote elsewhere, "since the coming of the Spaniards the natives are slower to do this, now contenting themselves with what they already have in the way of jewels and gold ingots, inherited from the past and from their ancestors."[80] Alzina, in the middle of the seventeenth century, wrote of a young Visayan bride who brought to the marriage approximately twenty-five pounds of gold in jewelry. The abundant use of gold jewelry among the natives was a surprise, but natives told him that gold was less abundant in comparison to the past.[81] The Igorots refused to divulge the locations of their mines, and the Filipinos extracted only the minimum quantity necessary to pay tributes or to make small purchases. Father Alzina bemoaned the abandonment of gold mining in Masbate, Bool, and other small islands of the Visayas and attributed it to a lack of ambition or laziness on the part of the natives, though he recognized that they were reluctant to mine gold due to their fear of extortion by Spanish authorities.[82] Considering the hardships of panning and mining and their fear of the colonizers, Filipinos were highly rational. The crown tried without success to encourage gold mining through low taxation. Despite the decline in gold production after the Spanish conquest, in the last years of the seventeenth century, the governor confided to the Italian traveler Gemelli Careri that all the metal collected by the natives was equivalent to 200,000 gold pesos.[83] Bullion percolated through the economic networks of the islands before reaching the international markets, of which India exercised the highest demand.

Filipinos also harvested cowry shells (*Cypraea moneta*) from the coasts, which they sold by weight to Siam, Cambodia, Malaysia, and Bengal, "where they are used as money and a means of trading, as happens in New Spain with the cocoa-bean."[84]

The Mediterranean Connection and the Long Post-1400 Trade Boom

In Southeast Asia, patterns of long distance trade were interconnected with regional networks in which Chinese, Javanese, Indian, Arab, and Malay merchants participated in "a long post-1400 boom" of trade.[85] Throughout the centuries, Islam had expanded across the Indian Ocean, and Muslim mercantile communities had appeared in East Africa, India, and Southeast Asia.

The crucial network of long distance trade connecting Southeast Asia with African, Middle Eastern, and European markets before colonization constituted, in Scott's words, the "Mediterranean Connection."[86] This "connection" originated in the Molucca and Banda archipelagos, the Spice Islands, south of the Philippines. From these islands, cloves and nutmeg arrived at the entrepôts of Malacca and Acheh in Sumatra. Atjenese, Arab, and Indian vessels delivered spices and other Asian products to Africa, the Red Sea, and the Persian Gulf. From Egyptian and Syrian ports (Alexandria, Beirut, Cairo, and Damascus), Venetians distributed these precious commodities to European markets.

Caliphate armies had invaded the Iberian Peninsula in 711, and since the ninth century, Muslims from Spain settled in commercial enclaves between Southeast Asia and Europe. An uprising in Córdoba against the emir caused the first wave of expatriates in 814. Later, the campaigns of Ferdinand III from 1228 to 1248 culminated in the conquest of Córdoba and Seville and caused further departures. The occupation of Granada by Isabel of Castile and Ferdinand of Aragon in 1492 sent Spanish-speaking Muslims to North Africa and the Indian Ocean. According to Gaspar Corrêa, a Portuguese chronicler of the sixteenth century, when Vasco da Gama arrived in Calicut in 1498 he sent João Nuz, a New Christian fluent in Hebrew and Arabic, to inquire about the city's business. There Nuz encountered a Moor who addressed him in Spanish and told Nuz that he was born in Seville. João de Barros, another Portuguese historian, called this Moor "Monzaide" and claimed that he was a native of Tunis. Both agree on his Spanish language fluency.[87] Approaching Goa, da Gama met another speaker of the same language: "This Jew, at the taking of Granada, was a very young man, and having been driven from his country he passed through many lands until he came to Turkey, and went to Mecca, from whence he passed on to India."[88] When the Portuguese bombarded Hormuz, they encountered a Spanish speaker who was also a native of Granada. In 1515 a fleet of Mameluks, Turks, and Spanish Muslims from Granada and Tunis—a North African commercial center—attacked the Portuguese in Calcutta. Members of the Magellan expedition spoke in Spanish with Pazeculan in Borneo and Uzman of Tidore in the Moluccas. After the War of the Alpujarras (a region north of Granada) from 1568 to 1571, thousands of Muslims who had remained in Spain, called *Moriscos*, were deported. In the following decade, Ottoman armies fought in the Balkans and Persia, and a Turkish fleet was defeated in the Battle of Lepanto in 1571. After all these disturbances, Mediterranean Muslims appeared in Sumatra, Borneo, and the Moluccas. Melchor Dávalos, a Spanish official in Manila, acknowledged their presence in 1585:

> Persians and Arabs and Egyptians and Turks brought [Muhammad's] veneration and evil sect here, and even Moors from Tunis and Granada came here, sometimes in the armadas of Campson, former Sultan of Cairo and King of Egypt. . . . And every year they say that Turks come to Sumatra and Borneo and Ternate, where there are now some of those defeated in the famous battle which Señor Don Juan de Austria won.[89]

In 1492, the Catholic king and queen decreed the expulsion from Spain of all Sephardic Jews, those who refused to convert, which increased the number of Spanish speakers in centers of trade. For instance, in 1510, two Castilian Jews were taken by Simão Martins in a vessel from Mecca to Calicut, and they were employed as interpreters by Afonso de Albuquerque, the governor of Portuguese India. One century later an English captain met a Spanish-speaking Jew in Mocha.[90] The Iberians' ability to converse in the places they visited enabled them to gather knowledge about local markets and to transmit information. Letters from Ignatius of Loyola, founder of the Jesuits, arrived in India from Cairo in one month. In the first decade of the seventeenth century, Morga observed that the Portuguese sent communications from India to the peninsula under the care of Spanish-speaking Jewish merchants. Following the Red Sea route, the letters crossed Arabia to reach Alexandria, and from there, merchant ships took them to Venice and Spain. Francesca Trivellato observes that Jews in Livorno, Italians in Lisbon, and Hindus in Goa participated in a stable, cross-cultural network of trade. Already in the 1620s, one Sephardic family had imported Indian diamonds from Lisbon and shipped them to Italy.[91] García Silva de Figueroa, Spanish ambassador to the Safavid court in 1617, praised the safety of the maritime and terrestrial routes from the Philippines to Spain, via Aleppo in Syria.[92]

An indication of the relative importance of Filipinos in this "Mediterranean Connection" was their economic role in Java. In Malacca, before the Portuguese conquest, Islamized Tagalogs were among the largest-scale traders and ship owners.[93] When Afonso de Albuquerque conquered the entrepôt, he nominated a Filipino governor to serve over the Muslim communities. Two Malacca merchants from Luzon were also important participants in the spice trade at the time of the Portuguese arrival: Regimo Diraja had active communications with Southeast Asia—Brunei, Pasai, Siam, and Sunda— and China, while Surya Diraja annually sent 175 tons of pepper to China; one of his boats went with the first Portuguese fleet to visit the Chinese Empire.[94] Other Filipinos were hostile to the Portuguese and collaborated with their enemies to remove the newcomers from Asian routes. Portuguese chronicler Fernão Mendes Pinto wrote in 1539 about a fleet sent by the viceroy of Cairo under a Turkish commander, Heredim Mafamede, to raise the siege of Atjeh. It was a multinational force of Muslims from Turkey, Ethiopia, India, and Luzon. After the victory, Heredim named the Filipino Sapetu Diraja commander of the garrison.[95]

By the time the Europeans arrived, Islam had already been present in Southeast Asia for centuries. By 1276, Islam was present in Malacca. In 1390, Rajah Baginda led an army of firearm-equipped Muslims from Sumatra to Sulu.[96] Muslim Malays overthrew the Madjapahit Empire in 1478 and established the Islamic government of Malacca. In the fifteenth century, Islam spread to Borneo, and soon the sultanate of Jolo emerged on the Sulu archipelago. In the early sixteenth century, the sultanate of Magindanao on the Pulangui River became the most powerful in Mindanao. Several years before Legázpi arrived in Luzon, Islam was gaining converts among its people. Antonio de Morga noted that the natives were becoming Muslim, "having themselves circumcised and taking Moorish names. Had the coming of Spaniards been delayed longer, that religion would have spread throughout the island and even through the others."[97] The process of Islamization was propelled by the fact that those who seemed most successful in the world of commerce were also those most attracted to Islam's ritual practices. Some

Filipinos imitated the Islamic taboo on pork, apparently believing it to be a ritual key to their fortune.[98]

The predominance of Muslim merchants in the Indian Ocean and Southeast Asia—Turks, Persians, and Arabs—lasted until the first two decades of the seventeenth century, at which point the spice route from Aceh in Sumatra to the Red Sea vanished. European powers, principally the Dutch, had displaced them.[99] By 1620, the "Mediterranean Connection" had ceased to exist.

China and the Islands before Spain

China, the dominant economic power in Asia and the most important trade partner in the history of the archipelago, exercised considerable economic pull in the region. During the Sung dynasty (960–1279), exchanges between the Philippines and China grew substantially, and junks visited Mindoro, the Visayas, Luzon, Palawan, and Polillo Island in northeastern Luzon. A Sung edict of 972 referred to Mindoro, and in 982 a Chinese source indicated that some Filipino merchants had arrived in Canton. Pirates from the Visayas raided the China coast in the twelfth century. In 1368, the Ming dynasty tried to exercise control over foreign trade by establishing a system in which only officially recognized missions could enter the empire, and imperial edicts banned Chinese merchants from officially going abroad. In 1373, under Emperor Hung-wu, the first embassy from Luzon arrived to pay tribute. The emperor, in return, dispatched an imperial official with presents of silks and porcelain vases. A Chinese mandarin visited Luzon during a 1405 inspection tour of Southeast Asia's trading ports during Yung-lo's reign as emperor (1403–1424). Islands like Pangasinan and Sulu, which were eager to achieve the same recognition as Luzon, dispatched embassies as well. The most prominent tributary mission traveled from Sulu in 1417. A large retinue accompanied the rulers, who brought a rich "tribute" of gold, pearls, precious stones, spices, and tortoiseshells. The Chinese bestowed on the Sulu chiefs the title of "princes of the realm." One of these princes died traveling on the Grand Canal, and given his status, his body was buried with the prescribed Chinese royal ceremonies. Zheng He's fleets diverted vessels to visit Lingayen, Manila, Mindoro, and Sulu.[100] The last embassy from the Philippines to Beijing arrived in 1421.

Tributary missions to China were costly, requiring the construction of large vessels, the collection of luxurious cargo, and considerable financial resources to support a large accompanying entourage. In addition to the status conferred by Chinese titles and royal seals laid upon Filipino rulers, future trade revenues were often immense.[101] Contextualizing the tributary missions within the political economy of the barangays, one scholar suggests, "An upsurge in tributary trade missions aimed at deflecting foreign trade wealth away from potential trade rivals" corresponded with "competitive interactions among numerous polities of similar complexity and scale."[102] The late fourteenth and early fifteenth centuries witnessed a peak in missions to the Chinese court. At the beginning of the fifteenth century, competition among northern communities in Luzon to control the Moluccas-Borneo-Luzon-Fujian eastern trade route, and rivalries in the southern Philippines for hegemony along the Moluccas-Java-Melaka route, resulted in the trade supremacy of Manila in the north and Sulu in the south. They were not isolated phenomena. Barangays, with powerful datus competing with each other, occupied the coasts of Luzon, Mindanao, and the islands of Leyte and Panay.[103]

Sultanates and chiefdoms in the Philippines and Brunei were intermediaries between China, the Moluccas, and the Banda Islands; Filipino traders frequently visited the Moluccas. From the Spice Islands, cloves, nutmeg, mace, and sandalwood arrived at Jolo in the Sulu Islands, where hardwoods, pearls, and forest and maritime products joined the cargo. These commodities followed a western route in the direction of Java and Malacca or traveled northward to the Philippines where local products—gold, wax, betel nuts, cotton goods, shells, animal skins, carabao horns, slaves, etc.—were added to the freight. Goods were loaded into Chinese junks in local ports or transported by Filipino boats to southern China. In return they received porcelain, ironware, lead, tin, glass beads, copper gongs, bells, silks, and "trade gold."[104] It was difficult for the bulky Chinese junks to navigate the waters south of Luzon, and ships from the Philippines and Sulu were in charge of collecting the spices and bringing them to entrepôts like Jolo and Manila.

Through the fifteenth and sixteenth centuries, relations among markets abroad and the Philippines intensified. Consequently, the same trend was apparent in the volume of exchanges between mountain peoples and lowland barangays; large quantities of luxury goods arrived upland in exchange for forest products.[105] This upsurge in trade is reflected in the importation of tens of thousands of porcelain Chinese pieces that have since been found at gravesites.[106] The datus' ability to mobilize labor and military forces required the distribution of goods to their subordinates and allies, and demand for porcelain corresponded with an increase in ceremonial feasts, in which the amount and quality of food was as important as its presentation.[107]

Commerce with Thailand and Vietnam also intensified during the Age of Commerce, evident in the amount of porcelain and earthenware jars recovered during archeological excavations. From the fifteenth century to the seventeenth, large quantities of pottery from Thailand and Vietnam entered Southeast Asian trade.[108] However, not all porcelain was equal. Filipino datus kept the best Chinese pieces, distributing the cheapest ones among the lesser nobles, commoners, interior tribal chiefs, and clients. The abundance of pottery from different regions reveals the increasingly prominent role played by ceramics in the political economy of the islands' chiefdoms. These gifts were necessary to extend a coalition's networks and to consolidate a datu's power before colonial times.[109] Intensification of trade attracted populations from the hinterlands to the coast and generated social and economic changes. Increasingly nucleated settlements developed, in which groups of homes clustered at the center of villages, and in places with adequate settings, agriculture evolved from shifting to sedentary.[110]

An increase in trade involving Southeast Asian societies began in the fifteenth century. The forces propelling the Age of Commerce—population growth and larger markets—formed part of a global trend in which Filipino societies were embedded. Tropical forest hunter-gatherers and upland tribal groups exchanged goods with more complex organized chiefdoms and participated in economic circuits encompassing states in Southeast Asia, as well as in China and Japan. After 1571, the galleon trade linked the American economies to the Filipino network of exchange across the Pacific, radically transforming the islands' societies and their historical trajectories.

CHAPTER TWO

~

The Origins of Spanish Settlement in the Philippines

Manila and the Origins of World Trade

The travels of Vasco da Gama and Ferdinand Magellan heralded the beginning of a continuous and lasting maritime connection among the earth's large landmasses. While Columbus's voyages initiated the Atlantic economy, the founding of Manila in 1571 was the origin of the Pacific world trade. During its first two centuries, this emergent global economy practically ignored the Pacific archipelagos and, to a large extent, Australia, with the exception of those peoples on its northern shores who interacted with Southeast Asia.[1] However, global trade truly emerged when all of the large, populated continents of the globe began to exchange products without interruption and in values sufficient to fundamentally influence all of the involved trading partners. In the words of Sanjay Subrahmanyam, "One can from the late sixteenth century speak of a commercial nexus that truly girdled the globe. This nexus was to become stronger, and commerce more intense in later centuries but the fundamental links had been established by 1600."[2]

This world trade was essentially dependent on the silver that was mined in the viceroyalties of Mexico and Peru in the Spanish Empire and to a lesser extent in Japan. Eminent economists had been aware of the white metal's fundamental role in mercantile transactions. Adam Smith, in *The Wealth of Nations* (1776), explains, "The silver of Peru finds its way, not only to Europe, but from Europe to China." Furthermore, he observes, "The silver of the new continent seems in this manner to be one of the principal commodities by which the commerce between the extremities of the old one is carried

29

on, and it is by means of it, in great measure, that those distant parts of the world are connected with one another."[3] John Maynard Keynes, in A *Treatise on Money* (1930), points out the crucial relevance of American bullion, particularly in the history of England and the world: "In the case of England, a large part of the imports of bullion were due to Drake's capture of Spanish treasure ships and many similar exploits by others. These expeditions were financed by syndicates and companies and represented business speculations, the success and fruits of which supplied a stimulus to enterprise of all kinds."[4]

Francis Drake's circumnavigation (1577–1580) resulted—in addition to the accumulation of geographic knowledge—in a handsome loot of thirteen chests carrying pieces of eight, eighty pounds of gold, and twenty-six tons of uncoined silver. Investors in Sir Francis's venture received a return on their money of 4,700 percent.[5] Keynes points out the consequences:

> Indeed the booty brought back by Drake in the *Golden Hind* may fairly be considered the fountain and origin of British Foreign Investment. Elizabeth paid off out of the proceeds the whole of her foreign debt and invested a part of the balance (about £42,000) in the Levant Company; largely out of the profits of the Levant Company there was formed the East India Company, the profits of which during the seventeenth and eighteenth centuries were the main foundation of England's foreign connections.[6]

The immense returns on these opportunities were only possible because previously unheard-of amounts of silver allowed Europeans to participate in the network of these recently inaugurated global markets. In Asia, goods from Europe generated little demand, bullion alone being sought by local merchants. Nonetheless, this incipient globalization was not an improvement for all concerned. Smith melancholically reflected, "To the natives, however, both of the East and West Indies, all the commercial benefits which can have resulted from those events have been sunk and lost in the dreadful misfortunes which they have occasioned."[7]

The political entity that realized the largest rewards from the silver industry was the Spanish Crown. The king of Spain reigned over the richest silver mine in history: the Cerro de Potosí. As early as 1602, Jesuit Matteo Ricci's world map, printed with legends in Chinese, already shows the Potosí Mountain on the American continent. The mine was located more than 15,000 feet above sea level in the Andes in the Viceroyalty of Peru (present-day Bolivia). The *cerro* accounted for 60 percent of the world's silver production in the sixteenth and seventeenth centuries, despite its decline after the 1640s.[8] Its deposits were extremely rich, and a new extraction technology—the mercury-amalgam "patio process"—made the Spanish American mines in Peru and Mexico the lowest-cost sources of silver in the world.[9] In addition to jurisdiction over America's silver mines, the Spanish kings enjoyed privileged control over mercury. Rich cinnabar deposits, like Huancavelica (Peru) and Almadén (Spain)—the largest producer of quicksilver in the world—supplied the American miners' needs. During the sixteenth century and until 1645, the Fugger family of Augsburg bankers administered Almadén in return for loans to the Spanish Habsburgs. On occasion, the mine of Idrija (Slovenia), located in Habsburg territory, also exported mercury to America.

To make sense of imperial Spain and its interest in Pacific trade, it is necessary to disentangle the country's economic resources, the monarch's seat of power, and the Spanish Empire as a whole. Spain was a small country of perhaps 7.5 million people by the middle of the sixteenth century, about half the population of France. Its trade, quite different from that in Western European states like France, England, and the Netherlands, consisted of exporting raw materials and importing manufactured and luxury products. Early modern Spain "was a backward country with poor resources, dependent on external markets and external supplies."[10] American silver provided the fiscal foundation to finance Spain's continuous hostilities against its enemies. A Spanish friar writing in 1630 clearly saw the role of mining for Spain: "Potosí lives in order to serve the imposing aspirations of Spain: it serves to chastise the Turk, humble the Moor, make Flanders tremble and terrify England."[11] In 1664 Thomas Mun, an English writer on economic issues, observed about American mines, "which are in the possession of the King of Spain: who thereby is enabled not only to keep in subjection many goodly States and Provinces in Italy and elsewhere (which otherwise would soon fall from his obeisance)." He concluded that the king was "ambitiously aiming at a Monarchy by the power of his Moneys, which are the very sinews of his strength."[12]

Between 1500 and 1800, according to calculations, Latin America produced 150,000 tons of silver. The Japanese provinces of Kai, Idzu, Iwami, and Sado Island had the second-most productive silver mines. Their output amounted to about 30 percent of the total silver mined in the sixteenth century and about 16 percent of the total mined in the seventeenth century.[13] For the Portuguese, Japan was the *Ilhas Argentarias*, or *Ilhas Platerias* (Silver Islands), and Luis de Camões wrote in his epic poem *Lusiadas* of "*Japao, onde nace a prata fina*," ("Japan, where the fine silver is born").[14] By approximately 1570, the differing ratio of gold to silver between China and Japan rendered it profitable to send silver for the purchase of Chinese gold. Alessandro Valignano, the "Visitor" or overseer of all of the Jesuit missions in Asia, explained in 1592 that "one of the major tribulations of the Jesuits in Japan was the importunity with which numerous *daimyo* (feudal lords) besought them to act as bullion brokers in this business."[15] Japan's silver in the modern era played an important role in Asian economic and political developments. The unifiers of Japan, Oda Nobunaga (1534–1582), Toyotomi Hideyoshi (1536–1598), and Ieyasu Tokugawa (1543–1616), financed their military campaigns against rival feudal lords with silver mines' profits; these earnings also paid for Hideyoshi's invasion of Korea and the consolidation of the Tokugawa shogunate.

Large quantities of bullion entering the global market were the key impetus to world trade. Meanwhile, from about 1520 a period of inflation called the "price revolution" surged worldwide. In Europe, prices increased an average of five times for foodstuffs and perhaps threefold for manufactured products.[16] The price rise was a reflection, in part, of the quintupling of silver production in central Europe between 1460 and 1530, but Japanese production and the influx of bullion after 1545, especially American silver, contributed mightily to a worldwide inflation trend. If the people's standard of living and the fiscal health of states suffered due to price increases, there were winners as well; in the words of Keynes, "Never in the annals of the modern world has there existed so prolonged and so rich an opportunity for the business man, the speculator and the profiteer."[17]

Atlantic Silver in the Sixteenth and Seventeenth Centuries

The Manila galleons traveled one of a number of routes connecting American mines with Asian markets. The galleon trade's economic course makes sense only when viewed within the network of transoceanic routes traversed by the white metal.

By law, all trade with America was centralized in Seville, a southern Spanish city on the banks of the Guadalquivir River, to facilitate tax collection. It was the site for the House of Trade, or *Casa de Contratación*; in the words of Clarence H. Haring, it was "a department of the government, a ministry of commerce, a school of navigation and a clearing house for colonial trade."[18] The institution collected all colonial taxes and duties, approved voyages of exploration and trade, kept information on trade routes, and licensed captains and pilots. After 1680, trade operations moved to Cádiz, a city with better port facilities located on the Atlantic coast, and by 1717, the new Bourbon dynasty had officially moved the "House" there.

Since 1503, Spanish authorities had regulated exchanges with America following a monopolistic model. Trade with overseas possessions was conducted under the supervision of a merchants' guild or *Consulado de mercaderes* founded in Seville in 1543; it worked in conjunction with the House and

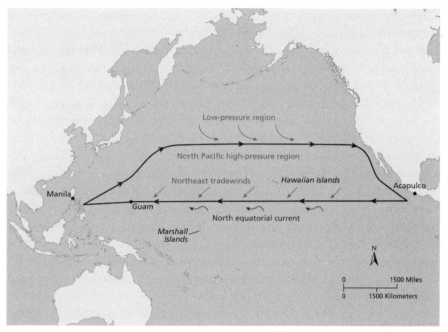

The Manila Galleons' Route

had close relationships with the Consulados of Mexico City and Lima, both established toward the end of the sixteenth century. These institutions represented merchants' interests and acted as courts of law. The Consulado was only established in Manila in 1769; before then, all important matters pertaining to the galleon's business were decided in the *cabildo*, an assembly of citizen-merchants—"city and commerce." Small business disputes were taken care of in Manila by lower tribunals, while large lawsuits were the purview of the High Court of the Philippines. The *Consejo de Indias* (Council of the Indies) presided over all colonial institutions in both America and Asia and ruled on all matters pertaining to administration, legal dispositions, and church business.

Domestic and foreign merchandise destined for the Americas accumulated in Seville while waiting for transport; in return, the city received goods produced in America, like dyes, pearls, sugar, and—the most coveted of all—bullion. The regulations of 1564 mandated the annual dispatch of two fleets protected by armed galleons. The first, called the *flota* (fleet), sailed to New Spain and other Caribbean destinations, and the second, with the name of *galeones* (galleons), sailed for Tierra Firme, Cartagena de Indias, on the Caribbean coast of today's Colombia and other ports of northern South America. The galeones would meet merchants coming from the Viceroyalty of Peru at Nombre de Dios or Portobelo in today's Panama. Merchants from the viceroyalties went to the fairs of Veracruz, Cartagena de Indias, and Nombre de Dios (after 1593, Portobelo) to buy the imported merchandise. The *Armada del Sur* (Fleet of the South) carried the goods that had crossed the Panama Isthmus to the port of El Callao near Lima in Peru. On the return voyage, both fleets met in Havana and departed together for Seville.

The fact that, legally, Seville was the central location for exchanges with America did not imply that Spaniards controlled the transatlantic trade. During the seventeenth century, more than 90 percent of the fleets' capital and profits belonged to French, Genoese, English, Dutch, and German shipping interests. Mun noted in his 1664 tract that the Spaniards had lost their hegemonic position in the American market: "But now this great profit is failed, and the mischief removed by the English, Dutch, and others which partake in those East-India trades as ample as the Spanish Subjects."[19] In addition, goods smuggled by Europeans other than the Spaniards fulfilled about two-thirds of the American demand, according to records from 1686.[20] Silver from the viceroyalties reached Europe through official and unofficial channels. Pyrard observed in the first decade of the seventeenth centuries that the Portuguese sold slaves at the Plata River, "where they obtain much silver."[21] European manufactures laded in Portugal were transported to Brazil and distributed in the Viceroyalty of Peru. Agents from Peruvian merchants were present in Brazil and Seville. New Christians of Portuguese origin arrived in Lima after 1636. This network of trade was called the "back door" of the Viceroyalty of Peru.

An understanding of the fleet system and its economic underpinnings is necessary if one is to understand, as well, why merchants in Seville opposed the Manila galleon. Silver that left from Acapulco was outside the purview of officials and investors in Seville, and textiles arriving from the Philippines were in direct competition with European manufactures. Meanwhile, merchants in Peru and Mexico considered themselves fortunate to have investment venues and sources of supply outside the control of Atlantic interests. Also relevant is that in moments of special penury during the sixteenth and seventeenth centuries, private silver arriving in Seville was in danger of being confiscated by royal officials in exchange for state bonds, *juros*; Acapulco was safe from such risks.

China and the Global Market in the Sixteenth and Seventeenth Centuries

On the supply side were the mines of Mexico, the Viceroyalty of Peru, and Japan; on the demand side, the Chinese market exercised the most powerful pull. In China, by the eleventh century, officially recognized merchant houses issued large quantities of notes, and by the twelfth century its use spread to the rest of the country. The late Yuan and early Ming emperors resorted to printing notes in large quantities to finance military campaigns. Trade required a medium of exchange to replace the devalued notes, and silver became the bullion of choice. Gold was too valuable and impractical for everyday use, while copper coinage was problematic. Silver could be assayed for purity, but testing copper coins would have required melting them, while their variations in weight and metallic content further complicated pricing. By default, silver became the favored monetary substance. Despite their determined efforts, the Ming emperors (1368–1644) were unable to reestablish the use of paper money as currency, and to no avail the imperial administration repeatedly attempted to interrupt the arrival of silver from the coast. Soon, local governments in maritime regions began collecting taxes in silver. Mark Elvin observes, "Partly as a consequence of popular pressure and partly because specie was cheaper to transport and store than grain, permission was given in 1436 for part of the land tax to be paid in silver; and by 1500 the practice had become widespread."[22] During the 1450s, the government began to pay officers' salaries in silver, and copper coins were used for small transactions. Gradually, imperial authorities accepted the precious metal's predominance; around 1570, the emperor implemented a critical change in economic policy by establishing the "Single Whip" tax system, consolidating a diverse array of levies into a single sum, paid in silver. This tax consolidation took centuries to be fully implemented— there were always exceptions. Nonetheless, everyone from merchants and landowners to poor peasants participated in the empire's commercial network because the tax system required payment in silver. From the sixteenth century onward, China was able to economically interact beyond the old pan-Asian circuits via trading partners such as the Portuguese, the Spanish, the Dutch, and later the British. Europe and the Americas were well within the range of Chinese economic influence.[23]

China developed its commercial and diplomatic relations under the umbrella of the "tributary system." Tribute missions to China were costly and lavish undertakings organized by political entities to pay homage to the emperor in Beijing. The arrival of these envoys was an occasion for gift exchanges and for the bestowing of titles. Meanwhile, business deals often took place alongside diplomatic formalities. Such arrivals were irregular and not a source of governmental revenues; the gifts given by the Chinese were more luxurious than the presents brought by foreigners. The reality was that the tributary system represented a vast network of economic exchanges with

China as the dominant partner. In the words of Takeshi Hamashita, "This system, encompassing East and Southeast Asia, was articulated with neighboring trade zones like those of India, the Islamic region and Europe."[24] The adoption of silver bullion by China and its neighboring countries as their main monetary substance had global consequences. In 1500, the population of Asia—where Asia is defined as the continent situated east of Egypt and limited by the Ural Mountains, the Caucasus Mountains, and the Caspian and Black Seas, located east of the Pacific Ocean, north of the Indian Ocean, and south of the Arctic Ocean—could be estimated to be between 200 and 225 million; by 1650, numbers reached around 300 million, in a world of approximately 500 million people. A century later in 1750, Asians constituted perhaps 60 percent of a global population of 700 million.[25] Within Asia's landmass, in the words of F. W. Mote, China "has always been the largest bloc of the human race, its population larger than that of any other ethnically, culturally, or politically defined unit in world history."[26] There were 155 million Chinese in 1500, 231 million in 1600, and 268 million in 1650.[27] During the late Ming dynasty, cities like Nanjing had over one million inhabitants, while Beijing followed closely with 660,000. When such a large percentage of the world's economy is committed to purchasing a particular commodity, especially one that is highly valued and relatively easy to transport between continents, that industry's impact is certain to be global.

European arrival on the Chinese coast occurred at a time when the Ming Empire was declining as an oceanic power. Factors partially explaining the abandonment of an imperial maritime policy included Mongol pressure in the north, the capital's 1421 relocation from Nanking to Beijing, Vietnamese resistance to Chinese occupation between 1406 and 1427, and Confucian officials' relentless opposition to Cheng Ho's costly maritime expeditions. However, there was another important reason: the remodeling in 1411 of the Grand Canal—1,705 kilometers from Hangchow to Peking and still active today—fitted it for transport during all seasons, rendering sea-based grain convoys superfluous. The shipbuilding capacity of littoral China was redirected to inland water transport. During the following centuries, maritime initiatives were in the hands of Chinese coastal peoples.

China was a manufacturing power without comparison in the world. Its population was able to produce enormous quantities of goods for export at very low prices, like gold, silk, cotton, and items carried as "ballast" by junks, including millions of porcelain pieces. In 1630, Fujian-born He Qiaoyuan remarked that silver acquired through foreign trade resulted in massive exports, thereby ensuring "employment for weavers, potters, and merchants, whose waxing affluence augured higher standards of living for all."[28] The Ming kilns at the southern town of Jingdezhen employed more than ten thousand workers. Using kaolin, clay from the area, and firing at temperatures higher than 1,300 degrees, they mass-produced the blue and white porcelain that would become an enduring symbol of Chinese craftsmanship. In the 1540s, the Lisbon elite were drinking tea from Ming porcelain services and placing special orders for porcelain with Portuguese decorations. By 1614, blue and white Ming pottery was in daily use by the common citizens of Amsterdam, as depicted in Dutch still-life paintings. Shards of Ming porcelain appeared on the shores of Lake Titicaca in the Andes at about fifteen thousand feet of altitude, indicating that Chinese porcelain was commonly used in Peru.[29] The Jesuit Xavier d'Entrecolles, who figured out the Chinese technique of porcelain manufacturing, estimated in the first half of the eighteenth century that the great pottery center of Ching-te Chen, a town near Nanjing of nearly one million people, possessed around three thousand kilns.[30]

Dutch East India Company ceramics exports are an example of the immense capacity of China's manufacturing. During the fifty-five years between 1602 and 1657, the company brought to Europe more than three million pieces of Chinese pottery, in addition to several million pieces transshipped at Batavia for reexport to Southeast Asia, India, and Persia. From 1729 to 1734, another 4.5 million items were imported, and finally the Dutch exported 42.5 million pieces between 1730 and 1789.[31]

Safavid Persia was the main source of silk for Europe during the sixteenth and seventeenth centuries, while Chinese exports of silk dominated Japanese trade (carried between Macao and Nagasaki) and the Manila galleons' cargo. Antonio Bocarro, an official Portuguese chronicler, estimated that China produced almost 2,500 tons of silk per year in the early seventeenth century, one-third of which (about 800 tons) was destined for markets abroad. Taking as an example the Manila market, a galleon in the 1630s would transport between 31.3 and 52.2 metric tons to Acapulco, and from the early eighteenth century, each galleon would carry back between 200 and 700 tons of raw silk to supply the silk processing industry of New Spain.[32] This textile remained a fundamental commodity in global commerce well into the eighteenth century.

The Discovery of the Sea: Iberians and Spices

During the two centuries after 1492, European navigators realized that all seas formed a single body of water. Maritime expeditions had visited most of the regions fit for human habitation and had established enclaves in territories where economic opportunity was assured and where local people offered little opposition.[33] The Iberians, followed by the Dutch and British, organized a series of expeditions in pursuit of the highest commercial returns, which were initially guaranteed only by trading in those spices that were, at the time, highly concentrated in tropical Asia.

The term "Spice Islands" encompasses the small Molucca and Banda archipelagos located in what is now Indonesia. Until the last decades of the eighteenth century, these islands were the only places in the world in which cloves and nutmeg grew. Exports of such commodities took off after 1470, coinciding with the emergence of Malacca (in Malaysia) as an entrepôt. The best cinnamon grew in Ceylon, and pepper came from Kerala on the Malabar Coast of India, but in the sixteenth century its cultivation expanded to other parts of the subcontinent and Indonesia. Pepper's price was only a fraction of the cost of nutmeg and cloves, but in terms of quantity, pepper ranked as the most important export of Southeast Asia.[34]

Depending on the monsoons, merchants often stayed in port cities, where they collected goods for their return trip and waited for the winds to change. Spices from the Moluccas arrived in Malacca, where the Chinese bought their share, and Muslim merchants—the larger number came from Gujarat in India—controlled the trade's western route. These goods went from Calicut to the markets of northern India, where vessels delivered their cargo and set sail once more from Aden in the Red Sea and Hormuz in the Persian Gulf. From there, these commodities traveled to Middle East ports in the Mediterranean to be collected by Venetian merchants who distributed spices in European markets. Changes in the Indian Ocean's trade networks were initiated upon the arrival of the Portuguese and intensified as the Spanish, Dutch, and English followed. Armed vessels featured prominently in these preexisting economic relations. Gun-carrying ships allowed Atlantic powers to "[break] down the bottleneck inherent in the use of human energy and [harness], to their advantage, far larger quantities of power. It was then that European sails appeared aggressively on the most distant seas."[35]

The Military Revolution and the 35 Percent of the World

Until 1800, European powers were able to control approximately 35 percent of the world as a result of changes in warfare initiated in the fifteenth century.[36] The products of this process of change, known overall as the "military revolution," "consisted of hardware of ships, cannons, muskets, gunpowder, and fortifications and software of drill, military engineering, logistical-bureaucratic apparatus, and financial systems."[37] The expenditures for such military apparatus required an ample tax base to finance armies and fleets, which in turn concentrated power in the hands of monarchs and made possible the consolidation and emergence of political entities. All states, including Ming China, Mughal India (founded in 1526), Muscovite Russia (1480), the Ottoman (1453), and Safavid Persia under Shah Abbas (1587–1629), employed guns of different sorts. New military technology was also behind the emergence of centralized kingdoms in Siam and Vietnam. The seventeenth century brought a drive toward building absolutist states, competing for trade and resources; examples include those ruled by Kings Prasat Thong and Narai in Siam (1629–1688), Iskandar Muda in Aceh (1607–1636), Ageng in Banten (1651–1680), Hasanuddin in Makassar (1635–1669), and Agung in Mataram, Java (1613–1646).[38] Carlo M. Cipolla points out that there was a crucial difference between these powers and those coming from Europe: "Western guns were always much superior to any non-European product and their superiority was universally recognized."[39]

Europeans were unable to defeat land-based Asian powers until the eighteenth century—when the British prevailed in the Battle of Plassey (1757) in Bengal and later in the Opium War (1839–1842)—or compel the Tokugawa to "open" Japan's ports in 1852. The Portuguese, Spanish, Dutch, and British resided on islands outside the control of land-based states or in coastal areas where local rulers tolerated them as intermediaries who connected their territories with far-flung trade networks.

The Spaniards' plans to expand further into Asia beyond the Philippines fell short in practice. However, the military technology that came with the galleons served them very well in their wars with European adversaries in Asian waters and in their subjugation of native populations. Manila was surrounded by walls and forts of European military architectural design, while its position relative to the Pasig River and the bay gave it an even greater strategic advantage. Father Antonio Sedeño, a Jesuit who had been a staff officer under the Duke of Feria, recommended the building of defensive works and the establishment of a regular army garrison. Philip II insisted to the viceroy that contingents recruited in Mexico for service in the Philippines should be competent soldiers, at least fifteen years of age, and provided with adequate equipment, implying that the troops already present in the islands were of inferior quality.

Governor Santiago de Vera (1584–1589), following Sedeño's advice, decided to begin fortifying Manila. The work was continued under Gómez Pérez Dasmariñas (1590–1593), who ordered the construction of a defensive wall surrounding the city. Governors during the Eighty Years' War (1568–1648) with the Netherlands invested large sums in fortifications and in restoring walls that had been damaged by the forces of nature. For instance,

Diego Fajardo (1644–1653) strengthened the land-facing side of Manila's fortifications at the cost of 300,000 pesos; authorities also erected a fort with forty cannons to protect the port of Cavite and built strongholds in Spanish outposts like Ternate in the Moluccas, Taiwan, and northern Mindanao.[40]

Spaniards taught military drills to their Filipino allies and commanded native troops in order to steel their resolve and keep discipline. While Spanish soldiers and officers usually held the positions in command, the inhabitants of the Pampanga province were exceptions. Pampango soldiers were garrisoned outside Luzon and in the Moluccas and usually served under officers from their own province.[41]

Obviously, guns and military organization helped the Spaniards deal with the more than one hundred uprisings and revolts that arose during colonial times, but until the conclusion of the Spanish regime in 1898, native upheavals ended disastrously. A Filipino historian attributes these defeats to the animosities among different native groups. "Thus the Pampangans aided the Spaniards in putting down the Tagalog uprising, and when the Pampangans themselves rose in rebellion, the Tagalogs retaliated by helping the Spaniards."[42]

Adam Smith and David Ricardo considered commerce a civilizing activity for all parties involved, in which partners in trade could accrue a net profit without predatory violence. Kirti N. Chaudhuri presents a contrasting view, noting that when Europeans arrived on Asian shores, they rapidly realized "that the profits from armed trading were higher than in the case of peaceful commerce."[43] Governor General Jan Pieterszoon Coen's letter of 1614 to the directors of the Dutch East India Company (Vereenigde Oost-Indische Compagnie, or VOC) is particularly illustrative: "You gentlemen ought to know from experience that trade in Asia should be conducted and maintained under the protection and with the aid of your own weapons, and those weapons must be wielded with the profits gained by the trade. So trade cannot be maintained without war, nor war without trade." Thirty years later Antonio van Diemen answered the VOC's Delft Chamber, "We are taught by daily experience that the Company's trade in Asia cannot subsist without territorial conquests."[44] Along the same line of thought, Josiah Child wrote in 1686 that, in order to protect the British against the Dutch and gain autonomy from the Mughals, it was required "to make this Company a formidable Martial government."[45] As was true for the Portuguese and Spanish, success for the Dutch was independent of a rational organization or a sophisticated understanding of market forces; instead, large profits were dependent on a military-enforced monopoly.[46]

The Portuguese and the Vasco da Gama Era

Since the middle of the fifteenth century, the Portuguese had organized profitable expeditions to the African coast, and in 1488 a fleet commanded by Bartolomeu Dias entered the Indian Ocean after sailing around the Cape of Good Hope. The following step was to build a fleet to reach India. In charge of the expedition was Vasco da Gama, who sailed from Lisbon in 1497. The ruler of Malindi, on the African coast, was coerced to provide da Gama with a pilot to cross the Arabian Sea to India. The Portuguese fleet arrived in Calicut on May 20, 1498, completing the 9,500-mile voyage in ten months. When the newcomers reached the Malabar Coast, the Indians did not appreciate the merchandise offered by the newcomers; nonetheless, the Portuguese were able to collect a quantity of pepper and other spices despite da Gama's refusal to pay the required custom duties.

The three Portuguese ships had sternpost rudders, three masts, rigging, square sails, and cannons onboard. Sturdy Portuguese carracks and galleons contrasted sharply with the relatively frail crafts employed in the Indian Ocean. According to Gaspar Corrêa in his *Legends of India*, written before 1563, these Indian vessels (*dhows*) had no cannons, and the hull planks were sewn together with coir.[47] The newcomers were the first to employ the naval developments of the military revolution on the Indian Ocean, and to their great satisfaction, Portuguese artillery was found capable of sinking unarmed ships and bombarding cities with deadly results. Arriving in Calicut, da Gama sent a convict ashore—condemned people were employed in dangerous missions—"and he was taken to a place where there were two Moors from Tunis, who knew how to speak Castilian and Genoese. . . . And they asked him what he had come to seek so far; and he replied: We came to seek Christians and spices."[48] Vasco da Gama's voyage inaugurated an era of European oceanic hegemony in Asian waters that lasted until the end of the nineteenth century, when the United States and Japan emerged as maritime powers. Control of sea-lanes in Asia was dependent upon the previous Atlantic economy: "Sea power, capable of deciding Oceanic policies, did not exist outside the Atlantic. The control of the Atlantic thus meant the mastery of the Indian Ocean and ultimately of the Pacific."[49]

Until the second half of the eighteenth century, with the exceptions of the Spanish in Luzon and the Dutch in Java, Europeans were strong only at sea and in attacks on coastal targets. "Agriculturally based inland states had little to fear from them; but the point about the age of commerce was that its centers of growth were accessible by sea,"[50] and the Portuguese, in order to tap into these economies, soon established a chain of trading outposts from Africa to Macao.

Da Gama's venture was followed in 1500 by the pivotal expedition of Pedro Alvares Cabral. Cabral sailed with 1,500 men in thirty-three ships armed with powerful artillery. After claiming Brazil for the Crown, Cabral arrived in Calicut, and with the acquiescence of the local ruler—the Zamorin—a factory, or trading post, was established. Relations between the Muslim merchant community and the newcomers were tense, and under the pretext that the king of Portugal was lord of sea and land, the Portuguese captured a number of ships. Enraged local merchants killed factory founder Aires Correia, as well as other Portuguese, and took their property. The sixteenth-century historian João de Barros wrote that in reprisal Cabral burned ships and bombarded Calicut, killing five hundred.[51]

In 1502, Manuel I decided to send another fleet "of great and strong ships which could stow much cargo, and which, if they returned in safety, would bring him untold riches."[52] In addition to ten large ships, Vasco da Gama added five caravels "because he hoped to make war with them, and he had the necessary artillery put into them."[53] Arriving in Calicut, da Gama took as prisoner a Brahman, sent as an ambassador by the Zamorin, and ordered the fleet to get close to the shore. "All day, till night, he bombarded the city by which he made a great destruction."[54] Meanwhile, two large ships and twenty-two small boats with rice, sailing from the Coromandel Coast, approached the port. The ships were plundered and, according to Gaspar Corrêa:

> Then the captain-major commanded them to cut off the hands and ears and noses of all the crews, and put all into one of the small vessels, into which he ordered them to put the friar, also without ears, or nose, or hands, which he ordered strung round his neck, with a palm leave for the King, on which he told him to have a curry made to eat of what his friar [the Brahman] brought him. When all the Indians had been thus executed, he ordered their feet to be tied together, as they had no hands with which to untie them: and in order that they should not untie them with their teeth, he ordered them to strike upon their teeth with staves, and they knocked them down their throats.[55]

Da Gama's sailors put the victims in a boat that was covered with mats and dried leaves and set on fire. On another occasion, "they hung up some men by the feet in the vessels which were sent ashore, and when thus hung up the captain-major ordered the cross-bow men to shoot arrows into them."[56] These were not isolated events; Portuguese historical sources collected numerous incidents of sadistic cruelty perpetrated by their navigators.[57]

The Portuguese built factories and signed treaties with local powers to guarantee a steady supply of spices at a fixed price. They required ships in the Indian Ocean to trade only if they bought a *cartaz* (license) and paid customs at Goa, Hormuz, or Malacca. The recipient could not have any dealings with Muslim competitors and was expected not to engage in unauthorized spice trading.[58] Custom revenues and sale of cartazes generated larger profits than trade with Europe by the end of the sixteenth century. "The model set up by the Portuguese admirably suited the purpose of the Dutch and English East India Companies," which, in turn, eagerly established similar institutions.[59]

From 1500 to 1530—the decades Reid calls "the period of disruption"[60]—Portugal replaced Syria, Egypt, and Venice as the main participant in the spice market. From Lisbon, carracks delivered cargoes of spices at Antwerp, a port and powerful financial center in the Low Countries. To strengthen his settlements in Asia, the king sent fleet after fleet from Lisbon. "To this system of continuous reinforcements, worked out by Dom Manuel with the assistance of Antwerp capital, must be attributed the success that attended the navies of Portugal on the Eastern seas."[61]

The Portuguese consolidated their enterprise when Afonso de Albuquerque conquered Goa in 1510 and made it the Portuguese administrative center in Asian lands. In 1511 he occupied Malacca, in what is now Indonesia. The city was a distribution center of spices and a port of call for the vessels navigating the circuit of winds in Java, the Indian Ocean, and the South China Seas. By the early sixteenth century, it was a port of call as well for Indian ships and Chinese junks, and contact with Japan, in particular the Ryukyu Islands, had been initiated. Tomé Pires in his *Suma Oriental* wrote, "No trading ports as large as Malacca are known, nor anywhere they deal in such a fine and highly prized merchandise. Goods from all over the East are found here; goods from all over the West are sold here. It is at the end of the monsoons."[62] Later, Spanish, Dutch, and English ships opened up a new route, by way of the Sunda Strait, that challenged Malacca's privileged position. In 1515, the capture of Hormuz secured Portuguese control of the Persian Gulf; Macao was founded on the coast of China in 1557, and Nagasaki in Japan received the Portuguese around 1570. The violent methods practiced by Portuguese navigators in the Indian Ocean failed in the China Sea. After being defeated by Chinese coastal fleets, the Portuguese accepted the terms of trade dictated by Ming authorities, and they never tried to confront the Japanese. All the Portuguese enclaves in Africa, the Middle East, and Asia received the name *Estado da India*.

By 1515, an official Portuguese fleet had already visited the Molucca Islands, where the rajahs of two islands, Ternate and Tidore, carried on a prolonged rivalry competing for the clove trade's revenue. In years to come, the Portuguese and Spanish became involved in the conflict.

The most valuable products brought by the carracks to Lisbon were spices. Vitorino Magalhaes Godinho observed that in 1515, the spice trade's profits were equivalent to all of the kingdom's ecclesiastical revenues and double the value earned by the trade in precious metals.[63] At that time, "from just over one *cruzado* paid for a *bahar* of cloves in the Moluccas," the price "had risen to 700 *cruzados* by the time it reached Lisbon." A *bahar* was about 600 pounds.[64] Such immense revenues explain why Europeans engaged in distance trade during the modern era despite all risks involved.

Ferdinand Magellan

Vasco da Gama's success did not receive uniform approval. Cristóbal de Haro, the Fuggers' representative in Lisbon, was quite upset about the treatment he had received from the Portuguese Court and moved to Seville when Charles I, then a seventeen-year-old adolescent, became king of Spain. In Seville, de Haro was in contact with Juan Rodríguez de Fonseca, bishop of Burgos and president of the Council of the Indies, the institution in charge of Spain's colonial empire. The Fuggers' agent had gathered information about maritime routes in Portugal and resolutely urged the Spanish to send an expedition following a course across the Atlantic. From his grandfather Maximilian, Emperor of the Holy Roman Empire, the new king of Spain had inherited millions in debt to the Fugger bankers. In addition, the American continent had not managed to yield, in the first decades of the sixteenth century, any commodities comparable to the spice trade in their economic benefits, and the Spanish Crown was eager to reach the source of cloves and nutmeg. "It was not Charles who made the decision to sign a commercial contract with Magellan, but a German banker by the name of Jacob Fugger."[65] Ferdinand Magellan received the charge to organize an expedition to the distant islands, and Charles I, with 10,000 ducats borrowed from the Fuggers, was the largest investor on the voyage.[66]

Magellan was a native of Portugal who, in 1505, went to India with the fleet of the first viceroy, Francisco de Almeida. During his eight years in Asia, he participated in the capture of Malacca with the army of Afonso de Albuquerque. Antonio Pigafetta—the expedition's chronicler—recounts that Francisco Serrão of Portugal, sailing in the service of the king of Ternate, corresponded with Magellan when he was in Malacca. "Therefore, when Don Manuel, King of Portugal, refused to increase his pension by a single toston per month, an increase which he thought he had well deserved, he came to Spain."[67] In 1517, he was in Seville.

Recruiting the crew proved quite difficult. About forty Portuguese joined a cosmopolitan group of Spanish, Italian, French, Flemish, German, Irish, and other sailors of diverse origins, including an English master gunner under the Spanish name Andrés Lombardero.[68] There were two interpreters—Jorge, a speaker of Arabic and Persian, and Enrique the Malay, who had been purchased in Malacca—as well as a small number of Africans among the 237 crew members. Seville in the sixteenth century was a thriving slave mart.

On September 20, 1519, the five small caravels sailed from San Lucar de Barrameda at the mouth of the Guadalquivir River, crossed the Atlantic, and began their eventful navigation down the coast of South America. There was a mutiny and a court-martial for sodomy. The defendants were the *Victoria*'s master, Antonio Salomón from Sicily, and a Genoese apprentice, Antonio Varesa. Magellan ordered Salomon's execution, and Varesa perished when he was thrown into the sea. Burning at the stake had been the penalty for these activities since medieval times. On Dutch ships, culprits were bound together and thrown overboard.[69]

A stop in Rio de Janeiro in Brazil interrupted Magellan's arduous voyage. Samuel E. Morison mentions a revealing incident witnessed in hiding by Magellan and Pigafetta. It seems that a native Brazilian girl entered the master's empty cabin and saw an iron nail. "With great skill and gallantry, she thrust it between the lips of her vagina."[70] The anecdote indicates the lengths to which native people, like the islanders that the Spaniards were going to meet in their Pacific navigation, would go to obtain iron.

Magellan finally encountered the strait that would bear his name and sailed out of the passage around November 1520. The sailors gave the name of "Pacific" to the body of water, "for during this period we met with no storm."[71] Despite the calm, the small fleet proceeded in harrowing conditions. Antonio Pigafetta described the fearful "three months and twenty days" it took them to cross the ocean in these terms:

> We only ate old biscuit reduced to powder, full of grubs and stinking from the dirt, which the rats had made on it when eating the good biscuit and we drank water that was yellow and stinking. We also ate the ox hides which were under the main-yard, so that the yard should not break the rigging: they were very hard on account of the sun, rain, and wind, and we left them for four or five days in the sea, and then we put them a little on the embers, and so ate them; also the sawdust of wood, and rats which cost half-a-crown each, moreover enough of them were not to be got.[72]

They suffered terribly from scurvy. "The upper and lower gums of most of our men grew so much that they could not eat."[73]

Magellan hoped to get supplies from an island that they encountered, but the natives "entered into the ships and robbed us, in such a way that it was impossible to preserve one from them."[74] In addition to their onboard pilfering, they took the smaller boat that was fastened to the flagship, the *Trinidad*. As a reprisal, Magellan "went on shore with forty armed men, burned forty or fifty houses, with several small boats, and killed seven men of the island; they recovered their skiff."[75] The natives were considered "great thieves, and for the sake of that we called these three islands the Ladrones Islands."[76] These "Islands of Thieves" formed part of the southern Mariana Islands. The name changed when, in 1668, the Jesuit Diego Luis Sanvictores landed in Guam, and the queen regent Mariana, mother of Charles II, endowed the mission with 3,000 pesos annually.

After entering the Philippine archipelago through the Suriago Strait, Magellan's ships landed on the island of Limasawa, where Enrique the Malay communicated with the natives. Morison observes, "West had met east at last by circling the globe. Enrique may have been the first man to do it."[77] Magellan named the Philippines *Islas de San Lázaro* after the saint's day on which the landing took place. Soon some boats from southern Samar in the Visayan archipelago appeared carrying fish, coconuts, and a kind of liquor called *arrack*. "The alacrity with which its inhabitants initiated trade with unknown foreigners reflected a common feature of Visayan life—all communities exchanged foodstuffs."[78]

When the Spanish reached the island of Cebu, the rajah demanded that the newcomers pay "tribute," citing a case from four days prior when "a ship called the Junk of Ciama (Siam), laden with gold and slaves had paid him his tribute."[79] To prove his point, he introduced to Magellan a merchant from Siam who had remained behind to sell gold and slaves. The merchant, taking the new arrivals for Portuguese, immediately explained to the rajah the advantages of allying himself with such powerful visitors. Enrique the interpreter corrected the misinformation with the claim that the king of Spain was much more powerful than the king of Portugal, who had been so highly praised by the merchant. Magellan signed a treaty, and the rajah, his family, and his subjects converted to Christianity. When the queen and the accompanying servants received baptism, she asked for "the little wooden boy to put in the place of the idols."[80] The image was the future *Niño Jesús de Cebú*. Political treaties and religious conversions took place alongside commercial exchanges. Iron was paid for in gold: "For metal, iron, and other big goods they gave us gold. . . . They gave us ten weights of gold for fourteen pounds of iron: each weight is a ducat and a half."[81] As was the case with the girl in Rio de Janeiro and later events concerning thieves in the Marianas, the Cebu inhabitants' desire for iron reflected its scarcity in these lands; the metal was highly valued by societies that lacked it.

Instead of following his given instructions—"that first and foremost, before any other part, you should go to the said islands of Maluku"[82]—Magellan became entangled in local politics. To make a show of power, he joined an expedition of Cebuans who went to attack Lapulapu, the rajah of Mactan. The defenders had muskets and crossbows and put up a spirited defense. Magellan's ships' artillery could not reach their opponents, and on the retreat, the natives killed the captain general.[83] The remaining crew continued to Brunei, where they encountered a prosperous society presided over by a Muslim prince: "They venerate Mohamed and follow his law."[84] The newcomers were given lavish gifts. They proceeded majestically on elephants with a retinue of "twelve men, each of whom carried a porcelain vase covered with silk for conveying and wrapping up our presents."[85] The potentate's residence had a fort with artillery; inside the compound they encountered the captain general of the sultan of Brunei, who was the son of the king of Luzon in the Philippines. Pigafetta inquired about the abundant porcelain: "I learned that it is made with a kind of very white earth; it is said if poison is put into a vessel of fine porcelain it breaks immediately."[86]

After taking by force two pilots in Sarangani in the Philippines, the crew finally reached Tidore. "We were so much rejoiced since we had passed twenty-seven months less two days always in search of Maluku, wandering for that object among the immense number of islands."[87] They were hospitably received, and the king allowed the sale of spices to them—"we bought cloves like mad,"[88] commented Pigafetta—and the sultan declared himself a vassal of the Spanish king. The Spaniards collected such a quantity of spices that, when the chief of the nearby island of Bachan presented one slave and ten "bahars" of cloves to Charles I, they could take only two because "our ships were so heavily laden, that we could not receive any more."[89] On their departure they passed by the Banda Islands and reached Timor, where they noticed the presence of merchants from Malacca and Java, as well as junks from Luzon that came to buy sandalwood and wax.

All this wandering took its toll; only two vessels remained from the original five. One was the *Trinidad*, which had been recaptured by the Portuguese. The survivors ultimately arrived in Lisbon in 1524. The *Victoria*, under the command of Juan Sebastián Elcano, sailed across the Indian Ocean.

Eighteen Europeans and three East Indians arrived in Seville on September 6, 1522. The voyage had taken three years, and the costs in human terms were staggering. Of the five ships in the original fleet, only the *Victoria* reached Seville. Out of the 237 original members, only 37 sailors survived; the majority had died or remained as prisoners of the Portuguese in Ternate. From a financial perspective, the voyage was not a particular success. The weight of cloves brought by the *Victoria* "amounted to three hundred and eighty-one sacks, with a net weight of five hundred and twenty-four quintals, twenty-one and one-half libras," and the cargo also contained small amounts of other spices.[90] Nonetheless, the *Victoria*'s cargo defrayed the expenses of the entire expedition.

Juan Sebastián Elcano, the ship's pilot, received a fitting coat of arms. Its symbols were three nutmegs, two sticks of cinnamon, twelve cloves, and a globe, surrounded by the Latin legend *"Primus circumdedisti me"* ("You were the first to circumnavigate me"). On both sides stood two Malay kings, each holding a branch of a spice tree. Pigafetta proceeded to Valladolid in Castille, where he presented the king with "a book written by my hand of all the things that had occurred day by day in our voyage."[91] The expedition empirically proved that all of the world's oceans were interconnected, and the Spaniards had gathered invaluable geographical knowledge of maritime routes and ports of call. In the words of O. K. H. Spate, "No other single voyage has ever added so much to the dimension of the world."[92]

Among the news brought back to Spain buttressing Charles I's claim to the Spice Islands was the fact that the Portuguese periodically visited the Moluccas but had not effectively occupied them. Shortly after the news of the expedition had reached Europe in 1519, Charles I was elected and crowned emperor of the Holy Roman Empire. The main contributor to the election was Jacob Fugger.[93] Portugal received news of these developments with great alarm.

Spanish Expeditions to the Spice Islands

In 1479, Portugal and Spain had signed the Treaty of Alcaçovas-Toledo, which allowed the Portuguese to pursue their expansion along the African coast and recognized the Spaniards' conquest of the Canary Islands. They were the first European powers to sign an agreement that distributed the world outside of their territories without taking into consideration the peoples inhabiting the lands. Pope Alexander VI, a member of the Borgia Spanish family, solemnized the agreement by the bull *Aeterni Regis* in 1481. In 1494, the Treaty of Tordesillas, a small town in Castile, followed this initial accord. An imaginary line of longitude, located 370 leagues west of the Cape Verde Islands, divided the world between the Iberian powers. To Portugal corresponded all the territories east of the line, including Brazil, and Spain could occupy all the lands to the west. In 1524, the negotiations between Portuguese and Spanish representatives to determine the location of the Moluccas, according to previous treaties, brought no satisfactory results, and Charles I decided to continue the enterprise. In fact, as soon as de Haro had sent the cloves brought to Europe on the *Victoria* to Antwerp, he urged the Spanish king to send one more expedition. A Fugger consortium financed this second voyage to the amount of 10,000 gold ducats, and four other investors contributed 4,450 ducats.

In the summer of 1525 an armada of seven ships commanded by García Jofre de Loaísa (with his nephew Elcano as a pilot) departed Coruña, a city in northwestern Spain. According to the plans, Coruña was to be the future center for the spice trade—a *Casa de Contratación*. Among the crew was the accountant Andrés de Urdaneta and three of the four natives brought by Elcano's *Victoria*, who had been taken to Spain as a present from the sultan of Tidore. They did not survive the voyage. The fourth remained in Spain because he was highly inquisitive about price differentials between Europe and Asia. Fernando de Herrera, the royal historian, observed: "He was so sharp that the first thing he did was to inquire how many *reals* a ducat was worth, and a real how many *maravedis*, and how much pepper was given for a maravedi; and he went from shop to shop to get information of the value of spices."[94]

Before reaching the Strait of Magellan, two ships were lost in a shipwreck and one more was deserted. Another vessel went back to Mexico after crossing the Magellan strait due to a shortage of food. Loaísa died on July 30, 1526, and Elcano passed away five days later. The next commander of the expedition expired on the island of Guam on September 15. Only the *Santa María de la Victoria*, with a complement of eleven natives picked up in Guam to work the pumps, was able to reach Mindanao. There, a native reported that junks from China arrived annually to buy gold and pearls. The expedition tried to sail to Cebu, but the winds blew them back to the Moluccas, where the crew joined some survivors of the Magellan expedition. The rajah of Tidore and his court, all arrayed in magnificent clothes, invited them to a banquet: "Their richly decorated canopies, their resplendent attire in cloth of gold, their necks adorned with heavy gold chains, their smooth, glossy hair entwined with gold filigree, told of their trade."[95] The next day, after loyalty ceremonies, the Spaniards with help from the natives began to build earthworks on which to place their artillery. This was the beginning of a war between the Spaniards, with Tidore and Gilolo as allies, and the Portuguese, who sided with Ternate, where the Portuguese had occupied a fort since 1512.

Imperial authorities continued their attempts to obtain spices, but they next decided to send expeditions from Mexico instead of from the Iberian Peninsula. Consequently, Charles V ordered Hernán Cortés to organize a fleet. In 1524, Cortés wrote to the king with a plan to occupy and fortify the Spice Islands in a manner different from the Portuguese factory system of establishing an enclave and trading for spices. In 1526, Cortés assigned the command to his cousin Alvaro de Saavedra Cerón and instructed him to sail to the islands, search for any survivors of the Magellan expedition in Cebu, inquire about the Loaísa expedition, and try to capture the Portuguese fort at Ternate. In each port, Saavedra should hire a "learned Jew" to translate the Latin letters of introduction to Asian potentates into Arabic or the local languages and to bring back clove trees to grow in Mexico.[96]

Magellan had found out that Cebu was a prosperous port of call for both Chinese junks and ships from the East Indies. In a letter addressed to the king of the island, Cortés explained the aims of Magellan's expedition: "You should know, that this so powerful prince, desiring to have knowledge of the manner and trade of those districts, sent thither one of his captains named Hernando de Magallanes with five ships."[97] He apologized for Magellan's conduct: "he grieved most at having a captain who departed from the royal commands and instructions that he carried, especially in his having stirred up war or discord with you and yours."[98] On October 31, 1527, the fleet departed from Mexico, and soon two ships disappeared in high winds and a third suffered a shipwreck. Only the *Florida*, commanded by Saavedra, crossed the ocean and reached Mindanao, where the crew encountered three survivors from the Loaísa expedition, who reported that the Cebuans had captured and sold to Chinese merchants eight Spaniards from Magellan's expedition. Saavedra tried to sail to Cebu, but the wind forced him back and he was unable to reach Mexico. He died on the coast of Tidore in October of 1529. After Saavedra's death, the *Florida* attempted to travel back across the Pacific but could not find favorable winds. All attempts to return had failed. The Portuguese governor of India, Nuno da Cunha, sent a ship to carry the remaining Spaniards home. It left Tidore in 1534, while Urdaneta and others stayed behind in Gilolo to collect a quantity of cloves. Finally, the accountant left the islands, arriving in Lisbon in June of 1536, where Portuguese officers confiscated all his maps and documents. Urdaneta and a companion reached Valladolid in Spain, where he wrote from memory a report of his experiences in the Moluccas eleven and a half years after Loaísa's fleet left Spain. The memorandum is highly enthusiastic about future prospects. "If your Majesty were pleased to order commerce to be maintained with the Moluccas, there might be brought from there every year over six thousand *quintales* of cloves, and there are years when there is a harvest of more than eleven thousand quintales."[99] Urdaneta also reported large quantities of nutmeg and mace available from the Banda Islands; he mentioned possible trade in ginger and cinnamon and added that there was gold on certain islands. Urdaneta concluded: "Your Majesty will also see, from this account, that there are many rich and valuable conquests to be made round the Moluccas, and many lands with much trade, including China, with which communication might be made from the Moluccas."[100]

Meanwhile, international relations amongst the Spanish emperor, Suleiman the Magnificent from Turkey, France, and the Pope soured, placing the dispute with Portugal over the Moluccas in a different light. Charles I needed all the allies he could get against such powerful enemies, so he approached Portugal. In 1526 Charles married Isabel de Portugal, the sister of João III, while his own sister, Catalina of Austria, married the Portuguese king. He signed the Treaty of Zaragoza, which provisionally relinquished the claim to the Spice Islands in exchange for 350,000 gold ducats until a more exact demarcation could be established between both empires.

The treaty did not impede attempts to cross the Pacific for long. In 1542, Ruy López de Villalobos, brother-in-law of New Spain's Viceroy Antonio de Mendoza, commanded another expedition. The objective was to colonize the Philippines and to establish trade with China and the Ryukyu Islands. The Spaniards spent a month in the east of Mindanao and incidentally explored the Leyte and Samar areas. Unable to reach Cebu, they were stuck on the eastern coast of Mindanao. Food was short, and the explorers abandoned the idea of establishing a settlement. The scarcity of provisions was an unintended consequence of the native islanders' practice of subsistence agriculture, which did not produce enough food to support newcomers. Villalobos's people moved to the island of Sarangani for seven months in 1543. The island benefited from its strategic position in a network of exchanges north of the Celebes Sea, "where the northbound spice route veered westward to Sulu, Borneo, and Melaka."[101] It had a sizable settlement, and the Spaniards encountered at their arrival four hundred boats on the shore exchanging cotton, silks, gold, porcelain, and aromatics for slaves and forest products, especially wax and rice.[102] Despite the port's affluence, the crew was deprived of sustenance and ate "horrid grubs and unknown plants, land crabs which sent people mad for a day, and a gray lizard, which emits a considerable glow; very few who ate them are living."[103] Ships went in search of food. Captain Bernardo de la Torre reached an island today identified as Leyte or Samar. Makandala, the local chief, welcomed the Spanish crew and gave them water and abundant food. Chinese porcelain and silk decorated Makandala's residence. Villalobos, thankful for the food, named the island *Felipina* to honor the future King Philip II; this naming was the origin of today's Philippines. Unable to find a route back to America, the Spaniards sailed as far as Tidore. Villalobos died in Amboyna in 1544, receiving his last rites from St. Francis Xavier, the famous Jesuit. A number of sailors remained in the Moluccas, and others returned from India to Spain on a Portuguese ship. Some of the Augustinian friars who had accompanied Villalobos went back to Mexico, and Urdaneta is believed to have obtained information about their navigation from one of them, Gerónimo de Santisteban.[104]

The dismal failure of Spanish voyages, in terms of human deaths and economic losses, nonetheless resulted in increased knowledge of the geography and commerce of Asia, gathered from natives and Portuguese traders. The Spaniards discovered that the Philippines were rich in cinnamon, ginger, and gold, and they began to grasp the economic importance of China and Japan. Thus far, this information was useless because they were unable to master the predominant currents and winds of the Pacific Ocean. Nearly twenty years would pass before a new attempt to establish a colony in the Philippines.

Miguel López de Legázpi

When Philip II became king in 1556, he ignored his father's reservations about the Portuguese, and plans to enter Asian commerce began to take shape. The European political landscape was quiet at the time. The king had signed the Treaty of Cateau-Cambresis with France in 1559, while from 1558 to 1565 the prices of spices—cloves, cinnamon, and pepper—rose notably.[105] A royal order charged Viceroy Luis de Velasco of New Spain to organize a fleet for "the discovery of the Western Islands toward the Malucos."[106] Andrés de Urdaneta, who was now an Augustinian friar, received a letter from the king asking him to put his knowledge and experience in the service of the planned expedition, to be commanded by Miguel López de Legázpi.

There were only a small number of pilots and able seamen in Mexico and even fewer willing to cross the Pacific, which explains the large number of foreigners in the crew: Flemish, Italian, Venetian, Greek, and French, in addition to ten or twelve Portuguese. Authorities allowed only twelve black servants onboard in order to conserve provisions.[107] Among the sailing group was a native of the Philippines, Jerónimo Pacheco, who had been brought to Mexico by Pedro Pacheco, a participant in the Villalobos expedition. The Filipino was a baptized Christian and a fluent Spanish speaker, which made him an invaluable addition.[108]

The Audiencia of Mexico gave detailed orders to Legázpi. He was told to respect the Treaty of Tordesillas and, consequently, to avoid the Moluccas: "Instead you shall enter other islands contiguous to them, as for instance the Philippines, and others which are outside said treaty and within his majesty's demarcation, and which are reported also to contain spice."[109] After reaching the Philippines, the crew was to collect information about the islands, including their wealth, trade relations with other countries, prices, and so on, and to deal with the inhabitants peacefully. Knowing the existence of slavery in the Philippines, Legázpi was told to buy some slaves and send them to Mexico, "so that they may serve as interpreters and from them may be learned the products of their lands."[110] In the process of gathering knowledge, they were to investigate Portuguese activities on the islands of Japan, some of which were supposedly on the Spanish side of the Tordesillas line. Of utmost importance was to discover the return route.

Under Legázpi's authority, and with Urdaneta acting as the chief pilot—in addition to his nautical experience he was able to speak Malay—two galleons, the *San Pedro* and the *San Pablo*, three pinnaces (small boats), and a *patache* (tender) of forty tons called the *San Lucas* left the port of Navidad on the Mexican coast on November 21, 1564, with a total of 350 soldiers and sailors.

When the patache lost sight of other vessels, Captain Alonso de Arellano decided to continue alone. The ship remained in Mindanao for five weeks waiting for the rest of the fleet, but due to the scarcity of provisions, Arellano decided to return to New Spain. The *San Lucas* sailed northeast to find the proper winds, and on August 9, 1565, the *patache* reached the port of Navidad in the Mexican coast, with a crew weakened by hunger and scurvy. Arellano claimed the reward for having reached the Philippines and for the discovery of the return route. There was a trial, and the court considered him responsible for abandoning the fleet, but he received no punishment.[111] In addition to Arellano's actions, there was the strange incident of Lope Martínez de Lagos, the pilot of a small boat in the expedition. He was condemned to death for fraud, but given his knowledge of the return route, he was sent back to the Philippines as a pilot carrying a sealed envelope with his death sentence addressed to the authorities. Somehow he discovered the contents, and instead of plotting the course to the islands, he led a mutiny that claimed the lives of the ship's other officers. This man appears quite unusual in that he was a mulatto who had risen to be a pilot, a position of authority usually denied to former slaves.[112]

The Legázpi expedition confirmed the reputation of the inhabitants of the so-called Islands of Thieves. It seems that the natives haggled about the price of foodstuffs, requiring payment in nails and pieces of iron; nonetheless, when the Spaniards emptied the baskets of rice, they were surprised to discover a thin layer of rice on top of a mound of sand. Incidents of violence took place between the natives and Spaniards.[113] A young seaman from the *San Pedro* remained ashore by accident, and when a search party returned for him, "they found the boy with thirty spears thrust in his body, the skin torn off his face, his tongue ripped out and a sharp stick thrust clear through the mouth, protruding through the back of his neck."[114] Retaliation was swift; the Spaniards hanged four natives and put fire to houses and boats. The chronicler reported, "In this way they will treat with more respect the next group of Spaniards that arrives and learn to keep more faithfully their promises of friendship."[115]

On January 26, Legázpi took formal possession of the *Ladrones'* archipelago. On this island, Legázpi signed a "blood compact" with the local chiefs. In a document to Philip II, he described the ritual in the following terms: "One from each party draws two or three drops of blood from his own arm or breast and mixes them in the same cup with water or wine. Then the mixture must be divided equally between two cups, and neither person may depart until both cups are alike drained."[116] Similar ceremonies took place on other islands, including Samar and Bohol. After leaving Bohol, Legázpi searched for a permanent base and sent ships to Mindanao and Cebu. On the Butuan River of Mindanao, the Spaniards exchanged silver for gold and spices, "The Moros being highly pleased with the Spanish silver *tostones*."[117] In spite of their commercial success in Mindanao, the Spaniards chose Cebu due to its anchorage and food supply.

The fleet, guided by Gala and Katuna, chiefs of Bohol, reached Cebu on April 27, 1565, where Chief Tupas and his warriors had lined up on the beach to confront the newcomers. Urdaneta tried to negotiate a peace agreement without success, and a confrontation ensued that defeated the natives. Previously, the fleet's artillery had burned houses to the ground. A Spanish soldier found an image of the Child Jesus in a remaining house, probably the same image that had been presented to the Queen of Cebu during the Magellan visit. After centuries, the statue stays in the Augustinian Church of the Holy Child. Cebu had an abundance of rice, fish, fruit, and game, and Legázpi decided to establish the enclave of *San Miguel* on the island. When the natives reluctantly decided to sue for peace, Cid Hamal, a Malay-speaking Muslim from Brunei, acted as a translator between Legázpi and the Cebu chief. Despite their previous hostilities, the people of the island accepted the Spanish terms and agreed to pay tribute as subjects of the crown, in exchange for protection against their enemies.

Legázpi called a council of his officers and friars to discuss the crucial matter of sending a ship back to New Spain. The councilors decided to prepare the *San Pablo* for the voyage. With Legázpi's grandson Felipe de Salcedo as commander and Andrés de Urdaneta as pilot, the galleon departed on June 1, 1565. The southwest monsoon carried the galleon up to northern latitudes, where the Kuroshio Current drove it along the coast of Japan, after which the ship entered the belt of westerly winds. Currents and winds drove the *San Pedro* along an easterly route. On September 18, the crew sighted San Miguel Island at the entrance of the Santa Barbara Channel of California. Finally, on Monday, October 8, 1565, after four months and eight days at sea, they reached Acapulco. Sixteen men had died during the voyage, and five more passed away upon reaching the port. Of the 195 men who survived, not more than eighteen were able to help maneuver the ship. The sailors had skin lesions and toothless gums as proof of their scorbutic sufferings. Urdaneta, after landing at Acapulco, marked a map with details of the winds and geographical features of the route. "In the history of cartography Urdaneta's chart was to become one of the most important, for the course he had laid down was to provide the route for the annual ship between Manila and Mexico."[118] A letter sent from Seville to Valencia in Spain narrating the events commented: "This is a great and very important achievement; and the people of Mexico are very proud of their discovery, which they think will make them the center of the world."[119]

Meanwhile, in the Philippines, Legázpi was waiting in Cebu in dire circumstances because the local chiefs refused to supply them with food and the local inhabitants refused to plant, hoping to get rid of the Spaniards. Expeditions to neighboring islands searching for victuals were unsuccessful. Luckily, Moro traders from Luzon brought rice, and the colonizers had a respite from privations, but it was not a sustainable solution.

During his time in Cebu, Legázpi had heard about the Island of Luzon, where Japanese and Chinese merchants came to trade every year. He knew from Portuguese reports about the profitable trade to be had with both Asian countries, and the Spaniards were familiar with the connections between Mindanao and Malacca, Borneo, and the Moluccas. The puzzling question for Legázpi was the presence of Chinese merchant junks in the ports of the archipelago. Fortunately, after a skirmish with a Bornean vessel, he received an answer. The Bornean ship was under Portuguese ownership, but the cargo was property of the king of *Brunei*. Legázpi explained that a misunderstanding had taken place, restored the vessel and cargo to its owners, and commenced a fruitful conversation with the Moro pilot, which Urdaneta translated from Malay to Spanish. By putting together new information and previous knowledge, a clear picture emerged of the Philippines's trade networks. Large Chinese junks went to Manila, and smaller ships throughout the islands delivered their cargo. Settlements in Mindoro guaranteed a Muslim—Moros to the Spaniards—monopoly on interisland distribution. Indian products arrived from Malacca to entrepôts in Butuan and Cebu. There was also a route to the Moluccas that bypassed the Sulu Islands and the island of Sarangani. This state of affairs dictated Legázpi's future strategy, aimed to eliminate Moro intermediaries in the island exchanges. He informed the king from Cebu in 1567, "There are some large islands called Luzon and Mindoro, where the Chinese and Japanese come every year to trade . . . the people of these two islands are Moros, and having bought what the Chinese and Japanese bring, they trade the same goods throughout this archipelago of islands."[120] Securing the route to Manila, the port of call for the China trade, required conquering Mindoro. Breaking connections with Malacca had necessitated counteracting Borneo's influence, and neutralizing the Mindanao and Jolo sultanates would be strategically necessary for gaining access to the Spice Islands. With varying degrees of success, the Spaniards followed this course of action between 1570 and 1582.[121]

In 1570, Legázpi wrote to Mexico, seeking guidance regarding the next step in Spain's strategy. Cebu was the ideal location to occupy if Spice Islands commerce were to be pursued, which implied a conflict with the Portuguese. Meanwhile, if trade with China were the aim, the settlement ought to be in Luzon. Tributes from the Visaya people subsidized military operations and encouraged further conquests, and soldiers continued in the expectation of future *encomiendas* (grants of land) from further occupation. Native contributions financed the Philippines's colonization to a large extent.[122]

Spaniards in Luzon

Martín de Goiti and Juan de Salcedo, Legázpi's grandson, sailed for Luzon on May 8, 1570, commanding a contingent of 120 Spaniards, 600 Visayan allies, and a captive Moro from Manila as a pilot. The Spanish captains made a blood pact of friendship with Manila's rulers, Lakandula and Soliman. Soon Soliman realized that the agreement implied vassalage and tribute payment to the newcomers. A conflict ensued in which the Spaniards and their Visayan allies defeated the local forces and killed about one hundred of Manila's inhabitants, among them a Portuguese artilleryman. They captured Soliman's cannons, gold, and prisoners, including some from China and Japan. Philip II, in letters arriving from Mexico, ordered the settlement of the islands and bestowed Legázpi with the titles of governor and captain general. In Panay, there was a shortage of rice due to a plague of locusts, and the Spanish commander decided to move the colony to Luzon, encouraged by the news of gold mines and abundant food. He left Guido de Lavezares in charge of Cebu and established military enclaves in Panay and on other Visayan Islands. Visayan allies accompanied the Spanish contingent of more than two hundred harquebusiers to Manila.[123] Lakandula, who did not share Soliman's qualms regarding vassalage to Spain, welcomed Legázpi, who received him and promised to forgive Soliman's actions. On May 19, 1571—the day of Manila's future patron saint, Potenciana—the governor took formal possession of the city. On June 3, Manila became a municipality, and a city council was established with two majors, twelve councilmen, a high constable, and a public notary.

A group consisting of Soliman's warriors, the *datus* (chiefs) of Hagonoy and Macabebe, and the barangays of Pampanga decided to confront the invaders. On June 3, 1571, a fleet of twenty or thirty *karakoas* (native craft) with small artillery attacked. Goiti ordered the Spanish boats to approach the enemy slowly; when they came in close range, the Spanish Infantry began to fire. Terrorized by the volleys, the natives leaped into the water. At that moment the Visayan allies also jumped, and "they slaughtered them because they are great enemies of the inhabitants of Luzon."[124] Soliman and approximately three hundred Filipinos died in the battle. The Spaniards captured several small pieces of artillery, and the soldiers received about five hundred natives as slaves plus "the *quinto* for his majesty."[125] The confrontation became known as the combat of Bankusay. Military defeat convinced the chiefs of central Luzon to accept the new status quo. In addition to their superior training and technology, the persistent conflicts between the scattered communities of the archipelago gave the Spaniards a crucial strategic advantage. The Jesuit Alonso Sánchez explained to Philip II that it was easy to subdue the Filipinos because each settlement welcomed the Spaniards to use them against their enemies, and in this way, both were conquered: "It seems that God disposed them as small morsels to be eaten one by one."[126]

To recognize the importance of the settlement in 1574, Philip II gave the city the honorific title of *Insigne y Leal* (distinguished and loyal) and named Manila *Cabeza de Filipinas* (head of the Philippines) in 1595. The new capital received a coat of arms that fittingly mixed military and maritime symbols. As Morga described it, "This is an escutcheon divided cross-wise, having a castle upon a red field; and below is a gold lion crowned and rampant with a bared sword in the dexter hand; one half of its body is in the shape of a dolphin upon the waters of the sea signifying that the Spaniards sailed thence with their arms to conquer that land for the kingdom of Castile."[127]

The Spaniards set out to occupy Manila's surrounding areas. Goiti, with the help of Lakandula, commanded expeditions to control the central region of Luzon and its bordering territories. They discovered near Manila that the inhabitants of Laguna de Bay and the Pampanga region were actively exchanging their rice and gold for cotton and other products and had been actively involved in Southeast Asian trade since pre-Hispanic times. "These vested interests gave Pampanga chiefs a special incentive for submitting to colonial authority once the superiority of Spanish arms had been demonstrated."[128]

Exploration of Luzon

Captain Salcedo imposed Spanish authority over the populations—"amounting to 24,000 or 26,000 men"—surrounding Laguna de Bay. He reached the southern Bicol region famous for the gold mines of Paracale, which were reputed to be "very good and very rich."[129] Another expedition continued north to Ilocos due to rumors of more gold mines. In reality, Ilocanos' precious metal originated from exchanges with the Igorots. Ilocos was highly valued by the crown for its large population and for the considerable quantities of rice and cotton produced. From there, Manila received its rice and cotton pieces, *mantas*, to manufacture sails for the galleons. The province was favorably located for overseas trade, and ships from China, India, and Macao visited its coasts when the weather made it impossible to reach Manila. Merchants from these countries did their business in Ilocos while waiting for the north wind, the *brisa*, to sail to the capital.[130]

During the first years of the conquest, the Spaniards used mercilessly systematic force to collect supplies and to subject rebellious communities. A clear example of these methods occurred during the initial occupation of the Island of Leyte. The datu of Limasawa, who had welcomed Legázpi to the Philippines in 1565, and his son Pagali persuaded six towns to revolt. The alcalde mayor of Cebu, Juan de Alcarazo, sailed with a fleet of forty ships and, to make an example and to stop the revolt from spreading any farther, pursued the rebels to a pocket in the hills, where all the men, women, and children were exterminated.[131] Bishop Miguel Benavides reported that companies of soldiers used to go to local villages and fall upon the population at dawn, taking the food, killing a number of natives, robbing them of their property, and seizing their children and women as captives: "We ruled in this way for a time."[132] The natives approached the governor with presents and offerings of friendship to avoid the pervasive violence, but the Spaniards interpreted these gestures as an indication of accepting their authority. Benavides clearly explained the colonizers' perspective: "We need to understand that to remain friends with the Spaniards meant to remain tributary vassals."[133]

Legázpi's expedition was the culmination of four decades of strenuous attempts initiated by Magellan and continued by Loaísa, Saavedra, and Villalobos. During these first years the Spaniards discovered the return route to New Spain and founded the capital of the Philippines. "The conquest of Manila, given its geopolitical situation, was fundamental to achieve the definitive consolidation of the Spaniards in the archipelago."[134] Before Legázpi died in 1572, the Visayas Islands and the central region of Luzon were under Spanish control. The rest of the islands had small military garrisons located in provincial capitals to guarantee the collection of taxes and to support missionary activities, while large parts of Mindanao, the Sulu archipelago, and the mountainous areas remained beyond Spanish authority until the late nineteenth century.

CHAPTER THREE

~

Spanish Settlement in the Philippines

The First Decades of the Colony and "The China Enterprise"

The Spanish arrived in the Philippines in 1565, a propitious period for the colonizers. The climate had improved since around the 1470s, and heavier monsoon rains had increased agricultural yield and encouraged cultivation of marginal lands.[1] The colonizers met fierce resistance from the sultanates in the south, but Islam had not yet spread widely throughout the archipelago, and the Dutch were still absent, giving the Spaniards four decades to consolidate their position. Moreover, the conquerors had accumulated a wealth of experience in administering and evangelizing to indigenous populations in America, which they applied to territories in Asia. Finally, yet perhaps most important, bullion production was increasing in Mexico and Peru, which enabled the newcomers to enter into established trade networks and expand them across the Pacific. The Spanish position improved further in 1567, when the Ming emperor rescinded the ban on private trade.

During their first decades in the Philippines the situation for the Spanish was precarious, but in the empire at large, portentous events were taking place. In 1578 Sebastião I, king of Portugal, had died fighting in Morocco. His successor and granduncle, Cardinal Dom Henrique, was advanced in years and in poor health, and he soon passed away, opening up a race for the Portuguese Crown. The winner was Spain. In January 1580, troops under the Duke of Alva arrived in Lisbon, and one year later, the parliament of Portugal recognized Philip II as their sovereign.

Initially the Spanish Empire's strategy in Asia was directed toward expanding Iberian territories in a manner similar to the American model of conquest. Voyages such as those of Augustinian Martín de Rada and Jesuit rector Alonso Sánchez, who traveled within the Ming Empire during the 1570s and 1580s, respectively, were undertaken with the objective of collecting firsthand information about China.[2] The king's cosmographer, Giovanni Battista Gesio, after reassuring the government that the Philippine Islands were within the demarcation assigned to Spain by the Treaty of Tordesillas, extolled Luzon's important strategic position, comparing it to the royal possessions in Italy or in the Low Countries and emphasizing Manila's strategic location for invading Japan and China.[3]

Meanwhile, Alonso Sánchez was given the delicate task of delivering the news about the union of Portugal and Spain to the Portuguese in Macao. Initially, the citizens were reluctant to accept this startling turn of events until a document from the viceroy of India arrived confirming the new situation; the Macao authorities took the oath of allegiance to their new king on September 18, 1583, albeit without the customary public festivities. Tact and prudence were required because the Chinese had banned the Spaniards from entering their empire and were alarmed by the union of the two Crowns. Regardless, the Portuguese made it clear to Sánchez that their economic viability was completely dependent on the mandarins' goodwill and that visitors from the Philippines should therefore avoid Macao in the future.

Upon his return to Manila, Sánchez discussed his experiences abroad with Governor Diego Ronquillo and Bishop Domingo Salazar; out of these conversations, la empresa de China (the China enterprise) came to the fore.[4] The idea was that, given China's refusal to allow missionary activities, priests should be sent from the Philippines with an army to protect them. If the Chinese denied their entrance, the expeditionary forces would use violence to establish Spanish civil and religious authority. This was not the first time Philip II had received a proposal of this kind. In 1567, the City Council of Mexico suggested dividing the lands of the Philippines and China among the colonizers; Rada, as well, recommended conquering China in a letter in 1569. Almost immediately after Manila's founding in 1571, Miguel López de Legázpi, with the encouragement of the Augustinian friars, conceived the first expedition into the region. Perhaps braced by the victory of Lepanto against the Turks in the same year, Philip II ordered the viceroy of Mexico, Martín Enríquez, to send Captain Juan de la Isla to the Philippines with orders to explore the coast, gather information about the Ming Empire, and take possession of Chinese lands. These imperialist impulses were not limited to China and the Philippines; in 1585, an official from Manila encouraged the king "to evict and expel the Muslims from all the Philippine islands, or at least to subject them and make them pay tribute, vanquishing those in Java, Sumatra, Acheh, Borneo, Mindanao, Sulu, the Moluccas, Malacca, Siam, Patani, Pegu and other kingdoms, which venerate Mohammed."[5]

For a second time, urgent matters required Sánchez's presence in Macao, and in 1584, the Governor Diego Ronquillo sent a document to the king about the conquest of China. Ronquillo wrote in glowing terms: the country was fertile and rich, the people were docile, and their tributes and taxes were worth more than all levies collected in the combined territories of the Spanish Empire. In addition, China did not border any powerful states, and on the northern frontier strong defenses protected it against the Tartars.

However, troubles were at hand—in this case, a grievous attempt at fraud. The crew of the galleon *San Martín*, with the complicity of their captain, traveled to Macao with a plan to take on additional cargo and sail to Peru, swindling their investors in Manila. When they arrived on the coast of China, there was a mutiny, and the captain lost his command. To the great satisfaction of Portuguese merchants, the mutineers decided to continue to Peru, loaded with merchandise. News of these events reached Manila, and before the crew could see their scheme to the end, Sánchez and the royal factor, Juan Bautista Román, arrived. The rebels were overpowered and the leaders executed, and with a new crew the *San Martín* finally set sail for Acapulco. That was not all; Spanish authorities became aware through this incident that the Chinese had allowed the Italian Jesuits Michele Ruggieri and Matteo Ricci to establish residence in Zhaoqing. This seemed an encouraging sign for negotiations with the Chinese to establish a Spanish trading post similar to Macao on the coast of Guangdong or Fujian, as well as to send an embassy to the emperor while keeping the Portuguese in the dark. The Macao business community was afraid of prices inflating if the Manila merchants entered the Canton fairs because the Portuguese did not have direct access to Mexican and Peruvian silver. Sánchez and Román's failure to achieve these goals moved the conquest of China to the forefront once more, and soon they sent documents to Spain requesting support for the venture. They were not alone in their dogged determination; the Portuguese rector of the Macao Jesuits, Francisco Cabral, wrote to the king to give his unconditional support to such military schemes and to offer his services as a gatherer of strategic information. Cabral's superiors did not welcome his activities. To protect the existence of the Jesuit mission in Zhaoqing, Alessandro Valignano, who was in charge of the order in Asia, prohibited all contact with the Spaniards coming from the Philippines. Jesuits in America, like the famous historian José de Acosta, were aware of Sánchez's military projects and strongly opposed them. News of the controversy reached Claudio Acquaviva, the general of the order in Rome, who wrote a letter to Mexico deploring Sánchez's bellicosity and suggesting his removal from the Philippines.[6]

In the midst of these schemes, the Spanish colony had reached a critical moment. Between 1580 and 1585, the cost of living rose as a consequence of lower agricultural production in the Pampanga province—the rice basket of Manila—and of a plague of locusts and lack of laborers in the Visayas. Natives had been levied for military action on the Moluccas and Borneo against the Zambals of northern Luzon. Meanwhile, the arrival of Chinese merchants in numbers of "more than three thousand each year," as well as demand from the Spanish colonizers, drove up prices for foodstuffs.[7] Inflation was not the only trouble; Spaniards had also suffered a series of embarrassing military setbacks. Interventions in Borneo in 1578 and 1580 proved unfruitful, expeditions to the Moluccas in 1582 and 1585 were unable to conquer Ternate, and in Luzon, the entire Cagayan Valley was up in rebellion. News of English harassment of Spanish shipping added yet another layer to a deep sense of unease.

In contrast to the gloom created by military threats and failures, trade with China was flourishing. Santiago de Vera, president of the Philippine Audiencia, wrote to the king in 1587 to report the arrival of a large number of junks, thirty of which had landed in Manila carrying cows, horses, and plenty of merchandise, in addition to more than three thousand Chinese visitors. Goods from China were able to meet practically all the Spaniards' needs at extremely low prices. To the chagrin of the Chinese, two Portuguese ships had also arrived and sold their cargo at a handsome profit. To counteract the competition, the Chinese proposed to de Vera the creation of a Spanish enclave in Fujian, adding that the governor of the province was interested in growing the tax base with the future fees paid by Spanish vessels. He wistfully added that, with the exception of the mandarins, all of China wanted a Spanish presence in their land. Trade was growing, and the only obstacle to shipping larger quantities of textiles to Mexico was the small number of vessels available. In a memorandum regarding the colony's economic situation from 1579 to 1586, the writer indicates that the Philippines was poorer than American possessions. The soldiers and *encomenderos*—settlers with land grants—suffered privations that were mitigated somewhat by the low prices of the food and clothing brought by the Chinese. After enumerating the variety of textiles taken to Acapulco, the author estimated that "in New Spain they gain two hundred percent and in certain goods much more."[8] Obviously, the junk trade and the Manila galleon appeared as profitable businesses.

The colonists were mindful of discussions in the Council of the Indies regarding the value of the Spanish presence in the Philippines and of complaints from Seville about the competition that Chinese silks presented in the American market. In their communications to Philip II, the Portuguese added their voices, arguing that the direct economic relationship between America and Asia implied that the viceroyalties in the New World would not be economically dependent on Spain, due to the abundance of all kinds of goods in China, and that revenue from Seville's taxes would disappear. Portuguese authorities were highly suspicious of Spain's activities and wanted to protect their economic interests from interference. The Council of the Indies responded in Spain's favor, noting that the businesses of both empires were already independent and that the galleon trade was the only means of support for the colony in the Philippines.

Manila's relationship with Mexico had reached a critical moment, too, as a result of Governor Gonzalo Ronquillo de Peñalosa's endeavors to establish a line of navigation to Peru, which implied that Acapulco would lose its privileged position. To address the colony's distressing predicament, de Vera gathered the main colonial interests in Manila on April 19, 1586. This meeting was the culmination of a series of conferences called the Synod of Manila, which had been organized since 1581 by the bishop Domingo de Salazar. Merchants, citizens, military men, the cathedral chapter presided over by the bishop, and the heads of religious orders all took part. They chose the Jesuit Alonso Sánchez as a *procurador*, or spokesperson, to carry their recommendations and findings to Philip II. Cognizant of the diverse interests of the colonists, a special committee drafted a memorandum, *Memorial general*, assessing the Philippines's precarious situation and suggesting possible remedies. Among the recommendations, the memorandum called for excluding Mexican merchants from trade in Manila and requested free trade with all the Portuguese possessions in Asia. Businessmen in Manila opposed the participation of Mexican traders because the latter were able to invest large capital, *encomiendas gruesas*, in the galleon, thereby raising prices and cornering the market. They proposed that Mexicans wanting to participate in the galleon trade relocate to the Philippines for ten years and exclusively use their own capital instead of acting as agents for other merchants. This requirement would prove unsuccessful, since representatives acting as proxy and other legal subterfuges circumvented legislation practically until the end of the line. Regarding exchanges with Portuguese territories, the king upheld the 1581 agreement under the Cortes of Tomar to maintain a separation between the economies of the two Iberian empires. Another suggested remedy was the establishment of the *pancada*, a system by which a board of citizens would buy merchandise wholesale from junks arriving in Manila and distribute it afterward among the interested parties. Soon the pancada was abandoned for free trafficking between the Spanish and Chinese.[9]

Furthermore, the bishop, the attorney general, the royal factor, and Alonso Sánchez met nightly to draft a plan to conquer China. The long document is a reflection of these authorities' assumptions and frame of mind. They estimated that the number of soldiers required was about ten to twelve thousand, to be recruited from the imperial European dominions (preferably Vizcaya in the Basque country), and the same number of Japanese soldiers plus five thousand warriors from the Visayas. The planners carefully detailed the supplies and the additional workforce that would be needed, including five hundred slaves from India, "since there are so many and so cheap." They asked the king to partner with the Portuguese, given their experience in China and their strategic location, which would allow for a two-prong invasion: the Portuguese army would enter from Canton and the Spanish forces from Fujian. Heedful of the destruction and depopulation that followed the conquest of America, the planners insisted on strong military leadership to keep discipline among the forces and avoid similar devastation in China. The rewards would be many. Towers of precious metals had accumulated in the Ming treasury; the document specified that silver was especially abundant, since, as the only bullion circulating, it "enters from other kingdoms and never leaves." Tributes and taxes would be plentiful, and given that the establishment of a Spanish colony would require bureaucrats and military men, many Spaniards would settle in this new territory. A large number of marriages were expected to follow between the newcomers and the local women; the grace, comeliness, and virtue of the Chinese women made them ideal partners to join the Spanish conquerors in creating a mixed population of Chinese Spanish offspring who would then occupy positions in the church, army, and government. The only sources of wealth in the American territories were mines, but in China, agriculture, manufacturing, and abundant resources would be more than enough to support a stable society of Chinese and Spanish citizens. The strategic political advantages were considerable, as well. Following a treaty with the Tartars and other Central Asian peoples, it would be possible to gather intelligence about the Ottoman Empire and exert pressure on the sultan from the east. After becoming the lord of China, it was inevitable that in short order the Spanish king would be declared the sovereign of the neighboring countries and archipelagos. Portugal's Indian possessions would gain additional security, and before long the Chinese merchants, now Spanish subjects, would arrive on the coasts of Mexico and Peru.[10]

Independently of the documents produced during the synod, Sánchez wrote a personal memorandum to the king—*Sobre la calidad y estado de estas islas en general* (About the quality and state of these islands in general)— describing the Philippines and advancing a series of recommendations. He rightly perceived that the islands' conquest had been possible due to endemic conflicts among native communities and compared the conquest to the drastically different situation the Portuguese faced in India, China, and Japan, all of them centralized states with powerful rulers. Sánchez warned the king about authorities and colonizers: the governor and other public officials lived a privileged existence, the bishop and the cathedral chapter were grumbling because they had not received their salaries, and the friars' only desire was to go to China and Japan instead of evangelizing the islanders. "If the merchants say anything, it is to cover up their profits, which are the largest known anywhere." In truth, Sánchez insisted, the Philippines had plenty of resources and occupied a privileged strategic position to defend all Christian enclaves and to further advance the religion in Asia, "whether by preaching or by the means that God disposes."

Taking into consideration the incorporation of Portugal under the Spanish Crown, Sánchez saw the Philippines as crucial for protecting communications between Portuguese Goa and Macao and Japan, given that the easiest routes were via the Straits of Malacca and Sunda. In addition, the Philippines was the closest point from which to help the Portuguese Moluccas and the city of Malacca in case of an attack and the only point from which the Spanish could launch any future expeditions, whether missionary or military, to China or Southeast Asia. He boldly recommended the conquest of Japan, "joining forces with the Christian Kings of Japan as they are asking now." Incidentally, in the year following Sánchez's explication of his project, a number of Japanese merchants from Hirado reached Manila. They declared that both Matsura of Hirado and the Christian daimyo, Konishi Yukinaga, would supply six thousand men or more for the invasion of China, Borneo, the Moluccas, or Indochina, without asking anything in return. Sánchez was aware that the Philippines's vast distance from Spain aggravated the islands' troubles, which were also compounded by the unhelpful attitude of settlers and bureaucrats who were looking for quick riches. He reminded the king of the military forces' precarious state and the scarcity of public funds to pay salaries and support the colony. To improve the situation he proposed to take advantage of gold's price differential between the islands and America, where the precious metal "ordinarily doubles its value." To carry out the necessary reforms, Sánchez suggested nominating a talented and honest governor and sending him to the Philippines with a significant military force supervised by able officers. To speed up the economic development of the new colony, he insisted on the prohibition of private trade between America and Manila; all merchandise and travelers should be transported in royal galleons, which would subsidize future freight and passenger rates and encourage investment and immigration to the islands.[11]

The first meeting between Philip II and Sánchez at El Escorial near Madrid lasted for two hours. Subsequently, in March of 1588, the king appointed chosen members from the main royal councils to examine the documents brought by the *procurador*. The royal audience and the committee nomination coincided with the Armada's arrangements to invade England, which indicates the importance given to these matters by imperial authorities. Upon the closure of initial deliberations, the news was received that the invading expedition against England ended in catastrophe, and as a result, the second audience between Sánchez and Philip II took place under gloomy circumstances. Sánchez decided to deliver the 1586 document on China without pressing the case for an invasion.

The Crown granted Sánchez's main requests, which were to secure the continuation of trade between Mexico and Manila and to issue a series of legal and financial decrees for the administration of the Philippines. As a consequence of the Jesuit's requests, Gómez Pérez Dasmariñas received an appointment as governor and captain general of the islands, with a higher salary than his predecessors and a knighthood of the Order of Santiago to enhance his standing among the colonists.

Settling Down in the Philippines

As soon as he arrived in Manila as the new governor, Dasmariñas ordered the construction of a wall enclosing the city, set out rules to govern the galleon trade, and initiated a course of energetic military activity. Under his orders, Spanish and Pampango troops struck against the Zambals with orders to destroy "everything in their path—villages, granaries, even the standing grain of the upland fields. All who resisted were to be killed; all who surrendered brought down to camps in the lowlands while their former homes were completely laid waste." Soldiers killed or captured more than two thousand Zambals, and hundreds of male captives became galley slaves in Cavite. The authorities relocated the survivors to places in which they could rebuild their villages under colonial supervision.[12]

Along the same lines, Dasmariñas planned an expedition to the Moluccas. The boats of the attacking armada were galleys, which required a number of rowers, who were difficult to recruit in Manila. To solve the problem, Dasmariñas decided to hire Chinese rowers at a salary of two pesos per month with the conditions that they would row only in emergencies, that they would not be chained to the oars like galley slaves, and that they would be allowed to carry their swords. These provisions did not sway their minds, and they refused the offer. Consequently, the governor threatened to conscript, among the Chinese of Manila, one able man out of every ten. In protest, the Chinese closed their shops, creating a shortage of essential supplies in the colony. At last, 250 men were gathered, and the Chinese merchants contributed 20,000 pesos to supplement the rowers' meager salary. International tensions presented additional complications. Rumors were swirling in the colony because the king of Cambodia had required assistance against an attack from Siam. The governor responded that he would consider the request for aid, though the Moluccas expedition had added to the ill will held by the Chinese, who were now afraid of being involuntary participants in a conflict between the Siamese and Cambodians. Under such ominous circumstances, Dasmariñas embarked on his galley *La Capitana*, manned by a crew that included a number of these reluctant rowers. At sea, the Chinese were forced to take the place of non-Chinese rowers. The Spaniards thought that they were not exerting themselves; they whipped them, and some died. The fleet was making slow progress due to rough seas, and the Chinese were kept at the oars. During the night of October 25, 1593, the Chinese killed all of the Spaniards onboard, including the governor. In Manila, as soon as the news arrived, Luis Dasmariñas (1593–1596)—son of the deceased and interim governor—ordered the demolition of Chinese houses and removal of this population from the city, aside from those required for basic services. Chinese non-Christians were allowed to conduct business only in designated places. When word of Japanese pirates reached Manila, the governor issued an order to expel all remaining Chinese, afraid that they would join them. A heightened climate of suspicion and mistrust grew against them, with tragic consequences in 1603.[13]

There were more plans to occupy territories beyond the islands. In 1593 an expedition tried without success to occupy Taiwan to monitor the junk routes from Fujian and Nagasaki to Manila. In 1626, under Governor Fernando de Silva, during the war with the Dutch, two forts were built in Keelung and Tamsui to protect Chinese trade from Dutch depredations. Spanish presence in Taiwan was short-lived, however, with the Dutch forcing the Spaniards to evacuate the forts in 1642.

The dream of an Asian empire was hard to forget, and soon some Spaniards were projecting further continental occupations. Hernando de los Ríos Coronel wrote to Philip II in 1597, proposing the conquest of the kingdoms of Cambodia, Siam (Thailand), and Vietnam. "It is very necessary and expedient that several expeditions and conquests should be made in these parts for the service of your majesty in view of the advantages that the Castilians would gain if they held a good post on the mainland."[14] The Portuguese entertained similar dreams; João Ribeiro Gaio, bishop of Malacca from 1581 to 1601, had put forward comparable schemes that would have required Portuguese and Spanish cooperation, like his plan of 1584 for the occupation of Aceh (in Sumatra)—at the time a crucial entrepôt in the spice trade—to be followed by the occupation of Siam, Cambodia, Vietnam, and China. From 1570 until 1610, Spanish and Portuguese archives accumulated documents containing similar proposals of territorial expansions.[15]

The Cambodian king's request to Dasmariñas in 1593 for Spain's aid against Siamese aggressions would return to Spanish attention in 1595. Siam had sent offers of friendship and trade to the Spaniards, as well as two elephants to be presented to the governor. Elephants were customary gifts in diplomatic negotiations among Asian countries during the modern centuries. The governor reciprocated the presents but postponed a reply due to existing engagements. Hostilities between Siam and Cambodia presented an opportunity in 1596 to send a Spanish, Japanese, and Filipino contingent to Cambodia. One of the advocates of this enterprise was the Dominican Fray Diego Aduarte, who went with the troops. The incursion was not successful. The Spaniards retreated down the Mekong River to the coast, after reaching the capital, Phnom Penh, and killing the king of Cambodia and a large number of Chinese.[16] There was another attempt in 1599, which similarly ended in disaster due to bad weather, sickness among the crew, and the refusal of the Philippines's governor to contribute reinforcements and supplies.[17] Siam sided with the Dutch during the war, and as punishment in 1626, Governor Fernando de Silva (1624–1626) led an expedition that was defeated by the Siamese. This was the last military action in the region until more than two hundred years later, when troops from Manila played an important role in the capture of Saigon by the French-Spanish expeditionary force in 1858, inaugurating the French Empire in Indochina.

Still in 1797, Governor Rafael María de Aguilar (1793–1806) wrote to Madrid that "a well-disciplined battalion could overcome armies of Chinese as numerous as those whom Alexander conquered." Delusions were long lasting.

The "Magellan Exchange" and the Islands

With the Manila galleon, plants and animals from America arrived in the Philippines as part of the "Magellan Exchange," which paralleled the "Columbian Exchange" across the Atlantic Ocean. The galleons carried to the islands maize, indigo, maguey, cacao, papaya, pineapple, peanuts, eggplant, cassava, tomatoes, sweet potatoes, and many more unknown cultivars. Conversely, the colonizers sent back plants to America.[18] Guido de Lavezaris informed the king, "I am sending also to New Spain shoots of the cinnamon and pepper trees, so that they may be planted there and benefit your Majesty. I have also sent previously a tamarind tree, and have been informed that it is already bearing fruit in New Spain."[19] Morga observed that some transfers to the islands were unsuccessful, such as olive trees and quinces, but he added that pomegranates and grape vines gave plenty of fruit in their new soils.[20]

In the obituary of Father Sedeño, one of the first Jesuits in the Philippines, a fellow Jesuit wrote, "He took great interest in planting groves and in laying out gardens, and was anxious that silk should be produced in the islands. . . . To this end he planted mulberry trees." Members of religious orders, particularly the Jesuits, were active agents in the Magellan Exchange, bringing new plants to the islands and studying the local flora.[21] In 1611, the Franciscan Blas de la Madre de Dios wrote *Books of Home Remedies*, followed in the second half of the seventeenth century by the Augustinian Ignacio de Mercado's treatise about the plants and trees of the islands and their healing properties.[22] A better-known example was Brother Georg Josef Kamel, who came to the Philippines in 1688. He had studied pharmacy before becoming a Jesuit, and in Manila he established the first pharmacy and a small botanical garden. Kamel wrote a Philippine supplement to the English zoologist John Ray's *Historia Plantarum*. As homage to his work, Carl Linnaeus gave the Asian flower *Thea japonica* the name "camellia" after Kamel.[23] Benito Legarda rightly evaluates the Magellan Exchange's significance: "Of greater future significance, although of inconsequential invoice value, was the carrying of plants and plant products from Mexico and Central America, some of which enriched the diet of Filipinos while others became important in trade and public finance."[24]

Along with plants, the conquistadors also brought deadly diseases that decimated native peoples. By 1500 smallpox was devastating populations in Indonesia and the Philippines. In the smallpox epidemic of 1591, which affected Manila and neighboring villages, natives died in great numbers while the Spaniards were unaffected. As Chirino described it, "There was an epidemic of smallpox (called by them *Bolotong*), which was killing off children and old men, although more fatal to adults than to the young."[25] Widespread illnesses of unknown nature resulted in large population losses in the years 1574, 1591, and 1595.[26] When the Jesuits arrived in Tinagon on the island of Ibabao, they found that "a plague, communicated from other districts, prevailed in that part of the island, causing the death of many people."[27] The Augustinian friar Casimiro Díaz mentioned a smallpox outburst in Cebu (1652) in which innumerable persons died. He observed, "These epidemics and plagues are very frequent in these islands, but smallpox is very punctual in causing general devastation every twenty years."[28] From Africa, Portuguese sailors brought yaws—an infection of the skin, bones, and joints—to Asia, and syphilis arrived with both Iberian peoples and African slaves.[29]

Even if geographical barriers offered some protection against the diffusion of foreign germs, interactions with newcomers were dangerous. Missionary activities and communications with the Igorots of Central Luzon intensified in the eighteenth century, and soon smallpox, measles, and syphilis spread among them. The road to Cagayan was completed in 1739; one year later, mountain people were suffering an outbreak of smallpox that lasted until 1741.[30] During prior epidemics, the Igorots protected themselves with radical quarantine measures. It was a common practice in Southeast Asia; populations from upland territories were aware of the dangers presented by contact with visitors from the coast.[31] An Augustinian friar observed, "As soon as they get the news or a hint this pestilence is spreading, they close up the mountain passes with such trees and underbrush they are absolutely impenetrable, and send word that if anybody should be as bold as to enter, they will kill him immediately."[32] The plague of 1740 is an indication that the Igorots' extreme precautions were not always effective.

Fortunately, the Filipinos avoided the demographic catastrophe visited upon American peoples. By the mid-seventeenth century, native populations in America had fallen to 4 to 5 percent of their former numbers, with the exception of highland settlements and Andean natives, whose populations declined only to 20 to 25 percent. The Philippines experienced less depopulation during the first 150 years of colonial rule, in comparison. Between 1565 and 1655, the numbers of Filipinos in Luzon and the Visayas diminished to around 33 percent. Lower population densities, widespread settlement patterns, and slow transportation diminished the impact of epidemics.[33]

A New Agricultural Regime

In 1604, Claudio Acquaviva, General of the Jesuits, received a long report from a member of the order in the Philippines, Pedro Chirino. The Jesuit described the economic potential of the islands in glowing terms: "These islands offer good inducements to the Spaniards, as well as for ecclesiastics and religious, to make settlements." There was a considerable population, and the people had a comfortable standard of living; they wore cotton and silk garments "and gold pieces (not merely of thin plate)." In addition, the land was fertile: "They have not only great harvests of rice (which is their ordinary bread), but also crops of cotton, with which they clothe themselves, and from which they manufacture quantities of cloths." He mentioned the case of an encomendero who, solely from the profits of *lampotes* (cotton fabrics), left an inheritance of more than 150,000 pesos gathered in a few years.[34]

To support the colonial regime, it was necessary to transform native society and adapt it to the new situation. The arrival of the Spaniards and large numbers of Chinese merchants and artisans required increased agricultural productivity to feed the newcomers and sustain their economic activities. This agricultural transformation took place after the introduction of the Chinese plow and the Asian buffalo, or carabao, as a draft animal. By 1589 Philip II instructed a new governor to encourage the domestication of native buffaloes for plowing, and in a detailed letter commented about the absence of horses, cows, and other domestic animals and told the governor that he had already directed the viceroy of New Spain to send two stallions, twelve mares, twenty-four cows, and two bulls and, if necessary, to get more animals from Japan and China.[35]

Philip II ordered the abolition of local slavery, initiating a protracted process of social transformation, culminating in the decree of 1692 that ended forced servitude, which was gradually transformed into debt peonage.[36] Incidentally, this measure was not universally embraced. In a document of 1790, the friar Agustín María de Castro criticized, in strong terms, a decision he believed to be based on reports "full of scruples and ridiculous enthusiasms." Freeing native slaves made the life of *principales* much more difficult, and the Spaniards, in addition to giving up their Filipino slaves, lost servants bought "with our own money to the Malabar and Chinese and sold later in Acapulco earning a profit of 100 percent."[37]

Missionaries taught new agricultural methods for preparing the land and insisted that the natives should reserve the best seed to plant. Success was achieved in the most productive areas, such as Luzon and the island of Panay; elsewhere, the slash-and-burn method was still in use through the middle of the eighteenth century.[38]

Increased agricultural productivity allowed the Filipinos to produce large quantities of rice to sell in Manila, and in the seventeenth century, the galleon would export rice to Mexico.[39] As in other Southeast Asian places, sources of supply developed close to major urban markets for rice. Manila was near to Pampanga in the delta of the Rio Grande—the "rice basket" of Luzon—which grew two annual crops. Ilocos contributed a substantial amount of rice to the city, as well. In the Visayas, Panay's harvest supplied the southern garrisons of the Moluccas and Mindanao.[40]

It was not only rice that the colonizers took into account. The islands of Panay and Mindoro produced abaca, a vegetable fiber used in the rigging of ships; Ilocos provided cotton, and other regions specialized in the manufacture of a variety of textiles. Tar came from the province of Tayabas, and wax was gathered widely but mainly from the Calamian Islands. All of these commodities contributed to support the colony or the galleon line or were taken to Acapulco as cargo.[41]

Reorganizing the Territory

Changing natives' settlement patterns was considered necessary toward transforming the Philippines's societies. The Dominican Diego de Aduarte explained, "The Indians in their heathen condition live in farmsteads and tiny hamlets, where it is difficult to teach them. . . . Hence, to make good Christians of them, it is necessary to gather them in larger villages."[42] Plans for concentrated communities appeared in the last decades of the sixteenth century, but progress was slow. By the end of the seventeenth century, there were a total of two thousand persons distributed in fewer than twenty villages on the whole archipelago. The majority of the Filipinos were subsistence farmers living in close proximity to the land they cultivated, and fishing and hunting were important sources of their diet; transferring natives to large villages threatened to destroy the ecological balance of their livelihood. In the Visayas, Moro raids targeted some of these new coastal or river enclaves, adding a powerful disincentive to assemble in large population units. New settlements achieved moderate success in the central plain of Luzon. Nonetheless, during the seventeenth century, there was a surge in the number of small population clusters with no more than ten families, called *sitios*, connected to a principal village (*cabecera*), the seat of the parish. Every parish had a series of chapels (*visitas*), attended periodically by clergy living in the cabecera. This *cabecera-visita* complex was modeled on Mexico's early missions. The colonists did not completely achieve their goals, but sufficient numbers of Filipinos entered into social contact with Hispanic culture.[43] Natives were attracted to church rituals, the pageantry of Holy Week, the procession of Corpus Christi, Christmas celebrations, and festivities during the village's patron day. Some built houses near the parish church to attend holy days, but these residences emptied after celebrations, and natives went back to their communities. Colonial authorities did not employ violent means to enforce their settlements' policies except in extreme cases, for instance when in 1680 a military contingent removed a number of Zambals from their mountains as retribution for their attacks on the Pampanga province. The relocated Zambals were settled in three villages and received instruction in sedentary agriculture under the supervision of the Dominicans. This was an expensive effort, however, with the friars paying 10,000 pesos for the establishment of these new communities.[44] The removal of natives from their original homes, along with deforestation as a result of the cultivation of new lands, severely disrupted the habitat and its populations, all of which led to an increase in locust plagues.[45]

The Colony's Finances

In his detailed study of the Philippines's finances, Luis Alonso Alvarez distinguishes between two kinds of expenditures to obtain colonial profits.[46] First there were costs related to the galleon, requiring the Crown to pay for the ships' construction and upkeep and the merchants to purchase Asian commodities. Additional costs were needed to maintain the Spanish presence, including protection costs, consisting of salaries to royal officials and expenses to support the military, and financial assistance to missionary activity. There was a powerful reason to support the church. Officials were temporarily assigned to posts in the islands while the friars' continuous presence contributed to the inordinate power exercised by the church in the Philippines. In addition to religious education, the friars performed a series of formal and informal administrative services. The Crown was aware that Spanish hegemony in the provinces largely depended upon the authority and prestige the religious orders had among the natives.[47]

There is a widespread assumption that the Philippines were a financial drain on the Imperial Treasury during the sixteenth and seventeenth centuries. Allegedly the metropolis outlays outweighed imperial profits, leaving only religious and political goals as the reason for the continuation of the Philippines colony. The historian John L. Phelan maintains that the abandonment of the archipelago implied either the return of the Filipinos to paganism or the occupation of the islands by the Protestant Dutch: "More than any other single factor a religious and missionary commitment kept the Spanish state in the economically profitless Philippines."[48] It was not the case.

It would have been impossible to send any missionaries to the Philippines at all, had the Crown not shouldered the majority of their expenses during that long and costly voyage from Spain to Manila. However, royal grants did not totally cover the disbursements of the traveling missionaries, which implied that the Philippine provinces of the religious orders made up the difference. Furthermore, the many deaths caused by tropical diseases required the continuous arrival of new clergy to the islands; without this frequent replenishment, the church would have disappeared. Thomas Gage, an English Dominican who became a Puritan divine later in life, was one of these priests destined to the Philippines. He observed, "The chief strength of the Church of Rome in the Philippines is of missionaries brought from Spain, and they are more frequently conveyed thither than to any part of Spanish America."[49] Nonetheless, their numbers were exceedingly insufficient. In 1655, the Philippines had 254 regular and sixty secular priests, and by 1722, there were 1,500 members of the clergy. Until the mid-eighteenth century, by and large Filipinos did not receive orders as priests, nor were they allowed to enter a religious order. In 1601, the Jesuits counted eight Filipinos among their members, but they were probably brothers, not priests. The Dominicans in Manila educated Chinese, Japanese, and Vietnamese young men to be friars in their seminary, but not natives.[50] Reluctantly, the orders began to ordain Filipinos as secular priests; by 1750, only 142 out of 564 parishes were under the native clergy's care.[51] Because of the population dispersion and the lack of religious ministers, for most of the colonial period, Christians might have received the sacraments every three years. The scarcity of priests was evident in Manila, as well. In the Jesuit Church, Filipinos sometimes had to wait two weeks for confession.

The daunting problem of sending missionaries from Spain explains why members of religious orders were always in short supply. It took approximately eight months to cross the Atlantic and the Pacific, but with delays at Seville and Acapulco, the journey usually lasted at least two years. Oceanic travel implied living for weeks in squalid circumstances and suffering grievous diseases. To regain strength, missionaries would spend some months in Mexico before embarking at Acapulco. Gage, on his way to Manila in 1625, wrote that those friars relaxed at properties bought by the islands' religious provinces: "It had been no small piece of policy in the friars and Jesuits of Manila and the Philippine Islands to purchase near about Mexico some house and garden to carry thither such missionary priests as they yearly bring from Spain for those parts."[52] In Acapulco, religious orders used to rent houses for the friars waiting to embark on the galleon. Ten years later than Gage, the Dominican Domingo de Navarrete paid 400 pesos to rent a single-floor house of mud walls and thatched roof for a few weeks.[53]

Gage and his friends encountered a friar who had come from Manila and who told them to avoid the islands, "where occasions and temptations to sin were daily, many in number, mighty in strength, and to get out of them, *labor et opus*, hard and difficult." Along with the fear of temptations, he and his companions entertained the less elevated thought of "what a slavish and uncomfortable life they should live in the Philippines, without any hopes of ever returning again to Christendom." Gage opted for a parish in Guatemala.[54] They were not exceptions. Ominous forebodings meant that many priests never reached the Philippines. Aduarte wrote of these frightened friars, "First, the climate begins to affect them. Some die. Others contract a thousand illnesses. The tales they are told about their destination are not better than what they heard in Spain; much worse, in fact, for they have them from eye-witnesses, both lay people and friars, and they scarce have the courage to go any further."[55]

Once missionaries landed at Manila, the problem was how to keep them on the islands. The hot and humid climate caused deaths and sickness among the new arrivals, and until the 1630s many friars considered the Philippines a stepping-stone prior to departure for Japan or China. Eventually, the hostility of Chinese and Japanese authorities stopped such attempts to spread Christianity in their lands.[56]

Friars in charge of parishes received a stipend. In addition to this remuneration, natives worked without payment as porters and rowers as well as providing manual labor for the construction of churches and other buildings, and often the clergy requested from their parishioners fish, rice, and free domestic labor. In 1603, the Jesuit Sánchez wrote to Acquaviva in Rome, explaining how Filipinos were constantly pressed "to act as bearers and oarsmen for encomenderos and missionaries, for there are no pack animals here, and so they must perforce be our beasts of burden." Diego de Bobadilla left an account of the reception given to a group of Jesuits in 1643, illustrating Sánchez's observation. The Jesuits had landed at Lampon, on the eastern coast of Luzon, and traveled to Manila overland. One hundred bearers carried their baggage up the slippery trail that climbed to the Sierra Madre passes and descended again to Laguna de Bay, where boats would take them down the Pasig River to Manila. Natives carried the sick on litters.[57]

With the exception of the Dominicans and the Jesuits, the religious orders charged heavy fees for the administration of sacraments. A number of ecclesiastics required their parishioners to sell products below market price; as a result, the friars took quantities of rice, wax, and cloth to markets in Manila and abroad at substantial profits. Villages close to Manila had to provide gratis domestic help for the convents, with the upside that these servants were exempt from the system of public labor known as the polo service.[58]

After a native uprising in 1621, Governor Alonso Fajardo (1618–1624) informed the king that Filipinos felt aggrieved by resettlement policies, exactions from the friars, and corporal mistreatment. The governor lamented that the rebels took into account neither the friars' protection against abuses from other Spaniards nor the many spiritual benefits received from the missionaries: "Of all of this they forget when the friars forced them to abandon their old dwellings and whipped them or their women, or cut their hair."[59] In a 1685 pamphlet, Alonso Sandín, a friar, justified the use of corporal discipline with psychological and moral arguments: "Everyone who has any understanding of the native character considers these punishments to be absolutely necessary, otherwise they would hardly be Christians at all; as it is, they are preserved from committing many faults."[60] Such penances were not suffered by the Filipinos alone. In the Visayas in 1615, a Jesuit convicted of sins against chastity before dismissal "was placed in stocks by his local superior and commanded to be whipped in the presence of the town officials as public reparation for the scandal he had caused."[61] As late as the second half of the eighteenth century (1766), Le Gentil witnessed, in a village close to Manila, how "a woman who had failed to go to Mass that day . . . was being taken to the church to be whipped."[62]

Despite abuses, a majority of lowland Filipinos converted to Christianity. Religious ideas were conveyed through church buildings, paintings, images, music, and theater, in addition to the pageantry of processions, rituals, and religious celebrations. The missionaries also instituted the systematic education of children and the organization of sodalities and confraternities. The publication of catechisms and religious tracts in local languages played an important role in the islands' evangelization. The large majority of Filipinos did not learn Spanish, and the friars were required to use indigenous languages in their missionary work. Evangelization was thorough in proportion to proximity to Manila. Pampangans and natives of Cagayan were more culturally and religiously assimilated than people from the Visayas, in which thirty Jesuits were in charge of fifty thousand or seventy thousand souls.[63] A syncretic Christianity emerged in which, despite friars' efforts, pre-Spanish beliefs and customs were still very much present.[64] Filipinos might have had difficulty with the institution of Catholic marriage and penance, but other sacraments and practices were accepted easily, such as baptism and coparenthood. Rosaries and crosses became new talismans. At the same time, Christianity conveyed a deeply comforting and predictable moral universe in which individual conduct determined an afterlife of reward or punishment.

There was an added benefit to the presence of friars; their lack of ties to kinship groups allowed them to act as arbiters in local conflicts with a degree of impartiality. In the words of Victor Lieberman, "Thus arose not only the Spanish state of the Philippines, but a Christian culture sphere, which after the Theravada, Neo-Confucian, and Muslim zones, was the last and smallest Southeast Asian cultural zone to cohere."[65]

Native Contributions to the Colonial Economy

Alonso Alvarez, after a detailed examination of colonial tax accounts, affirms that natives' fiscal contributions "constituted the largest sources of income that the Spanish power obtained in the Islands, by a large difference greater than the Mexican *situado*—the funds shipped in the galleon to support the colonial establishment—or any other levies."[66] Natives' taxes, along with exactions of labor and goods, formed the basis of the colonial economy.

Initially, the tribute consisted of a tax equivalent to eight reals per year paid by each household head; single men and women in their twenties paid half this amount, four reals. In 1595, the Audiencia in Manila issued a regulation of payments. Tributes thereafter consisted of money and an equivalent payment in products that were ordinarily plentiful in each province. In 1604 it was established that in the provinces, encomenderos collected four reals in produce, one fowl, and the remaining six reals in coin. During the seventeenth century the tribute was paid partially in money and partially in products (*tributo mixto*). Natives also paid tithes (equivalent to one real), another real for the community funds, and three reals for the church. To support defenses against the sultanates, a tax equivalent of half a real was collected from 1655 to 1850.

Related to the tribute was the institution of the *encomienda*. To compensate soldiers, the Crown named them *encomenderos* of a territory, an encomienda, with the privilege of collecting tribute from natives for a period of time; royal officials did the same in the territories under their jurisdiction. Native magistrates, called *cabezas de barangay*, collected these levies using a procedure called *cuenta cerrada*. They negotiated with Spanish officials an amount of products and money proportional to the number of tributes in each territorial unit, to be collected from natives and delivered to Spanish authorities. Legázpi awarded the first encomiendas in Manila in January 1571. The encomienda system had provided the Crown with the means to reward soldiers for their services. Initially, what made the encomienda especially lucrative was how blatantly the encomenderos abused the system, but during the first decades of the colony, the clergy actively exposed the encomenderos' violations of the law. The consolidation of the galleon trade and a gradual increase in rice production diminished the burden on the Filipinos, as well. As had happened in the Americas, the Crown rejected the colonizers' requests to make encomiendas hereditary. Gradually, the government eliminated them altogether. In 1621 there were 97,422 private encomiendas; in 1766, only 18,196 remained. The end of the institution officially took place by decree in 1721, indicating that vacant encomiendas would revert to the Crown and would not be assigned to anybody else. The tribute, now collected by the Crown, lasted until the end of the colony. In 1874, the tribute was fourteen reals, only four reals more than the amount established in 1589.

Tributes went to pay the missionaries' stipends, the transportation of merchandise to the provincial capital, and the salaries of colonial authorities, as well as local defense. With the produce of their territories, officials and encomenderos participated in the lucrative business of providing foodstuffs and supplies to government warehouses and the Manila market. This tribute was to remain in place until the second half of the eighteenth century, when these tributes came to be deposited instead into the Manila treasury.[67]

A further crucial source of revenue was the *bandala*, meaning "purchase" in Tagalog, which in reality was the compulsory sale of products to the government. Manila assigned an annual quota of goods to each province, and the *alcaldes mayores* distributed the quantity among the villages in their provinces. The collection went to provision the royal warehouses, the Cavite's arsenal, and the City of Manila. The governor established an official price, or *arancel*, for each required item, such as rice, timber, wax, and so on. However, in the provinces, the official in charge had the choice to pay for goods at the market or at the official price according to his own convenience; in addition, native authorities were responsible for collecting the assigned quotas, providing them with the opportunity to buy extra products at their own expense. Filipinos transported the goods free of charge to Manila, where they were sold. In reality, the bandala became an extralegal and burdensome form of taxation, since the hard-pressed treasury was in no position to pay; instead, the natives received promissory notes, and only from time to time did authorities make token payments.

A third native contribution was the *polo*, or the obligation to work forty days each year in public works for a small compensation that usually went unpaid. To support these workers, *polistas*, there was a stipend in rice paid by their community. These laborers cut trees, *cortes de madera*, and transported the logs to Cavite for the galleons' construction; they worked in the shipyards and were in charge of making cannonballs and other munitions. They served as rowers and porters, as domestic servants in convents, as sailors for the galleon, and as soldiers for the army. Through the institutions of tribute, polo, and bandala, native economies were integrated into the colonial market and the galleon trade.

War with the Dutch imposed an additional burden on the Filipinos. Of all of the provinces, Pampanga experienced the most pressure from the bandala and the polo, and its fertile territory and proximity to Manila meant that its rice and timber were in constant demand. In 1636, Domingo Navarrete commented upon the galleons' shipwrecks and other misfortunes that "the loss of so many ships was very afflicting but the greatest blow fell upon the Indians." Spaniards gathered six or eight thousand natives to cut trees and transport the logs to the shipyards. In addition, "under pretense of cutting for one, timber enough for two ships is cut, so that many persons make a profit of the labor of the Indias."[68] Many Filipinos fled the islands, and Navarrete concluded, "In all places whosesoever I was, from China as far as Surat I met with natives of Manila and its lesser Islands."[69]

The Situado

Three times during the reigns of Philip II, Philip III, and Philip IV the Council of Indies debated abandoning the Philippines. The archbishop of Seville was fearful of New Spain's independence based on trade stimulated by the galleons. In 1621 it was suggested that Panama become the American port for the galleon where the Audiencia could closely supervise its operations, and after the union with Portugal, the idea of exchanging the islands for Brazil was put forward. In the eighteenth century, the first minister of Philip V, Cardinal Alberoni (1717–1721), proposed to cede the Philippines and the galleon line to France. Competition with Seville-centered trade, Mexican political autonomy, and expenditures to the treasury were the arguments against Spain's occupation of the islands.

The Philippines were under the financial purview of New Spain (Mexico), which sent the Philippine situado to defray costs of administration in the Philippines. The situado was at first only the returns from the *almojarifazgo* duties—taxes paid over the exported merchandise—and other levies collected at Acapulco but later "became half-subsidy and half-commercial income; with the Mexican treasury making up from its own financial resources what the galleon trade could not adequately produce."[70] Corruption diverted situado monies to private pockets. For instance, in 1636, merchants in Acapulco made a shelter with boughs and leaves of palm trees to protect merchandise and people. "For a piece of work like this they have some years charged his majesty's account 8,000 pieces of eight for expenses; and this is defrayed out of the supply sent to the Philippine Islands." Similar outrageous charges, totaling some 800 or 1,000 pesos, were applied to the repairs of a small boat to carry goods and people aboard the galleon.[71]

The lion's share of funds from Mexico came from military expenditures in the war with the Dutch, particularly to gain control over the Moluccas. In 1621, according to Hernando de los Ríos Coronel (former procurator general of the islands), taxes collected in Manila totaled 255,541 pesos, compared to the expenditures for the Moluccas campaign, which represented 218,372 pesos. A report of 1637 indicated that the costs of the Ternate garrison produced a deficit of 290,000 pesos, charged annually against the Manila treasury.[72] Grau y Monfalcón, procurator general of the colony, reported (1640) that the colony's total revenue was 256,000 pesos, while expenses for the Moluccas reached 230,000 pesos. Receipts in the two years of 1621 and 1640 equaled 511,541 pesos combined, while 448,372 pesos were spent on the Moluccas. This means that only 12.35 percent of those taxes (31,585 pesos) was available for the Philippines's local costs during these two isolated dates.[73]

In addition to military expenses, widespread fiscal fraud contributed to the deficit until late in colonial times. Fausto Cruzat Góngora (1690–1701) proved to be an exception to this general corruption. Cruzat implemented a period of rigorous tax collection that resulted in 500,000 pesos saved to the Mexican treasury. With this capital, he began a program of public works continued by his successor Domingo de Zabalburu y Echeverri (1701–1709).[74] A few years after him, Governor Fernando Manuel de Bustillo Bustamante (1717–1719) infuriated citizens, friars, and the archbishop in his determination to collect large sums owed to the government. On October 11, 1719, a mob led by friars assaulted the governor's palace and killed him and his son.

In emergencies, governors requested loans without interest from the *Obras pias*. Quantities oscillated in the 1630s between 200,000 pesos in 1630 and 11,000 in 1635; the 100,000 requested during 1636 compensated for the low figure from the previous year.[75] The Philippine situado and the request of loans from the population were common features in the empire. The viceroy of Peru was in charge of the security of the west coast of South America from Chile to Panama; the protection of the Pacific coast of Mexico was the responsibility of the Mexican Treasury, and the Philippines was included in the Spanish Empire's global struggle for hegemony against its enemies in America, Asia, and Europe. As in the Philippines, fortresses and troops in America received situados.

The biography of Antonio de Morga vividly illustrates the life of an imperial bureaucrat during the Eighty Years' War against the Dutch. After leaving the Philippines in 1603 in command of the ships sailing for New Spain,

Morga became a member of the Royal Audiencia of Mexico City, where he was also advisor to the viceroy on military matters and counsel for the Holy Office of the Inquisition. Experience in the Philippines, Mexico, and Peru gave Morga a perspective on the Pacific in its entirety. He considered the ports on the west coast of America as interdependent with the Philippines and the Moluccas, with Manila serving as a crucial enclave for securing the Spanish position in the Pacific. In 1615, Dr. Morga predicted that the Dutch would make a strenuous effort to take the Philippines.[76] They knew very well that the exceptional harbors of Acapulco and Manila served as Spain's only gateways to the Chinese market, which explains the Dutch attempt to seize Acapulco in 1624, as well as their expeditions against Manila. Spain's Eighty Years' War in the Low Countries was no doubt its greatest financial drain, but struggles against enemy forces in America and Asia also imposed a substantial burden on the Imperial Treasury. In 1630, a Dutch observer wrote that the Spanish king spent 5 million guilders—about 2.5 million pesos—to defend the Indies every year, with the implication that this money was unavailable to finance military operations in Europe against the Netherlands.[77] Likewise, Dutch ships and troops were quite costly. Most of the remittances coming from Holland, in addition to a large proportion of the profits from trade, went to support the Dutch East India Company's garrisons and fleets.

The budgetary reality of the Philippines was quite different from appearances. Manila, like strategic places in America, received a subsidy, a situado—partly of the galleon proceeds—to defray military costs. Taxes previously collected on the galleon-transported silver from American mines earned a net profit for the Crown. In the islands, parishioners supported the church with their labor, products, and money. The galleons were built with native resources and the work of thousands of Filipinos, while tributes and bandalas went to maintain colonial administration. In fact, the Philippines was a highly cost-effective holding for Spain.[78]

The Role of Manila in the New Territorial Arrangements

Spaniards, like other Europeans in the east, suffered high rates of death from tropical diseases. A paymaster at Goa in 1634 stated that out of 5,228 soldiers who embarked at Lisbon between 1629 and 1634, only 2,495 survived the voyage.[79] In a study of the Cape route between 1500 and 1795, Jan de Vries calculates that European imports from Asia averaged fifty thousand tons annually ("ton burden" represents about a metric ton or 2,240.6 pounds), while two million men set sail to Asia but probably less than half of them ever returned due to fatalities at sea or at their destinations. Such figures indicate that during the course of three hundred years, Portugal and the companies lost one life for every 4.7 tons of Asian cargo shipped to Europe.[80] Given this high mortality rate, it is improbable that in any year between 1600 and 1740 more than 50,000 Europeans were living in Asia; by 1800 it could have been a total of 75,000.[81]

Figures of Spaniards in the Philippines correspond to similar trends. In 1650, 7,350 Spaniards lived within the walls of Manila; in 1702 the Spaniards were only 1,600, and by 1750 the city was inhabited by 7,000.[82] Manila was a cosmopolitan enclave connecting an array of markets, the single port that linked Spanish America, Imperial China, and Mughal India in a series of trading relations.[83] A Jesuit, in a letter to his general superior, Acquaviva, wrote in 1611 that eighty different nationalities took part in the festivities to celebrate the beatification of Ignatius Loyola; each group was "different from one another in language, color, region and usages, but all Christians."[84] In 1662, Bartolomé de Letona enumerated Manila's numerous trading partners—China, the islands and peninsulas of Southeast Asia, Japan, India, Sri Lanka, and Persia—and observed its assorted population: "The diversity of the peoples, therefore, who are seen in Manila and its environs is the greatest in the world; for these include men from all kingdoms and nations—Spain, France, Italy, Germany, Denmark, Sweden, Poland, Muscovy." De Letona added, "People from all the Indies, both eastern and western; and Turks, Greeks, Moors, Persians, Tartars, Chinese, Japanese, Africans and Asiatics. And hardly is there in the four quarters of the world a kingdom, province, or nation which has not representatives here."[85] Manila, like its counterpart Batavia or the British enclaves in India, was surrounded by walls and forts that both provided protection and functioned as prestigious symbols of its respective colonial system. Robert R. Reed characterized Manila and Batavia as centers of change that made possible the transformation of indigenous customs and facilitated social integration. In these cities, "men and women are concerned with the market, with rational organization of production of goods, with expediential relations between buyer and seller, ruler and ruled and native and foreigner . . . priority comes to be given to economic growth and the expansion of power."[86]

Indirect Rule: The Principalía

As in America, natives were considered legal minors protected by the Crown and church. They formed the *república de los indios* with their own laws, authorities, and languages; the majority of indigenous peoples spoke no Spanish. With the exception of the friar's lands, there was nothing in the

Philippines similar to the large *haciendas* of Mexico. Instead, the Spaniards implemented an indirect system of exploitation of the native population by co-opting the original Filipino upper class, the datus, to deliver local resources and a native labor force and basing the local government on the native kinship unit (barangay).

The archipelago was divided into twelve provinces; below these administrative partitions were the *pueblo de Indios*, which consisted of a cabecera and small settlement *barrios*, or *visitas*, as well as smaller divisions called *sitios*. Every pueblo was under its native petty governor, or *gobernadorcillo*, who was elected annually. Within the pueblos, the people formed groups of forty to fifty tributes called barangays, which were supervised by the *cabezas de barangay*. There was a second tier of authorities, of which the most relevant was the "lieutenant major," *teniente mayor*; and the three "major judges"—*policía*, *sementeras*, and *ganado*—in charge of keeping order and dictating agricultural practices. The gobernadorcillo performed some judicial functions, as well, which allowed him to prosecute and imprison culprits and to preside over lawsuits in which the quantity disputed was no more than forty-four pesos in value. A number of officers and ministers of justice assisted him in these widely varied functions.

Initially, the cabeza de barangay was a position inherited by the eldest son of the previous cabeza, but in time it became elective. This system of government was to remain unchanged until the legislation of 1786, when the hereditary succession of the cabezas de barangay ended and was replaced by a restricted electoral system. A cabeza's term of office was three years. Both father and son were exempt from paying tribute or performing labor services; cabezas and their wives received the honorific titles of *Don* and *Doña*, which came with symbols of authority, including canes, hats, and other regalia. They occupied seats of honor in church and attended all public functions in the pueblos together. After their tenure, gobernadorcillos and cabezas constituted a respected and influential group within the pueblo.[87] The electors of the gobernadorcillo were those who were or had been cabezas de barangay; after three years of service they became eligible for the office of petty governor. The families of the gobernadorcillos and cabezas, as well as the lieutenant major and the three major judges, received the title of *principalía* or *común de principales*, the class of notables. Their crucial role in the colonial system was to collect the pueblo's tributes and assign services. In practice, the missionary supervised this collection and was the most important person in the pueblo, the priest being the only Spaniard allowed by law to reside in the native villages; other officials, such as the alcalde, had to reside in the cabeceras.[88]

The parish priests received invaluable assistance from the principalía. They supplied bearers or oarsmen for transportation, assigned young people of the town in rotation to do the parish chores, manage the festivals, and set the tone for the parish. They were in charge of the community chest, which provided funds for charity works as well as the parish's public improvements.[89] In addition, these principales served as sacristans, *fiscales*, and celadores in charge of overseeing attendance of church masses and ceremonies and Christian indoctrination, as well as reporting on those who practiced native religion. Usually they were the leaders of confraternities and sodalities organized by missionaries. The friar often exempted these servants from the tribute and from the polos and secured a salary for them from the pueblo funds.[90]

This principalía performed two roles essential to the functioning of the colonial government. Foremost, they served as intermediaries between the material demands of the Spanish regime and the productive capacities of the population; the principales were the local political administrators. The principalía, in their role as intermediaries, had to negotiate between their own desire for enrichment, Spanish requests, and their fellow Filipinos' complaints. Only under extreme conditions did they abandon Spanish authorities to command natives into armed rebellion to redress local grievances.[91]

Colonial Administration

Above the native magistrates were the Spanish alcaldes mayores, in charge of the twelve provinces. They also presided over a provincial court, assisted by a lawyer and a notary. When a particular provincial territory was extensive, another Spaniard (*corregidor*) would rule smaller territorial units. Alcaldes and corregidores received a paltry salary, which they supplemented by extorting from natives. The *encomenderos* were the main authority in the territory in which they collected tributes, until the institution disappeared. The parish priest added his influence to this power structure, and his presence proved difficult to ignore.

The governor was also captain general and the main authority of the Philippines. His power was limited only by the control imposed by the Audiencia. He appointed all of the officials in the islands and was the president of the Audiencia, though one without a vote. A powerful deterrent that kept a governor from overreaching his authority was the inquiry, called *residencia*, at the end of his term of office. In the Philippines, the residencia for a governor lasted six months. His successor conducted the procedure, and all the resulting documentation went to the Council of Indies in Spain.

The Audiencia was composed of four judges, called *oidores*—fiscal, attorney general, advocates for the accused, and a defender of the natives—and other officials. The Audiencia was the highest court of appeals for criminal and civil cases. Through 1715, the Audiencia took charge of the civil administration in the interim between the death of a governor and the arrival of his successor, and the senior judge assumed the military command. The administration of Manila was the duty of a city council, consisting of two ordinary majors called alcaldes, eight council members, regidores, a registrar, and a constable. The alcaldes were justices who were annually nominated to the cabildo from among the city's Spanish householders. The regidores, notary, and constable held office in property. Imperial authorities sold permanent positions in the cabildo. Manileños could buy, sell, or inherit such posts, as was customary in imperial territories. The Archbishop of Manila held the highest position in the church; the other ecclesiastical authorities were the three bishops, one in Cebu, another in Segovia in Cagayan, and the third in Caceres in the Camarines. In addition, there were the provincial friars of regular orders including Dominicans, Augustinians, Franciscans, and Jesuits. The Episcopal court, which consisted of the archbishop, the vicar-general, and a notary, tried cases that fell under the canon law. A commissioner represented the Inquisition, though his authority was limited since its procedures were dependent upon the tribunal of New Spain. This commissioner first reported possible crimes to the tribunal in Mexico and, if a trial was warranted, the accused traveled by galleon to New Spain. In the case of a conviction, the guilty person returned to the Philippines to receive his punishment. Indians and Chinese were under the purview of the Episcopal court and exempt from the Inquisition's jurisdiction.

CHAPTER FOUR

~

The Seventeenth Century

The "Little Ice Age"

The eruption of the Huanyaputina volcano in southern Peru took place at the beginning of the seventeenth century. "In China, the sun was red and dim, with large sunspots." The summer was one of the coldest recorded in the Northern Hemisphere. Similar volcanic activity, followed by cold periods, occurred between 1641 and 1643.[1] Volcanic eruptions, which produced dense veils of emissions and fewer sunspots—the Maunder Minimum (1645–1715)—diminished the amount of solar energy received by the earth. El Niño—Southern Oscillation, or ENSO—also disrupted the climate. El Niño occurs in the Pacific waters of coastal South America when changes in the currents' direction produce a rise in ocean temperature; it constitutes the oceanic system most important in relation to Southeast Asia.[2] The decades from 1620 to 1640 witnessed the lowest temperatures on earth since 1000 CE. Cooler temperatures came with droughts, torrential rains, and unsettled weather patterns worldwide; for more than two hundred years, mountain glaciers advanced in the Alps, Iceland and Scandinavia, Alaska, China, the Andes, and New Zealand.[3] Populations suffered starvation, and death rates soared due to periodic famines, plagues of locusts, and epidemics. Large areas of Asia endured extensive and serious social disruptions.

In China, poor weather coincided with a deterioration of the Ming dynasty's budgets. China, like other countries, had felt the consequences of the Price Revolution, and the dynasty's fiscal foundation was consequently revealed to be faulty; all commodities had been valued in silver, which had lost its value, and the purchasing power of tax revenues diminished along with it. This inflationary trend affected the livelihood of almost everyone in the empire.[4] On top of these hardships, since 1584 northern and southern China suffered droughts, famines, and flooding. By 1594, "people in some parts of China were reduced to eating the bark of trees, the seeds of grass, or even seeds from the excrement of wild geese."

Drought was particularly severe during the years 1637 to 1641, with grain prices reaching extraordinary levels. There were reports of cannibalism and people disinterring corpses for food. Peasant uprisings spread throughout the Empire. In 1644 Li Zicheng, commanding an army of rebels, occupied Beijing. The Manchus defeated both the rebellious army and remaining Ming forces, installed a new dynasty, the Qing, and continued the occupation of China against Ming loyalists. Extreme climatic conditions in the northeastern territory had provoked Manchu attacks on China since the 1630s. "This explains why nearly all of the Manchus left their homeland and moved southward after the conquest."[5]

To confront the Ming loyalist Zheng Chenggong—Koxinga in western sources—the new Qing dynasty issued a decree commanding the relocation of coastal populations to inland territories, which halted the importation of silver and provoked a deflationary spiral of silver prices. Treasury official Mu Tianyan explained to the emperor that stopping the importation of silver was similar to "blocking a source of water while expecting to benefit from its flow."[6] The Qing lifted the prohibition in 1681, but all these events greatly upset the Manila market.

In Southeast Asia, the study of tree rings from teak forests in Java shows a period of below-average rainfall from 1600 to 1679. Dry seasons in areas of eastern Indonesia and the Philippines negatively affected populations whose survival depended on the balance between the wet and dry monsoons. The reduced precipitation led to poor harvests, which generated malnourishment and lowered resistance to disease; lack of clean water from wells and rivers due to drought aggravated an already dire situation.[7] Widespread plagues affected the Philippines and elsewhere. Casimiro Díaz reported, "The year of 1685 was a hard one on account of the general epidemic of smallpox which raged, not only in these islands but in all the kingdoms of China and Eastern India—especially on the Coromandel Coast, where many millions of Malabar died." Throughout the archipelago, children accounted for a large portion of the fatalities, but the heaviest losses were in the mountains of Manila among the Aetas, with "so many dying that those mountain districts were left almost uninhabited." Deer and wild swine perished in great numbers too. Moreover, "in China many millions of people died, so that there was no one to cultivate the fields; this caused great famine and mortality, after the epidemic of smallpox."[8]

The End of the Silver Cycle

By 1640, bimetallic ratios around the world converged. The relocation of metal from low-value areas (America and Japan) roughly equalized its value in all markets. In China, it took thirteen ounces of silver to purchase one ounce of gold in 1635, while fifty years earlier it had taken only six ounces.[9] According to Adam Smith, "Between 1630 and 1640, or about 1636, the effect of the discovery of the mines of America in reducing the value of silver appears to have been completed, and the value of that metal seems never to have sunk lower in proportion to that of corn than it was about that time."[10] Political entities like the Spanish Empire, the already mentioned Ming dynasty, the Ottoman sultans, and so on, saw the value of their revenues declining relentlessly during the sixteenth and seventeenth centuries, with devastating social consequences.

The drastic decline of the buying power of silver took place when political crises and wars blanketed the world, exhausting national treasuries and disrupting economies. It was much harder for the major participants in Asian trade to conduct business. The Dutch East India Company (Vereenigde Oost-Indische Compagnie, or VOC) built costly fleets and armies to enforce a strict monopoly of trade. Spanish, Portuguese, and English enclaves and Asian free-trading ports were continuously attacked. Local merchants in the Indian Ocean saw their fortunes deteriorating, and Turks, Persians, and Arabs ceased traveling "below the winds" in the first two decades of the seventeenth century. The Dutch systematically attacked their competitors and became the only winner at the summit of Southeast Asian trade.[11]

The Eighty Years' War with the Netherlands

During the seventeenth century, the economic and political situation was extremely difficult for the dual Spanish-Portuguese monarchy. This greatly enlarged empire was engaged in a protracted war with the Netherlands from 1566 to 1648. Spain's strategy in Europe implied intervention in Germany, confrontation with England, conflicts in northern Italy, and war with France.[12] Yet the tropical world was the decisive theater for warfare between the Dutch and the Iberians. Spices, sugar, slaves, and trade with China were contested markets in the global struggle with the Dutch. It was the first global war involving Europeans and third parties, like Congolese,

Persians, Indonesians, Cambodians, Muslim Filipinos, and Japanese at various times and places.[13]

Economic transformations in the Low Countries propelled the Dutch to exercise power beyond Europe. The Netherlands had dominated the European bulk-carrying trade in grain, timber, salt, and fish since the fifteenth century, with their position notably strengthening during the sixteenth and the first two decades of the seventeenth century. This carrying trade suffered a severe decline in the 1620s. The slump precipitated a shift within the Dutch maritime economy, from bulk transportation to the "rich trades" of East India, Spain, and the Levant. It was "the new high-value commerce which provided the wealth and, no less important, the rare materials and skills which made possible the astounding variety and sophistication of the Golden Age."[14]

The Dutch observed a truce with Philip III in Europe from 1609 to 1621 while consolidating and extending their possessions in Asia at Portugal's expense and threatening Spanish possessions in both the Pacific and the Atlantic. In 1615 they attacked the coast of Peru and sailed to Acapulco, where they exchanged prisoners for supplies and left the Mexican coast after missing the Manila galleon. In 1628, Admiral Piet Pieterszoon Hein captured a silver fleet in the Caribbean. During the 1620s, the Spaniards had the upper hand against the Dutch in Europe: General Ambrosio Spinola won the Battle of Breda—Velázquez painted the surrender ceremony—and a Dutch fleet was defeated near Gibraltar. However, expenditures for distant forts and fleets diverted resources from the armies in the Low Countries, resulting in increased fiscal pressure on all imperial territories. Poor harvests in Spain produced general inflation; subsequently, the Crown declared bankruptcy to its Genoese bankers. The Count-Duke of Olivares, prime minister to Philip IV, had already lined up a syndicate of Portuguese of Jewish origin called "New Christians" willing to do business with the Crown. There was opposition from the Inquisition, but the main obstacles were merchants in Seville and elsewhere who were afraid of the extent of Portuguese penetration into American markets and in the galleon trade. In 1627, Olivares arranged for the New Christians to receive an "edict of grace" from the Inquisition, and in 1629 they were allowed freedom of movement.[15] The years between 1621 and 1640 were the "golden age" for these Portuguese merchants and bankers.

Olivares proposed the "Union de Armas" in 1626, a project that would have required each imperial territory to raise fixed quotas of soldiers, proportionate to their size and population. Despite its appearance as a purely military plan, it reflected Olivares's desire for the elimination of individual regions' privileges and fiscal autonomy. However, Olivares had misjudged the climate of the times, and soon events took an ominous turn. When fiscal pressure increased, numerous popular revolts erupted in Spain, Portugal, and imperial territories.

During the 1630s, transfers of American silver to the Royal Treasury were discouraging. Peru, under the rule of the Viceroy Count of Chinchón, sent substantial quantities, but in Mexico, mine production was not flourishing as it had during previous decades. American economies had fundamentally changed. Silver remittances to Spain were affected by factors beyond the metal's production, including the large quantities taking the transpacific route from Mexico and Peru to China and its use as payment for defense against the Dutch, who were now well established in Brazil and the Caribbean.[16] The Spanish fleet's defeat at the Battle of the Downs (1639) in the English Channel signaled the end of Spain's role as a naval power in the north Atlantic. The Catalans, afraid of occupation by an imperial army, refused to collaborate with the central government, and a revolt broke out in May of 1640, with the rebels placing themselves under the authority of Louis XIII of France. Spanish troops took the Catalonian capital of Barcelona in 1652, and a Franco-Spanish peace treaty was signed in 1659. To add to the woes of the already beleaguered government, a 1641 conspiracy by the Duke of Medina Sidonia and the Marquis of Ayamonte tried to separate Andalusia from the Crown.

Dutch hostilities during the 1630s and 1640s inflicted enormous losses on the Portuguese territories, and it was clear that Spain did not possess the resources to be of any help. In the Atlantic, Johan Mauritius of Nassau took Pernambuco (1637) and moved against Bahia, Brazil's main sugar producer, the following year. Attacks in Brazil were followed by the conquest of Sao Paulo de Loanda in Angola—the source of slaves for Brazilian plantations—and the islands of Sao Thome and Annobom in the Gulf of Guinea. In Asia, the Portuguese suffered reverses in Hormuz, Bengal, Burma, and Ceylon, and the shogun expelled them from Japan. They also lost Malacca to the Dutch, who occupied part of Taiwan as well. It was the end of an era, not only in Asia but also in world history.

Fiscal pressures and territorial losses led Portugal to move toward regaining independence from Spain. The Catalonian revolt created propitious circumstances for the Duke of Braganza to declare himself King João IV of Portugal in December of 1640. Meanwhile, the Portuguese in Brazil, Mombasa, Mozambique, Goa, and Ceylon followed the example of their home country and rebelled against Spanish authorities. The French supported them, and João IV immediately ratified a treaty with England and signed a truce with the Dutch in 1641 that would allow Portugal to keep its empire in Brazil and Africa. Madrid officially granted Portugal's independence via the Treaty of Lisbon in 1668.

The Peace of Westphalia, a series of accords signed after the Thirty Years' War (1618–1648), acknowledged the demise of Imperial Spain as a European power, and Philip IV formally recognized Dutch independence by way of the Treaty of Munster (1648). These agreements represented the defeat of the Habsburgs of Vienna and Madrid. Despite its diminished power, Spain retained territories in Italy, the Low Countries, and other parts of Europe, but not for long. Carlos II died without an heir, opening up the War of the Spanish Succession (1702–1713), another global war with objectives ranging far beyond the dynastic conflict. The Habsburgs of Vienna wanted the Spanish domains in Italy and the Low Countries; England expected to extend its influence in the Mediterranean and to partake of American resources, while for the French king, "the main objective of the present war [was] the Indies and the wealth it produce[d]."[17] The Treaty of Utrecht (1713) concluded the war and recognized Philip V, Bourbon, as king of Spain and of the American Empire. The remaining European territories (southern Netherlands, Naples, Sardinia, and Milan) went to the Habsburgs; the Italian Kingdom of Savoy received Sicily; Britain took Gibraltar and the Balearic island of Minorca, as well as a contract, *asiento*, to supply slaves to America and the right to send a ship each year, *navío de permiso*, to trade legally with the viceroyalties.

The Philippines and the War with the Dutch

With respect to commerce in the Philippines, the Dutch had two main objectives: the control of the Molucca and Banda Islands and the elimination of the silk trade between Manila and China. During the 1630s, the Dutch East India Company estimated that profits on Chinese silk were 150 percent as opposed to 100 percent in the Persian arena, which encouraged them to monopolize the market for the product.[18] Jan Pieterszoon Coen, Governor General of the East Indies (1627–1629), initiated an openly hostile policy to control trade with China. An attack on Macao ended in failure, but the Dutch were able to occupy an enclave in the Penhgu Islands off mainland China, establish Fort Zeelandia in Taiwan, and blockade Manila to disrupt the junk trade.

During the war, the Dutch maintained forty to fifty armed ships in the Philippine waters in any one year, and since 1600 there were frequent naval engagements between the two powers. Two Jesuits, the rector of the College of Manila and the superior of the Ternate missions, sailed to Goa in 1615 to persuade the viceroy of the Estado da India to undertake a combined fleet operation against the Dutch in the Moluccas. The Portuguese viceroy would send four galleons to Malacca to encounter the Spanish fleet. Juan de Silva sailed with a large armada of ten galleons, including the 1,700-ton *San Marcos* as flagship, as well as four galleys and a number of small boats armed with three hundred cannons. The vessels carried five thousand soldiers, including a contingent of five hundred Japanese infantry. The fleet's purpose was to attack the Dutch in Java and the Moluccas, but such plans were in vain; the Dutch had destroyed the Portuguese ships before de Silva could arrive, and the armada returned to Manila on June 1, 1616, with sailors ill from fever; many died, including the governor. Dutch dominion in Southeast Asia was settled by this disaster in a manner comparable to the defeat of the Invincible Armada in 1588. Dutch fleets attempted to take the capital of the Philippines in 1618 and 1620, and there was a naval battle between a Dutch squadron and five Spanish vessels in 1624. The years 1644 to 1647 witnessed continuous naval hostilities, but on all occasions, the attackers suffered defeats. In addition to the relentless harassment of Spaniards, Chinese junks were systematically captured as well. Peter Nuyts, the Dutch factor in Taiwan, wrote to the VOC directors, "We must do our utmost to destroy the trade between China and Manila, for, as soon as this is done, we firmly believe that your Excellencies will see the Spaniards leave the Moluccas, and even Manila of their own accord."[19] Junks usually weighed 350 tons; due to Dutch hostilities the Chinese decided to use smaller boats provided with oars as well as sails. In 1616, only seven junks had reached Manila instead of the fifty or sixty of former times, according to a Jesuit observer; the next year, Admiral Lam captured three junks carrying silks and seven transporting foodstuffs, "fruit junks," because Manila imported supplies from abroad. In 1621, a combined Dutch and English fleet blockaded the city until May 1622, and in the same year a Dutch fleet destroyed eighty junks off the coast of China. The silk trade began to decline when assaults from Taiwan disrupted the route of Amoy junks. Coen's policy against the junks did not produce the expected results, but the damage inflicted had been severe.

At the time that the Peace of Westphalia ended the war, the Spaniards still occupied the Philippines; galleons continued sailing, and trade with China remained the colony's economic mainstay. However, losses had been frightful: Chinese and Japanese junks had been captured, transpacific trade had suffered heavy damages, and lives had been lost in great numbers, while in the Chinese market, Dutch competitors had removed Manila and Macao from their privileged positions. When a Fujianese delegation of merchants who traded with Manila visited Batavia during Coen's time as governor general, it was an indication of the new commercial configuration.[20]

Successful resistance against the Dutch inflicted a heavy toll on the Fili-pino population. The Spaniards recruited large numbers of natives from their villages and sent them to cut logs in the forests, haul them to the shipyards, and work on the construction of ships for long periods of time. These labors drew in natives from the Bicol region, Leyte, and Samar, and fell most heav-ily on the provinces of Central Luzon because of the Cavite shipyard, about which Captain Sebastián de Pineda (1618) informed the king, addressing the construction of galleons. Natives constituted the labor force and received pay according to their expertise. Woodcutters each received seven or eight reals per month and a daily ration of half of a *celemín*, which is equivalent to 2.3 liters of rice. The salary for a more qualified carpenter was ten or twelve reals per month. Wages for Masters—"the ones who lay out, prepare, round; and make the masts, yards, and topmasts"—was three or four pesos of eight reals per month and double rations (8.6 liters) of rice.

Supposedly, the government was responsible for paying these salaries, but given the Treasury's chronic deficit, payments were almost always in arrears. In the best of circumstances, the laborer did not receive any money until his arrival at the shipyard, and his salary ceased when he finished his service, with no compensation for the journey back to his town. It was com-mon knowledge that a regular worker needed at least forty reals each month to survive. To compensate for the difference, the natives' villages provided funds to raise the government wage to the minimum survival requirement. Occasionally, authorities recognized these contributions as loans made to the state.[21] Between 1610 and 1616, the Treasury owed the Pampangos ap-proximately 70,000 pesos; by 1660, the figure was 200,000 pesos. During the same years, the accumulated debt from the polo and bandala to the Filipinos subjected to tribute amounted to 300,000 pesos.[22]

Pineda indicated that at Cavite, the construction of a fleet required 1,400 carpenters. He also referred to the losses caused by the 1617 raid from Mindanao. The Moros burned one galleon and two pataches, captured more than four hundred workers, and killed two hundred, "while many have died through the severe work in the building" of ships at Pantao. The Moros and Dutch were allies against the common Spanish enemy. The captain repeated the workers' complaints about salaries already five years in arrears, which explained why "many have fled from the land; and so few remain that when the last ships sailed from the city and port of Manila last year, 1618, there were not two hundred of those Indians in Cavite."[23] The Treasury often left wages unpaid for lack of funds, but the situation was aggravated by the cabezas of barangays, who often kept the salaries for themselves. Labor services damaged local economies: "When they worked for the Spaniards, the Filipinos could not work their own fields; if they did not plant, their families had no food, fell sick, and sometimes died; they would have no products or money to pay the tribute; and if they did not pay their tributes they suffered even more."[24]

Hernando de los Ríos Coronel, who served as agent for the city of Manila at Madrid, wrote that it took six thousand laborers three months to haul the masts of one of Governor de Silva's galleons from the mountains to Laguna de Bay, whence they were transported by water to Cavite. They received forty reals per month from their own villages and had to purchase their own rations out of that sum. This was not sufficient for sustenance, and many laborers died, others ran away, and still others killed themselves. In his "Reforms Needed in the Philippines," the same priest petitioned the king to bring galleons from India and pleaded on behalf of the workers that "inasmuch as the Indian natives have been so ruined by the past shipbuilding, and your Majesty is indebted to them, for personal services and things taken from them by Don Juan de Silva for your royal service," they were owed "more than one million pesos."[25] There were a number of uprisings in the provinces due to the cortes de madera and other grievances. In 1621, the island of Bohol witnessed a rebellion, which was easily suppressed by an expedition of fifty Spaniards and more than one thousand Cebuans; in Cagayan, another uprising was prompted by tributes and a resettlement policy; as of 1628, a large part of the area remained in revolt; an expedition of soldiers and two thousand Filipino auxiliaries confronted the rebels and burned eight villages.[26]

Philip III suggested that the governor explore the possibility of building the galleons outside the Philippines. In 1629, Governor Juan Niño de Tabora commissioned a galleon in Cambodia at a cost of 100,000 pesos, but a storm wrecked it while it was sailing to Manila. The project did not continue, and Pampangos and Tagalogs continued to build galleons. The Jesuit Annual Letter of 1706 described the appalling conditions at the Cavite shipyard:

> While the skimpy rations given them are scarcely sufficient to sustain life, the work demanded of them is heavier than bodies more robust than those of these natives can bear. They are turned out for work at three o'clock in the morning and are given no rest until almost eleven. They are back to work at one and do not stop until ten at night. There is neither Sunday nor holyday for these wretches, and their quarters are some ruined sheds open on all sides to wind and weather. They slip on the hard ground.[27]

Although Spain's confrontations with the Dutch had ended, work continued at the same unrelenting pace. Ships were required for trade with

Acapulco, to protect Chinese junks as they sailed to Manila, and to build the small navies necessary to counteract the Moros' raids. Wages for native laborers, which usually went unpaid, were temporarily forsaken. By 1657, government debt for foodstuffs and supplies reached more than 200,000 pesos, and the accumulated liabilities of the colonial treasury had reached the enormous figure of 1,000,125 pesos.[28]

The government decided in 1649 to conscript natives from the Visayas to mitigate the conditions for the Tagalog and Pampango provinces, which had provided the bulk of the labor force. Recruitment for work in distant Cavite precipitated a revolt in Palapag on the island of Samar. From Samar, the outbreaks spread across to Leyte, to the provinces of Albay and Camarines, and then the rebellion reached Caraga, Cagayan, and even Zamboanga in Mindanao. Under the governor's orders, a force of Christians from Zamboanga in Mindanao suppressed the insurgents of Palapag, and other rebellions were ruthlessly crushed elsewhere. However, the labor draft stopped. Revolts in the Visayas were quite uncommon: between 1565 and the British invasion of 1762, only three major uprisings took place. This relatively small number could be attributed to the fact that the Spanish military provided the natives' only protection against the Moros' yearly raids from Mindanao and Jolo.

Central Luzon's labor force and resources had guaranteed the continuity of the colony during such critical decades. In recognition of such contributions, Philip IV instructed local authorities in 1636 and 1642 to express his royal gratitude to the inhabitants of the Tagalog, Pampanga, and Bicol provinces for their loyalty. However, worrisome events took place in 1660 when the Pampanga, Pangasinan, and Ilocos revolted in protest against the arrears on many levies of rice and the request for laborers to cut trees for four months in the Bataan forests. The uprising lasted two months. Governor Sabiniano Manrique de Lara ended the conflict by paying an initial installment on the debt of some 200,000 pesos and promising to reduce the woodcutting service. In the symbiotic relationship between the colonial government and Pampangos, Manila protected the province from the fierce Zambals, and Pampanga provided the capital with rice, timber, labor, and soldiers.[29] Uprisings in Pangasinan and Ilocos were soon under control.

The Hispano-Dutch war drastically affected the total number of subjects under Spanish control. O. D. Corpuz, using colonial population records, provides the following numbers for the Filipino population: in 1591, there were approximately 667,612 natives, compared with 500,782 in 1608 and 456,868 in 1635; in 1655, documents show only 433,098 inhabitants under colonial authority. By 1662, the total Christian population had increased to 600,000 Filipinos.[30] Deaths of natives account for some of the diminishing numbers, while others escaped Spanish tax officials; both factors correlate with the falling numbers of taxpayers.

The Moro Wars

The Spaniards had uprooted Islam from Luzon and the Visayas, but Sulu and Mindanao remained independent entities under Muslim rulers. In 1635, under the supervision of the Jesuit Melchor de Vera, the Spaniards built a fortress in Zamboanga, a peninsula in northern Mindanao, to protect the Visayas against the Moros' raids. Morga had written about the teachings of "their *gaçizes* and other *morabitos*, who often come to preach and teach them, by way of the Strait of Malaca and the Red Sea, through which they sail to these islands."[31] From the last decades of the sixteenth century until the colony's demise, the Spaniards fought the Muslims of the south in what was called the Moro Wars. The Moros raided the Visayas from their seats in Jolo and Lake Lanao in Mindanao and took captives to slave marts in Indonesia and Batavia, the capital of the Dutch East India Company. Slave raiding had a long history in the Philippines, but as Muslims were forbidden from enslaving their coreligionists, the spread of Islam made non-Muslim Filipinos a major source of captives.

Despite their history of hostility with the southern sultanates, Scott asserts, "Whatever success the Spaniards enjoyed during their first fifty years in the Philippines was obtained through cordiality with Moros"; in fact, they were their interpreters and advisors, and Muslims from Manila brought foodstuffs to the starving Spaniards in Cebu.[32] This had been a regular commercial procedure when the Spaniards appeared to be like any other merchant group. However, as soon as they showed themselves to be intent on displacing the Moros from their commercial networks, violence erupted. The first sparks in this long-lasting conflict began with the Spaniards' capture of Manila, which was linked to Borneo and the destruction of the Muslim enclaves in Mindoro. In 1578, Governor Francisco de Sande sailed for Brunei in the north coast of Borneo and commanded an expedition that was able to capture the capital. After ransacking the main settlement, he burned houses, took all artillery, and brought the doors and objects of their mosques back to Manila. Sande declared Brunei a vassal state of Spain but "abandoned the place and returned to Manila, both on account of sickness among his crew and also because he could not support and maintain the Spaniards in the island."[33] Natives tried in 1589 to organize an uprising in connection with Borneo. A number of Filipino datus engaged in negotiations with the captain of a Japanese junk and sent envoys to the sultanate. The insurgents also tried to establish contact with the Englishman Cavendish, who had attempted to capture the galleon *Santa Ana* without success. Because the Japanese did not arrive, the datus decided to count on the participation of a Bornean fleet to join local insurgents. A Filipino servant of an enco-mendero, Antonio Surabao, revealed the plot. Governor Santiago de Vera imprisoned the conspirators and ordered the beheading of seven members of leading families and of the Japanese interpreter Dionisio Fernández. The lesser datus suffered diverse penalties, and eleven of them were condemned to exile. However, there was no galleon that year to transport them, and the punishment did not take effect.[34] None of the Tagalog villages attempted to save their former lords, and the inhabitants of Pampanga similarly refused to join the uprising: the conspirators belonged to the previous noble class, which had lost the support of its subjects.

At the time of Spanish arrival, the Magindanau society of Mindanao Island had a social hierarchy similar to that of the Tagalogs and the inhab-itants of the Visayas. However, they had added a prince, or *kachil*, to the traditional Filipino social structure. The institution of kachil came from the Moluccas, and the power of these princes gave the Magindanaus a social cohesion unknown by other societies in the archipelago. Rice and sago palm were the main sources of food for the Magindanau, but their territory did not produce goods for trade, which partially explains their practice of slave-raid-ing—slaves were the only available commodity allowing them to participate in trade networks. In a letter to the Governor of Manila, a Spanish captain wrote, concerning the project of conquering the island, "that it will be of but little advantage to his Majesty, but a source of great expense. It has far fewer inhabitants than was reported, and all are very poor." The land was swampy and "there is no chief who can raise twenty taes of gold. Rice is very scarce; in the tingues is found a small amount, which is used for food by the chiefs only."[35] The peoples of the southern coast of Mindanao and the Sulu archi-pelago had similar social and economic situations.[36] They used harquebuses and small artillery, but what gave them a fundamental advantage were their boats. A number of rowers on each side propelled their karakoas, which were extremely well adapted to an insular sea full of reefs, rocks, and dangerous currents. The Jesuit Francisco Combes (1667) compared karakoas favorably to Spanish craft: "The care and technique with which they build them makes their ships like sail birds, while ours are like lead in comparison."[37]

In 1578, the Spaniards failed to make vassals of the chiefs of Sulu and Magindanau; this event was followed by unsuccessful attempts to establish a permanent settlement in Mindanao as part of Spain's plan to conquer the Moluccas. Finally in 1591, the Manila government decided to colonize Mindanao. For this purpose, "orders arrived from Spain, ratifying an agreement made by Captain Esteban Rodríguez de Figueroa with Governor Gómez Pérez Dasmariñas under which the former was to pacify and colonize the island of Mindanao at his own expense." The people of the Mindanao River, however, put up a fierce fight; Figueroa died in battle, putting an end to the campaign.

The Mindanao peoples were not alone in their enmity toward the Spaniards; Muslims from Ternate contributed significantly to their resistance. A Spanish captain, for instance, encountered in Mindanao a Muslim teacher from Ternate, "a *casis* who instructed them in their religion." To continue Figueroa's undertaking, the governor sent another expedition under the command of Captain Juan de Ronquillo. In a letter to the governor, Ronquillo explained the difficulties of conquering the land and the lack of economic resources, but he was aware of the strategic value of Mindanao for conquering the Moluccas. In conversation with local chiefs, he demanded that the Magindanao "break the peace and confederation made with the people of Terrenate, and must not admit the latter into their country."[38] Ronquillo did not achieve his expedition's aims; instead, following Governor Tello's instructions, he punished the Moors before leaving the islands "by destroying as much as he could of one of the region's principal sources of food. He cut down or set fire to all the coconut and sago palms within reach of his patrols, to the number of 50,000 trees."[39]

The Spaniards had a significant victory in the Moluccas with the capture of the Ternate sultan in 1606; soon the Moors of Mindanao sent a letter to Manila as a sign of friendship. It seems that this agreement worked, given that for more than two decades raids from that quarter stopped. If Mindanao kept the peace, there were other adversaries ready to take their place. In 1616, the Sulu, alerted to the presence of a Dutch squadron near Manila, decided to attack the shipyards at Pantao in Camarines. They entered Manila Bay, burned the Cavite navy yard, and carried away a number of Spanish prisoners. It was an effective strategy; they repeated the attack in Camarines in 1627. Muslim cooperation with Spain's enemies added a new dimension to the Moro Wars. The Dutch sent an ambassador to Muslim territories in 1628 for the dual purpose of discussing a common strategy against Spain and gathering commercial information. The Dutch encouraged the Magindanaus and the people of Jolo to raid the Visayas, urging them to destroy shipyards and burn ships under construction.

Coastal outposts were established to protect their colonial subjects and to negate the collaborative efforts between the Muslims and the Dutch. For instance, the absence of large-scale raids for the twenty years following the 1609 establishment of a Spanish garrison at Caraga in northeast Mindanao suggests that the garrison may have obstructed the Magindanaus' traditional escape route. The communities of the Great River of Mindanao were also passing through a period of reorganization that contributed to the decline in piratical activities. In 1634, when the Magindanaus resumed their raids, the old confederation of datus had taken the form of a unified sultanate.[40] The government built the fort of Zamboanga (1635) to neutralize the sultanate of Sulu. Immediately, the sultan wrote to the Dutch about the establishment of the garrison and requested guns and military assistance.

Governor Gustavo de Corcuera commanded two successful expeditions in 1637 and 1638 against Mindanao and captured the city of Jolo in the Sulu archipelago. He received a triumphant welcome in Manila, but the scarcity of resources for occupying the territories implied that the strategic balance between the Spaniards and Muslims had not changed. Expeditions against the sultanates had the unexpected consequence of leaving the Spanish fort in Taiwan largely neglected, and in 1642 the Dutch captured the garrison.

Japan and the Friars

Mercantile exchanges between the islands and Japan began in the fifteenth century. Export items from the Philippines included forest products, gold, pearls, deerskins, and earthen jars used for tea ceremonies. Morga did not think much about these pots, noting that "in this island of Luzon, especially in the provinces of Manila, Pampanga, Pangasinan and Ilocos the natives have ancient earthenware jars which are brown in color and not especially attractive to look at." Nonetheless, in "Japan these jars are regarded highly as being the most precious jewels of their inner rooms and chambers." Morga asserted that the price for some of these jars was 2,750 pieces of eight.[41] The friar Jeronimo de Jesús (1595), in a letter to Manila, mentioned that shogun Toyotomi Hideyoshi, in need of resources for the Korean campaign, confiscated all tea jars coming from Manila. According to the friar, the total value of these precious objects was 80,000 taels—at the time one tael was equivalent to eleven Spanish reals—or 110,000 pesos. The letter added that after selling the tea jars, the shogun would add another 55,000 pesos of earnings. Such profits, the friar observed, are the reason "why the Japanese are dying to go to Manila."[42]

The missionary activities of friars from the Philippines dramatically changed relations between both countries. Their presence in Japan led to a heated confrontation with the Jesuits, which required the issuing of papal documents and rendered no significant results. The active role of the Jesuits in the silk trade between Macao and Nagasaki entangled religious disputes with economic and political considerations in the Philippines, Macao, and Japan.

Prior to unifying, Spain and Portugal agreed to the independence of both administrations, which would allow the Portuguese to retain their *padroado*, or religious patronage, in Asia. The padroado had demarcated China and Japan as a practically exclusive field of evangelization for Jesuits under Portuguese jurisdiction. Soon after the consolidation of the Spanish conquest of Luzon, Spanish Mendicant orders—Franciscans, Dominicans, and so forth—attempted to enter the Chinese mainland and Japan without success due to fierce local opposition. Alessandro Valignano, the head of the Jesuits in Asia, realized that Japanese feudal lords, *daimyos*, were fearful after the union of both crowns because "if they allowed the conversion of Christians in their fiefs, we could afterwards use them to raise a rebellion on behalf of the [Spanish] King who supports us."[43] Obviously, the arrival of friars from the Philippines increased Japanese alarm.

To illustrate the success of their missions, the Jesuits of Japan organized an embassy to Rome of four young envoys under the care of Nuno Rodrigues. The group reached Lisbon in August of 1584, two and a half years after leaving Nagasaki. In Spain, Philip II received them in an audience at the Monastery of El Escorial. They continued their tour with visits to Pisa, Florence, and Sienna before arriving in Rome in March of 1585, where the pope received the Japanese in a solemn audience. In Venice, the embassy held a grand reception before their return to Spain. Before departure for Portugal, Philip II had another audience with them, and the party finally sailed from Lisbon on April 18, 1586.[44] While these exciting events were taking place, Governor Gómez Pérez Dasmariñas had a visit in Manila from a Japanese envoy (identified as Faranda Quiemon in the Spanish sources) carrying a letter from Toyotomi Hideyoshi. The document demanded vassalage from the Philippines and contained threats of an invasion should the Spanish refuse to comply. The Spanish governor, to gain time, sent an ambassador in the person of the Dominican Juan Cobo. Hideyoshi received the friar, and during the course of diplomatic business, Cobo showed Hideyoshi a globe with the position and extent of the Spanish Empire, which made clear the formidable power of the Spanish king. Hideyoshi replied to the governor of Manila, but unfortunately, Cobo disappeared in a shipwreck on the return voyage. One more time Faranda made a visit to Luzon. His arrival coincided with distressing rumors about an imminent Japanese invasion, with the added fear that the Chinese and Tagalogs would join the attacking force. The governor sent another envoy to Hideyoshi, including Franciscan Pedro Bautista and three companions, all of whom the shogun cordially received. Hideyoshi's warmth stemmed from his plan to use the Spaniards as commercial competitors against the Portuguese. He wanted to break the Macao-Nagasaki trade monopoly so that Japan could acquire Chinese silks and gold at cheaper prices. The four Franciscans remained at Kyoto, hoping that their presence would encourage the arrival of Manila traders. They began openly celebrating Catholic rituals, despite advice from the Jesuits and Japanese officials to temper their zeal since the practice of Christianity was not legal in Japan. The Jesuits had been focusing their efforts on converting feudal lords while cautiously interacting with the authorities, assuming that they could remain in Japan so long as they carried out their work unobtrusively. For the sake of Portuguese trade, indeed, Hideyoshi was prepared to allow the missionaries' presence as long as they outwardly respected his prohibition. The Jesuit Luis Frois put it this way: "Although he is well aware that we are all in Japan, he still pretends not to know this."[45] In contrast, the newly arrived Franciscan friars engaged in their activities among commoners, built churches in Meako, Osaka, and Nagasaki, and openly conducted services in defiance of the shogun's explicit prohibition.

In the middle of this unstable state of affairs, the incidents surrounding the galleon *San Felipe* added a further level of tension. Forced ashore by a typhoon, the *San Felipe* made landfall off the Japanese coast on October 19, 1596, and the local samurai confiscated the cargo, valued at 1.5 million pesos. The Spaniards sent a delegation to Kyoto, hoping that Hideyoshi would intervene in the matter. In the meantime, the Spanish pilot, Francisco de Olandía, in an effort to impress Japanese officials with the majesty of the Spanish king, told them that the Spanish conquests had been greatly facilitated by the friars, who had prepared the terrain before the arrival of military forces. The Japanese took such observations extremely seriously, and Hideyoshi summoned the Jesuit João Rodrigues, who spoke Japanese, to discuss Olandía's remarks. The shogun "traced out with his fan the relative positions of Spain and Mexico, and mentioned that the Spanish king had built up a large empire by sending missionaries ahead to prepare the ground. This was how the Philippines had become Spanish."[46]

Hideyoshi, pressed for funds due to the war in Korea, decided to confiscate the galleon's cargo and, to make an example, ordered the execution of a number of Christians. Six Franciscans, seventeen Japanese converts, and three Japanese Jesuit lay brothers suffered martyrdom at Nagasaki on February 5, 1597. Of the twenty-six martyrs, four were Spanish, one was Mexican, and another was Indo-Portuguese, while the rest were Japanese. Given these disturbing events, Governor Francisco Tello sent an envoy, Don Luis Navarrete, with a rich gift consisting of a portrait of himself, 3,000 pesos, and an elephant who received the name of Don Pedro. Hideyoshi showed some disenchantment with the animal's color. In a letter of reply to Navarrete's embassy, he wrote, "Thank you for the black elephant. Last year the Chinese promised to send me a white elephant."[47]

The object of Navarrete's visit was to claim the confiscated cargo of the *San Felipe* and to inquire about the martyrs. Hideyoshi told Navarrete that the executions in Nagasaki were justified, "for having, in his own capital, broken the law forbidding them to make converts or to teach their religion; they had paid little heed to this command." The ruler's suspicions were not unfounded. One of the martyrs, Fray Martín de la Ascensión, had written to the Spanish court criticizing the Jesuits for their lack of loyalty to King Philip II and pointing out the possibility of conquering Japan: the Jesuits "in Nagasaki alone . . . could have armed thirty thousand trustworthy musketeers, all of them Christians from the villages possessed by the fathers around Nagasaki." With these Christians, Spaniards "could conquer and pacify all of Japan" and make the Christian daimyo Konishi Yukinaga the ruler of the whole country.[48] Both sides wanted to keep the established relationship; Hideyoshi was mindful of the profits from Iberian trade, and the Spaniards were fearful of an invasion. To show his appreciation, the shogun invited Navarrete to eat at the palace three times and showered him with rich and costly gifts.

After Hideyoshi's death in 1598, his successor Tokugawa Ieyasu maintained for a time a benevolent tolerance with respect to Christianity. During this period of peace, the Japan-Philippines trade continued with profits for both parties. Public accounts from 1600 to 1603 show that Japanese junks brought wheat flour, hemp, iron, powder, foodstuffs like pears and tuna, and decorated screens, small desks, boxes, and other goods.[49] At the time, the Japanese were sending to Southeast Asia ships called *Go-shuin-sen*, or August red seal ships, officially licensed by the shogun to trade with a document bearing the red seal. The Philippines were a common destination for these vessels, surpassed in popularity only by Cambodia, Tongking, and Siam. About thirty ships took out licenses for the Philippines between 1604 and 1606.[50] Meanwhile, in Manila, Japanese merchants received privileged treatment: they paid only 3 percent instead of the full 6 percent of the almojarifazgo duties charged to the Chinese; in addition to this lower rate of duty, they negotiated total exemption from taxes when their cargo was destined for the royal warehouses.[51] According to a Spanish officer, trade between both countries consisted in pepper and raw silk from China, which were exchanged for saltpeter, hemp, flour, iron goods, copper, and "silver refined to a fineness of 65 rials per mark."[52]

Ieyasu's attitude toward trade with Manila appeared quite different from that of his predecessor. The Mexico-bound galleon *Santo Espíritu*, forced off course by the weather, entered the port of Hirado in Tosa in 1602, the same place of the *San Felipe* misfortune six years earlier. The galleon crew fought her way out of the harbor, to which Ieyasu commented that the people of Tosa were pirates, rightfully punished, and gave the Spaniards a document authorizing them to trade with Japan. Manila authorities remained distrustful; nonetheless, they sent a ship from the Philippines to the Kwanto every year at Ieyasu's request, bringing Chinese silks and other merchandise in exchange for Japanese products. According to the Spaniards, this voyage had the purpose of keeping Ieyasu's good graces so he would tolerate the friars' presence. Exchanges were highly profitable, according to official tax accounts. In 1605, silk shipments were valued at 63,500 pesos, and the following year their value reached 111,300 pesos. However, there was a progressive displacement of Japanese merchants from Manila with dire consequences. Juan Gil observed, "It is understandable that given this economic confrontation, boiling passions exploded into the conflict of 1608."[53] In this uprising, the Japanese fortified themselves in a building close to the Chinese Parian, rejecting any pleas of negotiation. The Spanish infantry was able to control the revolt, and the Audiencia ordered the demolition of the Japanese quarter and the expulsion of its inhabitants.

The increase in interactions with Japan is reflected in the growing numbers of Japanese living in Dilao, a district within Manila. In 1593, there were between three hundred and four hundred residents; by 1606, that population exceeded three thousand. After the rebellion, a number of the Japanese were deported, and modest trade continued until Ieyasu's final prohibition of Christianity in 1614. Takayama Ukon and some three hundred Japanese Christians arrived in Manila at the end of that year, forming the nucleus of a soon-to-be-repopulated Dilao district. In only a few years, the Dilao settlement probably constituted the largest group of Japanese outside of Japan, with Hernando de los Ríos Coronel giving their number as two thousand in 1619.[54]

Rodrigo de Vivero, nephew of Luis de Velasco, the viceroy of New Spain and then-interim governor of the islands (1608–1609), wrote to the shogun expressing his desire that trade might continue despite the turmoil in Manila. When Juan de Silva (1609–1616), the new governor, arrived, de Vivero prepared for his departure. The course of events was against the Spanish because in 1609, both the Dutch and Spanish appeared in front of Ieyasu, offering their respective services to trade with Japan.

The Japanese were able to manufacture thousands of guns; however, ship construction along European standards was a different matter. Ieyasu wanted to obtain naval architects and miners from among the Spaniards, and another shipwreck provided the opportunity to discuss the matter. On July 25, 1609, the galleons *San Francisco* and *San Antonio* and a smaller ship, the *Santa Ana*, left Manila for New Spain. The *Santa Ana* arrived in Mexico, but the *San Francisco*, on which the former interim governor de Vivero was sailing, was wrecked off the Kwanto coast. In a letter from Mexico, Viceroy Luis de Velasco sustained that the galleon had "one thousand tons," which indicates that it was beyond the legal capacity, and after bemoaning the financial loss to Manila's merchants, Velasco added, "All the damage has resulted for leaving the Philippines so late." The observation at first appears innocent enough despite the fact that there were seven pilots onboard and that the other ship, the *Santa Ana*, was able to reach the safety of a Japanese port. Juan de Cevicos, the ship's captain, gave a different version of events; according to his testimony, the accident occurred not because of errors in navigation but because the galleon was too close to the coast as it was covertly sailing to a Japanese port to sell silk. Juan de Silva agreed that the reason for the disaster was approaching the Japanese coast "because the ones in charge of the ship wanted it."[55] Ieyasu, who was still most anxious to foster trade with Manila, kindly received the survivors. Rodrigo de Vivero met with high Japanese officials and began by petitioning for freedom for the friars' evangelization; the second request was to ban the Dutch from Japan. In answer, the shogun offered a European ship, built by the English shipwright William Adams, to convey the survivors to New Spain, and in his petition insisted on miners being brought from Mexico to improve silver refining in Japan. In a series of demands called *capitulaciones*, presented in writing to shogunal authorities, Vivero reiterated his previous petitions for religious freedom and added that, should the Mexican silver miners come to Japan, the king of Spain would receive 25 percent of the silver produced. In addition, he requested a port for the Spanish galleons to take shelter in case of an emergency or to trade with the country free of interference from local authorities. There was never a definite answer from the shogun. The miner business was inconclusive, but Vivero wistfully wrote that if the shogun agreed to his requests, the Spanish king would receive 1 million pesos from the mined bullion; he regretfully acknowledged that the shogun refused to banish the Dutch.[56]

Ieyasu named the friar Alonso Muñoz as an ambassador in charge of carrying his answer to the Spanish authorities and loaned Vivero a ship and 4,000 ducats for the voyage to New Spain. Vivero optimistically assured Ieyasu that ships from Manila could substitute for the Portuguese carrack and provide the same amount of silk year in and year out. Spanish imperial powers did not receive his diplomatic approach favorably. The Jesuits were against the possible treaty, the Portuguese were outraged against the interference in their privileged market, Manila merchants were worried about a possible secondary role in the trade between Japan and New Spain, and the governor of the Philippines was against teaching western naval technology to the Japanese. Juan de Cevicos, in a memorandum to the Council of Indies, insisted that the Japanese were "useless on the sea because they don't know the art of navigation neither how to build strong ships."[57] He agreed with Morga's opinion: "For the Islands' greatest security from Japan has always been that the Japanese have no ships and are ignorant in matters of navigation." Cevicos opposed the idea of sending workers and master builders to make Spanish-style ships, "and to teach the Japanese to make them for themselves, it would be equivalent to giving them the very weapons they need to destroy the Philippines."[58] To the surprise of the people in Mexico, Rodrigo de Vivero arrived on the *San Buenaventura* with a Japanese contingent. Some of these Japanese visitors received baptism with joyous celebrations, and the viceroy hired three Japanese who went with him when he left for Spain in 1611.[59]

What preoccupied Ieyasu, like his predecessor, was not the possibility of a Spanish occupation of Japan; his real fear was that the Iberians would provide military aid to a Christian daimyo who might be a threat to the Tokugawa shogun. The activities of Sebastian Vizcaíno in 1611 and 1612 were worrisome in that respect. This navigator, known for his surveys of the California coast, received permission from the shogun to map out the east coast of Japan to facilitate the use of Kwanto ports by the Manila galleons in case of bad weather or other emergencies. Ieyasu's correspondence with the viceroy of Mexico about Vizcaíno's mission clearly illustrates the shogun's position. "It is best, therefore, to put an end to the preaching of your doctrine on our soil. On the other hand, you can multiply the voyages of merchant ships, and thus promote mutual interests and relations. Your ships can enter Japanese ports without exception. I have given strict orders to this effect."[60] When Vizcaíno finally set sail back to Mexico in October 1613, he carried with him an unexpected embassy, the Franciscan Luis Sotelo and a group of Japanese sent by Date Masamune of Sendai, as envoys to the king of Spain and the pope. The entrepreneurial Luis Sotelo hoped to negotiate trading privileges for the Japanese in exchange for the continuation of the Franciscan mission in Japan.

Crossing Mexico from Acapulco, they arrived in Seville, where a letter from Masamune was read with great joy. Masamune promised that his subjects would become Christians and proposed the establishment of a direct commercial line between Japan and Seville. This project coincided with ideas presented by the Portuguese merchant Pedro de Baeza in a memorandum to the Council of Indies, in which he suggested that trade with Asia should follow the Cape of Good Hope route.[61] It was not a far-fetched idea; in 1613 a fleet under Rui González Sequeira departing from Cadiz and sailing the same course brought support to Manila. After sorting out some protocol issues—Masamune was neither the emperor nor the shogun—the Court in Madrid received the embassy with the same protocol reserved for Italian dukes and similar potentates. From the capital, they traveled to Rome, where a formal welcoming ceremony took place, followed by an audience with the pope. After the Italian tour, they returned to Spain, and finally, in July of 1617, Father Sotelo and the Japanese embarked for New Spain. The enterprise did not achieve anything, as political events were against it. Richard Cocks, the head of the British East India Company in Japan from 1613 to 1623, had written in September 1613, "It is also said the Emperor will banish all Spaniard and Portuguese householders out of Japon, and suffer none to stay but such as come and go in their shipping, to prevent entertaining of padres." Ieyasu ordered the missionaries to gather at Nagasaki and await ships to carry them into exile.[62] The Jesuit writer of the *Annual Letter* of 1614 estimated that, at the time, the number of Japanese Christians was more than 250,000.[63]

Tokugawa Iemitsu (1623–1651) had studied a number of European globes and maps to obtain some idea of the relative size and importance of foreign kingdoms. Already in 1615 Tokugawa Hidetada had sent Ibi Masayoshi abroad to study foreign lands. When Masayoshi returned to Japan in 1622 after seven years of wandering, Hidetada summoned him to the palace and listened to him for three consecutive days and nights. Before Hidetada, Ieyasu and the daimyo of Satsuma had dispatched emissaries for similar purposes.[64] Masayoshi had seen the close connection between church and state in the Iberian territories and must have transmitted his misgivings to arouse the suspicions of the shoguns. Authorities banished the Spanish in 1624 and Portuguese residents some years later. Laws against missionaries, however, did not imply the interruption of trade. Japanese merchants continued their visits to Manila, but after 1620 they reached the Philippines from Macao. A colony of Japanese continued living in the islands under the Franciscans' pastoral care, but diplomatic relations came to an end when Governor Fernándo de Silva sent an embassy to Iemitsu at great expense but with no results. Not a single Japanese ship appears in the Manila tax records for 1627.[65]

In addition to taking advantage of every opportunity to tell Japanese authorities about the evil purposes of the Spanish and Portuguese, the Dutch encouraged the Tokugawa to attack Macao and Manila. The shogun finally decided to act in 1637 during the northeast monsoon. An expeditionary force of about ten thousand men was organized that should have been sufficient to overwhelm the Spanish garrison, and the Dutch received a request to supply some armed vessels to protect the transports against Spanish galleons.[66] The invasion did not take place because the Shimabara rebellion disrupted the plans. In the years of 1637 to 1638, the peasants of the Shimabara Peninsula and the Amakusa Islands suffered from heavy taxation while enduring a period of grievous famine. Religious persecution against local Christians ex-acerbated their grievances, and such turns of events led to a rebellion against their lords. In the wake of the rebellion, persecution of Christianity became strictly enforced. The *sakoku*, Japan's national seclusion policy, received new justification, and formal persecution of Christianity reached new heights. The issuing of red seal licenses stopped, and only certain ports in Japan were open to trade. Relations with the Portuguese ceased, as they had previously with Manila. However, there were exceptions to Japanese interactions with the world. Chinese merchants and the Dutch East India Company, confined to the artificial island of Deshima, traded at Nagasaki, but exchanges also continued with China, with Korea, and with the Kuril and Sakhalin Islands, as well as with the Ainu people of the Hokkaido Islands. The English com-pany, unable to do business in Japan and expelled like the Spaniards had been from Bantam in Java, decided to establish direct trade with China, and in 1685, the *China Merchant* arrived in Amoy as a harbinger of things to come.[67] Since Qing China used copper coinage in large quantities, the government decided to send a fleet of junks to Nagasaki to exchange silk and sugar for Japanese copper in 1685. A Sino-Japanese trade developed, which was to compete with the Dutch trade in Japanese copper and reduce the exports of silks to the Philippines.

The Portuguese in Manila

In Manila, the union of Portugal and Spain did not result in any advantages to local businessmen. Governor Diego Ronquillo (1583–1584) welcomed a Portuguese junk with wine, oil, and Chinese merchandise and encouraged the Portuguese to come every year. Trade with America was a completely different matter. When, in 1590, a Portuguese vessel from Macao went to Acapulco, authorities in Mexico confiscated the cargo, arrested the mer-chant, and charged him with violating the regulations banning foreigners from trading with the American colonies of Spain. Antonio de Morga in-dicated that Portuguese ships from the Moluccas, Malacca, and India sailed

each year with the southwest winds, bringing spices, cotton goods, and precious stones—diamonds, rubies, sapphires, topaz—from India, tapestries from
Persia and Turkey, and Portuguese preserves from Goa, as well as "blacks and
Kaffirs," that is to say, slaves.[68] After 1619, ships arrived regularly in Manila
from Macao carrying Chinese merchandise. The profits for the Macaonese
were more than 60 percent in Manila, and for the Chinese in Canton, profits
were between 25 and 30 percent. "That arrangement is so agreeable to the
Sangleys, with the said profit in their own land and without trouble that
they have ceased to come to this city as they did formerly." To secure their
monopoly, the Portuguese acted as brokers for Chinese merchants, charging
5 percent on each transaction. They brought goods valued at "more than one
hundred and fifty thousand pesos on the account of Sangley merchants of
Canton." To add insult to injury, some Portuguese remained in Manila and
dispatched their silks to Acapulco "under the names of persons of this city."
The city's inhabitants also saw their profits diminish due to Mexican merchants' agents charging a fee of 10 percent on the goods purchased.[69] Because
these intermediaries received a commission on the invested value, they did
not concern themselves with the actual prices, a disregard that contributed
to depressing business in Manila. Tax receipts suffered; in the thirteen years
from 1606 to 1618, the Chinese paid 574,627 pesos in duties. Since the Portuguese entered the trade, the incoming sangley merchants paid only 90,641
pesos from 1619 to 1631. Obviously, the Portuguese were controlling the
lion's share of the market. Spanish authorities were not particularly pleased
with this state of affairs, and in 1633, the king prohibited trade between
Macao and Manila, claiming that merchants from Macao took three times
the amount of money usually carried away each year by the Chinese.[70] The
royal prohibitions had no effect; forty junks brought such quantities of silk
to Manila that the galleons of 1634 could not take it all.[71] Silk imports from
Macao amounted to 1.5 million pesos per year during the 1630s.[72] Given
this brisk business, the independence of Portugal implied a serious blow to
silk importers, which explains why Corcuera, the governor of the Philippines at the time, proposed the union of Manila and Macao under Spanish
sovereignty. Another governor, Manuel de León (1669–1677), reestablished
contacts with Macao, and Portuguese ships came to Manila periodically, but
they never recuperated their previous place in trade with China.

The European Companies

The Portuguese and Spanish were not the only Europeans enticed by the
Asian markets. In the seventeenth and eighteenth centuries a number of

European countries established commercial firms, including the Danish, Swedish, and French East India Companies, along with the Austrian-Flemish Ostend Company. The most important ones were the English East India Company (EIC), founded in 1600, and the Dutch East India Company (VOC), established in 1602. These companies' charters granted them a monopoly on trade with Asia as well as military and political powers.

Commerce requires information, and the Dutch had access to it with the 1595 publication of Jan Huyghen van Linschoten's *Itinerary*, in which he summarized the experience of his six years (1583–1589) living in Goa as an agent of the Fugger bankers. Through his records, a substantial collection of Portuguese information about Asia became part of the public domain. "His book was a veritable merchant's manual of routes, commodities and conditions in the East Indies."[73] Another instrumental figure in the diffusion of knowledge was Cornelis de Houtman, who also gathered commercial intelligence. In 1592, Amsterdam merchants had sent him to Lisbon to report on the Spice Islands. His return to Amsterdam coincided with Jan Huyghen van Linschoten's arrival from India.

A development of fundamental importance related to the VOC operations was the opening of a new Indian Ocean route. After passing the Cape of Good Hope, Dutch East India men sailed the westerly winds, the "roaring forties," almost as far as Australia, where they were propelled by the Great Australian current, which pointed the ships straight to the north toward the Sunda Strait. This direct and much faster route from Europe to Asia enhanced the VOC's position in the spice trade. The immense distance from Holland to Java explains why the Dutch established an enclave on the Cape of Good Hope in 1652. In the words of Felipe Fernández-Armesto, "Holland's Golden Age became affordable. A growing proportion of the world's spice trade, which the Portuguese had never been able to shift out of its traditional grooves, spilled into European hands."[74] One of the reasons for Dutch predominance in the seventeenth century was a dynamic business class that incorporated bankers, merchants, and capital from Antwerp and that had moved to Amsterdam during the war with Spain, as well as a population of Portuguese Jews who had arrived in the late 1590s and specialized in importing East India commodities from Lisbon.[75] Amsterdam became a business center in a web of trading houses and business connections that covered large parts of the world.

Coen's 1619 founding of Batavia placed the capital of the Dutch East Indies in a strategic point on the Sunda Strait, on the island of Java. The plan was to set up a monopoly over the production and trade of cloves and nutmeg; consequently, Coen used the naval power at his disposal to further his designs. Through brute power and commercial policy, the Dutch tried to balance spices' supply and demand to guarantee high prices. VOC forces burned down clove farming villages and uprooted tens of thousands of clove trees. Production was concentrated on the islands of Ambon and Ceram, and the Dutch forbade the remaining islands from growing them. They applied similar procedures to control nutmeg cultivation: villages were demolished, and the indigenous people ended up as slaves in Java. By the late seventeenth century, the Dutch company had control of the main ports of Java and the Spice Islands.

The Spaniards did not forget the Spice Islands, and between 1582 and 1603, four more expeditions traveled to the Moluccas without success. Such persistence is easy to understand. Merchants coveted the islands because they were "where they find that brown gold that they call cloves."[76] In 1606, Governor Pedro Bravo de Acuña established a base in Ternate with a garrison of two hundred men; there was also an outpost in Tidore with only 150 men.

The Dutch did not just exercise a monopoly over clove production in the Moluccas; it seems that they had an agreement with merchants in Cadiz to prevent Manila from engaging in the spice trade, "for the Spaniards had to pay the same prices at Batavia as in Cadiz." The American colonies received spices from the fleets that sailed to Veracruz, in addition to the considerable quantities brought by smugglers.[77] Since 1615, the Spaniards had an agent in Makassar, a port in the south of Sulawesi, Indonesia, to continue their trade in such a unique commodity. Ships from that city landed in Manila until 1667, when all European merchants except the Dutch were expelled from Makassar.[78] It was not until 1662, when Ming loyalist Zheng Chenggong (Koxinga) threatened the Philippines from his Taiwan base, that forces in Zamboanga, Mindanao, Ternate, and Tidore were redeployed back to Manila. Historically, trade in spices had never been profitable for the Spaniards.

Dutch preeminence and Portuguese decline are attributed to the company's nature as a capitalist enterprise, while the Estado da India did not qualify as such. However, that is not the case; the VOC's success did not depend on a more rational organization, a better control of market forces, or a "capitalistic" functioning. Instead, its prosperity resided, first, on the export of silver from Tokugawa's Japan and, later, on copper, which found a wide market throughout Asia until 1715, when shogunal authorities limited its export. A second source of revenues came from exclusive access to Indonesian spices, ensured by the use of violence. Trade in metals and spices accounted for the largest fraction of VOC profits in seventeenth-century Asia. Subrahmanyam commented: "Force and diplomacy, rather than the laws of supply and demand, thus play a crucial role in the Dutch success."[79]

The English decided to concentrate their efforts in India, given the inferiority of their resources compared to the Dutch and their marginal position in Southeast Asia. In 1612, James I sent an ambassador to the Mughal emperor to sign a commercial treaty that would give the company exclusive rights to settle in India and build factories, in exchange for European goods. The British created trading posts in Surat (1615), Madras (1639), Bombay (1665)—given by Portugal to the English as part of Catherine of Braganza's dowry when she married Charles II—and Calcutta (1690). With the authorization of the Mughal emperor, the English extended their activities to the region of Bengal in 1634. In the Indian subcontinent, Gujarat, Coromandel, and Bengal were the most profitable regions for the English; the EIC export of Indian textiles to Europe had already begun to show a profit by the middle of the seventeenth century.

Merchants in Manila were kindly disposed to exchanges with the British. In 1644 and 1645, two EIC ships visited Manila, where authorities told them that regular exchanges with European powers in competition with Britain would not be authorized. These two voyages were not particularly successful, but the directors in London considered large profits to be possible in the future.[80] Following company promptings, the English government opened up direct negotiations with the Spanish Crown in Madrid during the 1650s and 1660s, but the Council of Indies refused to allow trade with any of Spain's traditional enemies. As always, in Manila there were ways to circumvent the ban. Ships going from European enclaves on the subcontinent to the Philippines used the flag of an Islamic state and a crew of Muslim sailors. The sultan of Bantam, Abdull Retama (1633–1666), collaborated with the British on mercantile operations. In the last decades of the seventeenth centuries, private merchants established trade relations between the Coromandel Coast, Madras, and the Philippines. After the Dutch expelled the EIC from Bantam in 1682, trade with Manila became a substantial part of Madras's economic life. Passing as "Moors," company servants, and "country traders," Portuguese, Armenians, Muslims, and Hindus eagerly exchanged Indian goods for bullion. By the 1680s, the amount of silver extracted from Manila by English interests varied between 10,000 and 100,000 pesos per year.[81]

The Armenian Diaspora

When authorities in the Philippines exercised rigorous surveillance against European vessels, Armenian intermediaries lent their services. Armenian territory was situated across from the main overland trade routes between Europe and Asia, and Armenian merchants rose to prominence in the seventeenth century, when Shah Abbas I (1587–1629) gave them a monopoly on Persia's raw silk export trade. Silk became the most important commodity in this thriving commercial climate and was carried over land and maritime routes that traversed Europe, the Levant, the Middle East, Central Asia, India, and the East Indies. Armenians profited from an extensive web of communities related by ties of kinship, religion, and commonality of language. An Anglo-Armenian agreement in 1688 allowed these merchants to establish themselves in British-Indian territories. "They could trade to and from British Indian ports, travel on Company ships and share indulgences obtained by the British Company, like Englishmen in Asia."[82] Father Casimiro Díaz wrote in 1718 about a *huerta* (house of recreation) in the vicinity of Manila built by an Armenian merchant at a cost of 100,000 pesos. As an indication of their commercial relevance, there was a quarter reserved for Armenians in Manila when their ships were in port.[83]

The New Christians' Mercantile Diaspora

A powerful diaspora of merchants and financiers emerged after the Catholic kings expelled the members of the Jewish population who did not convert to Catholicism, and the Inquisition began the persecution of New Christians—Jews and their descendants officially converted but were accused of practicing Judaism in secret. This mercantile community, from 1580 to 1630, "literally girdled the world. . . . The New Christian network worked by the principle of integrating several circuits of trade and finance, which had hitherto remained poorly connected."[84] These merchants were present in the main European commercial centers as well as in Africa, the Americas, and Asia. One notable case is that of the merchant Diogo Fernandes Vitoria, whose activities in Manila began in 1580 and ended in 1598, when he was condemned by the Mexican Inquisition. Fernandes Vitoria invested in Mexico, Brazil, and Asian countries from his base in Manila, but the main source of his profits was the American silver exchanged for goods he shipped to Peru, Mexico, and the Caribbean. His Chinese agents purchased silks on his behalf at the Canton fairs, and Japanese junks brought them to Manila. He received spices from the Banda Islands and Ambon in the Moluccas, along with products from the Coromandel Coast in India, Sri Lanka, Burma, and Indonesia. The Inquisition encountered references to investors and correspondents from Mexico, Macao, Malacca, and the Moluccas. His patrimony gives a glimpse of the galleon trade in those decades. Raw silk and fabrics represented 89 percent of his capital (about 64,536 cruzados; a piece of eight was the equivalent of 0.8 cruzados); 4,707 cruzados were in spices, 2,200 in slaves, 212 in rubies and diamonds, and 68 in gold. Precious stones were easy to conceal, and the galleons carried these gems in considerable quantities. The Pacific route was an alternative to the Portuguese carracks for taking diamonds to Europe; however, since the second half of the seventeenth century, New Christians began to use the men of British India for this purpose.

Fernandes Vitoria's business placed the islands in an intricate web of mercantile exchanges and investments covering a large part of the globe. New Christians participated in the slave commerce of Africa and Asia, sent textiles to America, invested in Asian trade, and shipped goods to Europe using the most convenient route to avoid taxation and state regulations. The duke of Lerma, chief minister under Philip III (1598–1621), first began signing contracts for naval supplies with Portuguese New Christian bankers. From 1626 to 1640, under the aegis of the count-duke of Olivares, Portuguese New Christians achieved a privileged position as bankers of the Crown in Madrid, receiving roughly half of the Spanish Crown's financial contracts. In 1628, Philip IV granted Portuguese New Christians the freedom to settle in any part of the empire, an opportunity they eagerly pursued, as demonstrated by the arrival of New Christians in the Viceroyalty of Peru. The Spanish Council of State discussed a plan to secure the return of Jews of Spanish and Portuguese origins from Holland, France, and Hamburg, promising full pardons and protection from the Inquisition if they kept the practice of their religion in private.[85]

During the 1620s, New Christians in Seville began to invest in the Manila galleons and increased their penetration in the economies of Mexico and Peru, strengthening their links with the Philippines. A good example of this practice is the case of Martins d'Orta of Seville, who in 1629 received the astonishing sum of 200,000 cruzados in pearls, amber, and musk. During the seventeenth century, New Christians sent at least 450,000 cruzados (about 360,000 pesos) to Asian markets, almost a third of the total Portuguese investments.[86] In exchanges from Acapulco and Peru to the Philippines, these New Christians had an important position.[87] Olivares's fall from power and Portugal's separation from Spain dealt a heavy blow to these financiers, and many of them left Spain.

In America, the arrival of Portuguese merchants after 1628 presented unwelcome competition, and when economic conditions worsened, the Inquisition took matters in hand. A number of New Christians received heavy penalties, saw their wealth confiscated, or were burned at the stake. In Mexico, more than one hundred persons were charged with practicing Judaism in secrecy between 1642 and 1645. A document signed in Lima on May 18, 1636, by officers of the Tribunal and addressed to the king summarized the proceedings of the largest inquisitorial trial in the history of the viceroyalty. The record began by pointing out that since six or eight years prior to the trial—coinciding with the royal edict of 1628—a large number of Portuguese merchants had entered the Viceroyalty of Peru from Argentina, Brazil, New Spain, and Central America, and soon they had controlled all of the wholesale and small retail business in Lima. "They had become the lords of the trade: From brocade to sayal and from diamonds to cumin every-thing was in their hands." They purchased the whole cargo of galleons from Spain "with credit" and distributed the merchandise all over the viceroyalty through their agents. The inquisitors acknowledged that the prosecution of such merchants aggravated the already critical economic situation in the viceroyalty, but authorities decided to continue with the proceedings. As a result, businesses were severely damaged by the imprisonment of merchants and the sequestration of property. Procedures concluded in an auto-da-fé in 1639, in which more than fifty New Christians received diverse penalties in addition to ten being condemned to death by fire.[88]

The End of the Century

After 1640 there was a "catastrophic and exponential decline" in economic activity in the Philippines,[89] while Manila's municipal activity "decayed clearly after the sangleys' uprising in 1639 and the 1645 earthquake."[90] In fact, the galleon trade suffered endless misfortunes. No ships were dispatched from the Philippines in 1636 and 1637, the *Concepción* was lost in the Ladrones in 1638, and the Dutch intercepted a large number of junks headed for Manila in 1640. Bad weather compelled one of the outgoing galleons to return to Manila in 1643. In 1645, the loss of the incoming galleon off the coast of Cagayan was compounded by the tragedy of the disastrous earth-quake that reduced the city to a pile of rubble. No ships came from Mexico in 1647, 1648, and 1652; in the following years four galleons were lost. The century concluded with another disaster. On July 3, 1694, four hundred per-sons drowned in the shipwreck of the galleon *San José*. "No larger or richer galleon had plowed the waters of the sea, for the wealth that it carried was incredible," wrote Casimiro Díaz.[91] Despite the *San José* disaster, businesses improved in the last decades of the seventeenth century following an upward economic trend that began to take off in the 1680s.[92]

CHAPTER FIVE

The Galleons[1]

Gemelli Careri, an Italian globetrotter, relating his adventures in his 1699 *Giro del Mondo* (*Travels around the World*), described the crossing from Manila to Acapulco:

> The voyage from the Philippine Islands to America may be called the longest and most dreadful of any in the world, as well because of the vast ocean to be crossed being almost one half of the terraqueous globe, with the wind always ahead, as for the terrible tempests that happen there, one upon the back of another, and for the desperate diseases that seize people in 7 or 8 months, lying at sea sometimes near the line, sometimes cold, sometimes temperate, and sometimes hot, which is enough to destroy a man of steel, much more flesh and blood, which at sea had but indifferent food.[2]

A Jesuit in 1574 considered the *Carreira da India*—the round trip between Portugal and India—"without any doubt the greatest and most arduous of any that are known in the world." In the best conditions, the complete voyage, including the time at Goa or Manila, took about a year and a half for the Portuguese carracks and a year for the Manila galleons.[3] The dangers and hardships of both routes were similar, though the journey from Acapulco to Manila was considered quite pleasant compared to the voyage around the Cape of Good Hope in either direction.[4] The English East India Company's ships took between seven and eight months to reach India. No matter the route, until the era of steam, intercontinental voyages took months, were extremely uncomfortable, and presented many dangers.

In 1565, the first galleons sailed from the Philippines to Acapulco, and for the 250 years that followed, their crossings kept open the lines of trade and communication between New Spain and the Philippines. The galleons remained in operation until 1813, when King Ferdinand VII, who was restored to the Spanish throne after Napoleon's defeat, decreed their elimination. In 1811, Mexican patriots had taken away the silver that was then ready to be sent to Manila, and months later, the last galleons arrived in Acapulco. In 1815, one final vessel departed from Mexico, heading to Manila on the line's final voyage. Its name was *San Fernando*, alias *Magellan*.

The *galleon* was a term used in the sixteenth and seventeenth century to describe a European high-sided vessel with a stern castle—a tall superstructure divided into levels—at the rear and a shorter superstructure, the forecastle, at the front. Usually, the ship's hull had three levels, or decks. The lowest part of the ship held the ballast of sand and stones; the hold stored most of the cargo and supplies; another deck stored cables, ropes, and sails and served as additional cargo storage space. The next level up was the gun deck, followed by the upper deck and castles. The galleon's hulls slanted inward from bottom to top, and this narrowing continued into the stern castle; this distinctive shape made the ship a stable platform for artillery, and the castles provided elevated positions for infantry in close-range fighting. Its decorative features included painted and adorned galleries around the back of the main cargo and gun decks.

The galleon had a main mast and a foremast, both carrying three squared sails; at the stern of the vessel the mizzenmast had a triangular or lateen sail and two square sails. The lower sails on the fore and mainmast provided the main forward motion for the ship. In good weather, a removable bonnet was attached to the lower edge. Sails and bonnets were painted with the letters A M G P, corresponding to the words "Ave Maria, gratia plena"— the opening of the Hail Mary prayer. By matching the letters on the sail to the bonnet, sailors could quickly attach the two together.[5] At the prow, the bowsprit pole carried two sails, and under it, projecting from the hull, the beak head supported the figurehead of a rampant gilded lion with a crown, a distinctive feature of Spanish royal ships. The captain's cabin and quarters for officers and passengers occupied the stern castle, while the highest part of the castle contained a smaller cabin for the pilot. On the upper deck, the whipstaff and compass allowed the helmsman to steer the vessel; the ship's wheel appeared around 1700.

As in other ships at the time, cooking with firewood took place on the lower deck in a pit built of bricks with sand at the bottom. Hernando de los Ríos Coronel, procurator of the Philippines, complained to the king about such cooking arrangements; it seems that such pits were located in the waist and not "in the first part of the forecastle," and during the first storm, the sea carried the pits away; passengers and crew then had to resort to cooking their food where they ate their communal meals, as it was the only other place they "can make a fire (and it is a miracle from God that the ships are not burned)." The reason for this limited space was "that the officials appropriate the largest storerooms of the ships."[6] De los Ríos Coronel's complaint indicates that careful regulations and controls about fire on the galleons had exceptions. According to the rules, only the officer in charge of foodstuffs could carry a lantern into the hold or light a fire in the cooking area, the use of candlesticks and lamps was restricted, and passengers and crew could smoke only in certain areas. During storms or in rough waters, the crew extinguished all of the ship's candles, lanterns, and oil lamps, and meals consisted of cold rations. Everyone on board was terrified of a fire getting out of control, a nightmare that came true in 1552 when, off the coast of New Spain, a lantern initiated a conflagration on the *Nuestra Señora de la Concepcion* that caused the deaths of more than three hundred passengers. In 1639 the *Santo Cristo de Burgos*, sailing to Acapulco, sank after an onboard fire. Its charred remains later washed up on the shores of the Marianas Islands.[7]

Latrines for sailors were at the prow, on a wooden framework projecting over the sea. In the Atlantic, galleons, passengers, and officials had their facilities—named *jardines* (gardens)—on the corridors surrounding the stern deck; it is possible that Pacific ships had similar accommodations.[8] Nonetheless, according to French sailor Pyrard of Laval, who traveled in a Portuguese carrack to India in 1610, "These ships are mighty foul and stink withal; the most men not troubling themselves to go on deck for their necessities, which is in part the cause that so many die. The Spaniards, French and Italians do the same; but English and Hollanders are exceedingly scrupulous and cleanly." There were exceptions, like the case of one Dutch Indiaman that arrived at the Cape in 1774 with eighty sick crew members: "She was between the decks so choked with filth, that some of my officers assured me, they had never seen so much dirt, not even aboard of any French ship."[9]

Like any other vessel at the time, galleons had pumps to remove the bilge or water that accumulated in the lower part of the hull. The bilge released an awful smell that mingled with the stench of animals, food, unwashed bodies, dirty clothing, and other offending substances; well-to-do passengers carried ampoules of perfume to conceal the stench.[10] On the Manila galleons, two or three pumps usually operated almost continually throughout the journey. Andrés Urdaneta, one of the survivors from the Loaísa expedition, described the dreadful experience of operating the pumps in rough seas. Stormy weather had damaged his ship, and large volumes of water leaked into it: "If we went two hours without working [the pumps], we spent another two hours working them, and we were also hard pressed by the sea and by the scant and spoiled rations and little water, and many died from overwork."[11]

In addition to navigational instruments like the compass—held in a wooden case called the binnacle and illuminated at night by its own lamp—pilots had at their disposal the astrolabe and the forestaff (*ballestilla*) to gauge the altitude of the sun and the North Star, tables for the daily declination of the sun, and the hourglass to measure time. The log line helped to determine the speed of the vessels, and the plumb line was used to measure the depth of shallow waters. Pilots were familiar with Pedro de Medina's famous 1545 navigation manual, *Arte de Navegar* (*Art of Navigation*). It was the best in Europe for the time, and "the Dutch for long depended on translations of the classic Spanish work."[12] There was not a mode of transportation in the modern era that could surpass the galleon in velocity or carrying capacity. Carlo M. Cipolla summarizes the historical relationship between European expansion and the galleons: "The gunned ship developed by Atlantic Europe in the course of the fourteenth and fifteenth centuries was the contrivance that made possible the European saga. It was essentially a compact device that allowed a relatively small crew to master unparalleled masses of inanimate energy for movement and destruction."[13]

Master shipwrights from America or Spain were in charge of naval architecture in the Philippines. To build the galleons, they used mathematical proportions to measure and cut the pieces of the ship according to precise specifications. The main rule of construction was a ratio of 1:2:3, which required the length of the keel to be three times the length of the beam, and the beam to be twice the depth of the hold.[14] These ratios implied that the galleons were slow and cumbersome to maneuver.

During the seventeenth century, there was a tendency to build ships with lower castles and longer keels, which were in proportion to the beam and the draft, the distance between the water line and the bottom of the hull. In the Pacific, innovations were slower to emerge in merchant ship construction, since business favored vessels with large cargo volume. The *Santísima Trinidad*, captured by Thomas Cavendish in 1762, had a 156-foot-long keel, a width of 56 feet, and a hold with a depth of 26 feet; these figures are closer to the proportions of the seventeenth-century galleons. Changes in ship construction produced the Dutch and English ship-of-the-line battleships and merchant vessels, called *frigates* (a word that first appears in Spanish documents after the middle of the eighteenth century), indicating a new kind of liner plying the Pacific.

The typical container for transporting cargo on Spanish ships was the cask, *tonel*, which had a capacity of 443.5 liters (approximately 117 gallons). Two *toneles* were equivalent to a *tonelada*, or ton, of 234 gallons.[15] The tonnage of the Manila galleon determined its carrying capacity. According to a law of 1593, the size of the galleon was decreed to be 300 tons, but as with most regulations, this one was not enforced. By 1589 there were ships of 700 tons, and by the seventeenth century 1,000-ton vessels crossed the ocean. In Governor de Silva's fleet, which sailed to Malacca to attack the Dutch in 1616, the flagship was the 1,700-ton *San Marcos*. There was another galleon of 1,600, two of 1,300, and four more with tonnages above the 300-ton limit. De Silva's vessels are a good example of the fluid boundaries between trade and warfare, in that Philippine galleons were both merchant ships and warships indistinctively. Fernando Manuel de Bustillo Bustamante, Governor of the Philippines, reported in 1718 that the three galleons of the line at the time were respectively 612, 900, and 1,000 tons. The *Rosario*, which was in service from 1746 to 1761, was 1,710 tons with a cargo capacity of 18,867 pieces, although the legal maximum was 4,000 pieces. The *Santísima Trinidad*, captured by the British in 1762, was the largest ship built in the islands at 2,000 tons. When the ship docked in Plymouth, it became a tourist attraction. The *Scots Magazine* described it "as one of the largest [ships] ever seen in Britain"; the *Annual Register* gushed that "she lay like a mountain in the water."[16] The Portuguese had traditionally built ships of 1,000 tons in the sixteenth century, like the 1,600-ton *Madre de Deus*. In India, between 1600 and 1640, the British had four ships of 1,000 tons and fifteen ranging between 700 and 900.[17]

There was an economic rationale behind such large merchant ships. A vessel of seven hundred tons was much more cost-effective than one of three hundred; the larger ship, with a crew of eighty or ninety, would demand stores of foodstuffs and other supplies that would only occupy 10 percent of its capacity; the necessities for fifty or sixty men on the smaller vessel would need 13 to 15 percent of the storage space. Such economic realities explain why large ships dominated the East Indian and Atlantic trades.[18]

At least two thousand trees were necessary for the construction of one galleon. With the passage of time, forests in the proximity of the shipyards were depleted, and transporting logs from long distances soon turned into a considerable problem, which explains the practice of building galleons near a ready supply of timber.[19] The main shipyard during the Spanish regime was Cavite, close to Manila; however, galleons were built in Iloilo, Cebu, Camarines, Pangasinan, Bicol, and so on. In 1617, Muslim raiders burned three ships under construction in the Masbate shipyard. Some galleons were made outside the Philippines, including the *San Lorenzo* in India, the *Nuestra Señora de Guadalupe* or *Mexicana* in Thailand, and another in Cambodia. These exceptions were frowned on by the government, and in 1679 a royal order required that ships intended for the Acapulco line be built only in the Philippines.[20]

The islands were generously wooded with high-quality trees. Two contemporary geographers praise this abundance: "The Philippines forests are the source of so many kinds of woods with so wide a range of color, grain, texture, ease of working, hardness, weight, and strength properties that there is a wood suitable for any use."[21] This picture is consistent with Captain Pineda's report to the king in 1619, which described the extraordinary properties of the *maria* hardwood employed in galleon construction. "If a ball be fired into it of the size of eight libras or less, it does not pierce the wood; and if the ball is large, the wood is not splintered." Domingo Fernández Navarrete reported that after a 1647 battle between the *San Diego* and the Dutch, "Above 1,000 bullets were found in her, and of above 2,000 that were fired at her, not one went through."[22] A timber called *arguijo* was commonly used: "From it are made the keels, beams, false keels, wales, mast heads and pumps, of whatever size required. For that tree, as above stated, grows very tall and straight. Gunstocks, gun-carriages, and wheels for the artillery are also made from that wood." Pineda concluded, "There are many other kinds of woods which are also used for the above purposes," like *molave*, which was employed for the galleon's ribs and knees.[23] In maritime construction, all of the timber needed to be seasoned at least for a year; however, in the Philippines, sometimes "the vessels were being built while the wood was cutting," with the consequence that "one must tear up the decks every two years and put down new ones, for they are rotten. Likewise, the planks along the sides must be changed, with the exception of the futtock-timbers and top-timbers made of the wood maria; for that wood, although cut and not seasoned, never rots, because it is always durable, in one way, without rotting."[24]

To make cordage and rigging, the Philippines provided *cabo negro* and the well-known *abaca*. Caulkers used the local coconut husk fiber. In Europe, pitch and tar impregnated the rigging to make it water-resistant, but in Cavite, cordage remained in its natural state, which accelerated its deterioration.[25] The sails were made of Ilocano cotton cloth, which was better, more durable, and cheaper than sails imported from Mexico. Due to the long and arduous voyages across the Pacific, however, "The ships sailing from Manila to New Spain carry sails for the return voyage and nevertheless have to make others in the port of Acapulco."[26] Shipwrights used wooden pegs and iron nails to attach planks to the hull. Iron came from China, Japan, India, and

Mexico. Chinese and Filipino blacksmiths forged the iron items required for the vessels. Sheets of lead protected the hull against leakages and damage from insects and shipworms, the mollusk *Teredo navalis*. Captain Pineda recommended, "It would be of the highest importance to cover the ships with lead at Manila, which would obviate careening them every year. Don Juan de Silva neglected to do that, because he was always in haste to resist and attack the enemy."[27] However, in less stressful times, shipwrights applied sheets of tin or lead to the hull as an added precaution against shipworms. The entire process of building a galleon could take two years, although there were exceptions like the *San José*, at the time one of the largest ships in the world. Its construction began in 1693 and was completed in a record nine months, to general surprise.[28]

Galleons were royal property, and the Treasury financed the cost of building the liners and the expense of careening and refitting them. Royal ownership opened the door to all kinds of corruption. In 1587, Governor Vera constructed a 500-ton galleon at a cost of 8,000 pesos. Timber, cordage, and other building materials were cheaper in the Philippines, and Filipino labor and supplies subsidized galleon construction. During the eighteenth century, the cost of galleons increased enormously. For the *Filipino*, which escaped from the British in 1762, the Crown disbursed 95,857 pesos, and for the *Santísima Trinidad*, the cost amounted to 191,000 pesos; a frigate of thirty cannons cost more than 100,000 pesos. The 1766 narrative of Le Gentil concerning the *San Carlos* and the *Santa Rosa* shows the customary construction and upkeep of liners. The *San Carlos*, after leaving Cavite, returned to port, "for the people on board were afraid that she might go to the bottom of the sea, as she could not carry her sails." Fortunately Captain De Caseins, a knowledgeable French officer, responded to the merchants' concerns by noting that the problems had originated "in her superstructure, which was too heavy and too high. . . . Señor De Caseins had the stern castle pulled down and left the vessel flat like a frigate." The ship's voyage to Mexico was successful. The merchants on the *San Carlos*, however, insisted on spacious accommodations, and the stern castle was rebuilt. The remodeled galleon was unable to make the voyage because "it was found impossible to navigate her" after having encountered some bad weather in the South Sea. Another revealing case was the *Santa Rosa*, the first vessel to restart the line after the British had captured Manila. Upon its return from Acapulco, it required repairs, which, according to shipbuilders at Cavite, would amount to at least 40,000 pesos. Caseins offered to put the galleon in seaworthy condition for only 10,000 pesos—"The governor did not oppose as he knew that Caseins would report back to the king." He took charge of refitting the *Santa Rosa* even though, in his opinion, "There is no lack of shipbuilders in Manila. The work of docking and overhauling the vessels is admirably done there." Caseins left Manila on February 12, 1767. As soon as he departed, the attorney general ordered a new inspection and deemed the ship unseaworthy, and repairs began anew, "undoing all of Caseins's work. The ship was caulked and the main deck was raised higher to allow for greater storage space," for a cost of 50,000 pesos, greatly inflated by official corruption.[29]

Le Gentil observed that after construction, the ships typically remained in the Cavite shipyard without periodic maintenance. Returning vessels from Mexico baked under the tropical sun and were battered by rains. Galleons remained unattended from July to February, at which point extensive repairs were needed to restore the vessels to seaworthy condition. "This is the Governor's great opportunity—this is when he gathers in his crop. He is the head of the Marine Department and of the Treasury, and from every quarter gold flows into his pocket."[30]

The Line

The route followed by Urdaneta became the customary course for the Manila-Acapulco run. Oskar C. H. Spate observed that in the late seventeenth century, the route was moved between thirty-two and thirty-seven degrees north in order to avoid the colder, stormier, higher latitudes. However, here the westerlies were less reliable, making the voyage longer and adding privations for crew and passengers.[31]

The galleon's route from Acapulco to Manila was guided by the northeast trade winds. These airstreams reliably carried the ship across the ocean at good speed. The galleon from Manila followed the westerlies north, aided by the Kuroshio Current, which propelled them toward Acapulco. This current originated off the east coast of Taiwan and flowed northeastward past Japan, where it merged with the North Pacific Current. There was a critical zone of variable winds, between the prevailing northeast and westerly airstreams, where disasters occurred. It was essential to clear the Philippines before the baguio season between July and October because a late sailing meant encountering a typhoon. June was the best month for departure, as ships encountered winds that pushed the galleon from Cavite to the Strait of San Bernardino—the *Embocadero* in colonial times—where the expected monsoon would propel it northward. After departing from Cavite, the galleon followed a winding channel that connected Manila to the Embocadero. It usually took the galleon about two months to reach open sea. Gemelli Careri left Cavite on June 28 and did not clear the strait until August 10. There were exceptions like the *San Carlos Borromeo* in 1766, which took only three weeks to reach the open Pacific. Squalls and currents tossed the galleon on a course that was full of sandbanks, rocks, and low-level islands, with days of fog presenting additional perils to navigation. In the words of William L. Schurz, "a lost galleon is associated with almost every step in the way out of the straits."[32] Along this dangerous course, Le Gentil observed, "she picks up many things from the alcaldes and the friars to be transported to Mexico."[33] In 1613, Philip III recommended a northward course that followed the west coast of Luzon up to Cape Bojeador. Despite royal interest, there were no changes to the route, and repeated efforts during the eighteenth century to substitute the customary track were unsuccessful. After the galleon sailed the San Bernardino Strait, the monsoon carried it on its way, but a zone of storms and variable winds often required the galleon to turn back to the Philippines before it could attain the necessary latitude.

A historian from colonial times, the Jesuit Jose de Acosta, wrote about the voyage, "they mount a great height, until they come right against the Islands of Japan, and discovering the Californias, they return by the coast of New Spain to the port of Acapulco." He added, "They sailed easily from East to West within the Tropics, for that there westerly winds do reign; but returning from West to East they must seek the Western winds without the Tropics in the height of seven and twenty degrees."[34] Cape Mendocino in northern California was the mark to turn southward to reach Cabo San Lucas. When the ship arrived at the Navidad port, the galleon dropped anchor and procured provisions and water. A courier took documents to the viceroy in Mexico City, and sick people were left in the care of the local mission. However, the pilots tried to avoid the vicinity of the California coast, given the fog and the navigational hazards. Captains tried to time their arrival in Acapulco during December or the first weeks of January.

A number of heterogeneous conditions had to be met to allow a galleon's departure from Manila. A crucial factor was the timely arrival in Manila of the Chinese junks, as well as the Acapulco ship with the silver from the previous year's sales. Cargo had to be loaded and all bureaucratic procedures completed. Contrary winds or enemy vessels could postpone departure or even delay the galleon's sailing until the following year.

When all was ready, authorities wished farewell to the departing vessel with solemn ceremonies. The galleon approached the city walls as closely as the water level allowed, the governor delivered to the officers the ship's papers and the royal flag, and the command of the galleon was entrusted to the captain general. Meanwhile, a procession of friars carried the statue of the line's virgin-patroness along the walls and delivered it onboard, accompanied by a salvo of gunfire. The archbishop gave his blessing as the ship sailed for the open sea. At all of the churches in Manila, members of religious orders and parishioners prayed for a successful voyage. Casimiro Díaz explained the emotions surrounding the departure: "All are interested in the prosperous voyages of the galleons; and it is one of the greatest troubles of these islands, if not the worst, that all are dependent on two bits of wood, and those entrusted to the fickleness of the sea—the one that goes [to Acapulco], and the other that is expected."[35]

A galleon's sailing time was not predictable, and changes in wind circulation altered the speed of crossings between Acapulco and the Philippines. The time depended on the strength of the trade winds west of the date line and on the position of the monsoon trough—a "line in a weather map showing the locations of relatively minimum sea level pressure in a monsoon region"—during June.[36]

The worsening climate of the seventeenth century affected each voyage's duration. Sailing was speedy between 1590 and 1630 but slowed greatly between 1640 and 1670. A study of the galleons' logs from 1591 to 1750 reveals that voyages from Acapulco to Manila in the middle of the seventeenth century were 40 percent longer—over forty days on average. It is likely that sailings from Manila to Acapulco suffered the same delay. Longer sailing times coincided in large measure with the Maunder Minimum of the seventeenth century, when sunspots became exceedingly rare; these events are associated with "a shift in atmospheric circulation in response to changes in solar activity."[37] Alterations in the monsoons and trade winds' patterns made the crossings slower and more dangerous, as well. Voyages returned to their customary duration toward the last decades of the seventeenth and eighteenth centuries.

The route corresponded with the Pacific's typhoon belt, which explains the long list of shipwrecks and catastrophes that punctuated its history. As early as 1568, the *Capitana*, commanded by Felipe Salcedo, departed from Cebu to New Spain with 130 persons and a load of cinnamon. Upon arriving at the island of Guam, after Salcedo and the passengers had disembarked, "a heavy storm broke out that carried away the ship and dashed her against the coast, where she was smashed to pieces, with a total loss of all her cargo."[38]

Miguel Selgas's catalogue of typhoons that crossed the Philippines is also a record of the galleons' hardships and misfortunes. In 1576, five years after the occupation of Manila, the *Espíritu Santo* sank in the Catanduanes Islands, and passengers and crew were drowned or killed by the natives. Pedro de Chavez punished the natives in such a way that afterward they were "tamed and regretful," according to Casimiro Díaz.[39] The *Santa Margarita* ran aground on one of the Mariana Islands in 1600 after eight months of wandering during which the ship suffered a succession of storms. Of the 260 people who had embarked, only fifty were still alive. Natives plundered the galleon and killed many; only twenty-six survived. The *Santo Tomás*, which bypassed the island and stopped for provisions, refused to delay its departure to collect the stranded seamen. Such urgency proved worthless; due to fog on the Embocadero, the *Santo Tomás* shipwrecked on the Catanduanes. In 1602, a different galleon named the *Espíritu Santo* suffered stormy weather near Japan. In a report, Pedro Anciondo said, "We met with a storm which obliged us to lighten the ship of everything on top deck, and of 300 boxes and bales from below deck." With difficulty, it made its way to Cavite. Only eight persons survived on the galleon voyages of 1603, the same year of the Chinese uprising. The *Nuestra Señora de los Remedios*, without masts and with its cargo lost in the heavy weather, went back to Manila; its companion, the *San Antonio*, disappeared without a trace with all of its passengers, crew, and cargo.

Antonio de Morga left his position in Manila's High Court in 1604 and crossed the sea to Mexico on a galleon also named *Espíritu Santo*, which was accompanied by the *Jesús María*. Things went badly from the outset. The *Espíritu Santo* ran aground on a shoal close to Manila. Chinese junks came to its aid, pulling cables at high tide and tugging the large ship to deep water. On November 10, along the coast of California, a furious gale almost drove the galleon against the shore. It lost its rigging, and twelve days later lightning struck it. After two more trying months, the badly damaged galleon reached Acapulco with its exhausted crew.

In August of 1620, a violent typhoon raging over Samar wrecked the *San Nicolás*, which was carrying 330 people, and a second galleon foundered near Palapag. After a typhoon and a series of hurricanes, the two galleons of 1629 returned to the islands. A baguio in 1638, near the island of Rota in the Mariana Islands, wrecked the flagship *Nuestra Señora de la Concepción*; the cargo was totally lost, and many died. The following year two ships coming from Acapulco were broken on the coast of Vigan, resulting in 150 deaths. In 1639, two of the five ships that had left Manila for Acapulco sank near Cavite, and six hundred Chinese perished. The year 1649 witnessed the destruction of the *Nuestra Señora de la Encarnación* by a typhoon in the San Bernardino Strait, with over two hundred persons lost.

Pedro Cubero Sebastián was a Spanish priest known for his travels around the world from 1670 to 1679. His missionary work took him in 1670 to East Asia, which eventually led him to complete an eastward trip around the world. A storm lasting eighty hours lashed at his galleon while it crossed the Pacific. All of the crew and passengers confessed to him, and he finally calmed the weather by throwing relics into the water.[40] In 1694, the biggest galleon built in the islands, the *San José*, perished in a storm.

Galleon voyages became more stable after 1670; however, disasters continued to strike. The *San Francisco Xavier* of 1705 vanished without a trace. In 1750, the *Virgen del Pilar* was taking on water while leaving the port of Cavite. When the alarmed passengers petitioned the captain to go back, the reply was, "To Acapulco or Purgatory!" They reached the latter destination; pieces of wood and other remains from the galleon later appeared along the shores of Luzon. The *Santo Cristo de Burgos* crashed into the rocks of Ticao Island on the way to Acapulco in 1726. The passengers and crew survived, but when the sailors were taking the cargo to shore, a conflagration set alight the ship and had to be quickly extinguished by the crew. The next day another fire destroyed the galleon and the remaining cargo. Merchants indebted to the obras pias were suspected of starting the blaze. According to the law of the time, if the cargo was damaged, the merchants were required to pay back the loans, but if the merchandise was lost by an act of nature, like a fire, they were clear of their debts. The cause of the flames remained a mystery. Official inquiries took place, and the authorities imprisoned the galleon's captain general and his officers and confiscated their property. Other European lines suffered comparable disasters. As one historian recounted the Dutch experience, "The tale of shipping disasters during a hundred and fifty years is too long to unfold here, but passing mention may be made of the spectacular tragedies of 1697, 1722, 1728, 1737, and 1790, when many richly laden homeward-bound Indiamen were lost, several of them with all hands."[41] Portuguese shipwrecks were "staggeringly heavy" for the century spanning 1550 to 1650, with between 112 and 130 ships lost. The number dropped steeply by 1650, and during the eighteenth century, a voyage to Goa was only as risky as one to Bombay or Batavia.[42]

In addition to the threat of shipwrecks, the *arribadas*, or returns to port, presented an additional hazard. In 1602, the *Jesús María* and the *Espíritu Santo* retraced their route after five months of terrible weather and drifting in the ocean; almost all of the people onboard perished. Four galleons in the years 1616 and 1617 pulled back to port, as was the case for the galleons of 1655, 1666, 1672, and 1687. In the eighteenth century, the *Santísima Trinidad*, unable to ride the storms, was captured on the way back to Manila by the British during the Seven Years' War. In 1795 the *San Andrés* turned back to Manila, as did the *Magallanes* in 1806.

The return of a galleon to the Philippines was a human and economic catastrophe. Usually, the vessel was greatly damaged, and many onboard had died. Storms tangled the galleon's masts and rigging; heavy seas broke the rudder and opened up leaks, ruining the cargo. In emergencies, bales and other merchandise were thrown overboard to lighten up the ship. Financially, an arribada was nearly as damaging as a shipwreck. Even if the bales of silk could be kept undamaged until the following year, a double landing was not permitted or sometimes, for lack of space, not possible.[43]

Schurz asserts that between 1777 and 1794, the galleon was required to change its route and make stops at San Francisco and Monterrey in California, but Vera Valdés Lakowsky found no evidence of such a detour in Mexican archives. A number of ships bound for the Philippines departed from the port of San Blas on the Mexican coast or stopped there back from Manila before and after 1796. After 1768, San Blas was the anchorage that connected the missions and presidios of California with New Spain and was the port of departure for voyages of exploration to the Pacific Northwest.

The Voyage

Richard Walter, whose *Voyage Round the World* narrates George Anson's expedition from 1740 to 1744, is highly critical of the galleon's navigational procedures: "The instructions given to their captains (which I have seen) seem to have been drawn up by such as were more apprehensive of too strong a gale, though favorable, than of the inconvenience and mortality attending a lingering and tedious voyage."[44] The Dutch admiral Johan S. Stavorinus put forward a similar complaint in 1793, attributing the decline in Dutch navigational skills to the East India Company's bureaucratic routine.[45] Both ignored the nature of such enterprises, in which profit was the merchants' main concern and caution overruled other considerations.

The frigate *Fama* in 1798 and the *San Gerónimo* two hundred years earlier sailed from Manila to Acapulco in a record time of three months and twenty days, but these vessels were the exception to the rule, as the journey generally took much longer. The whole voyage averaged four or five months, with some longer passages of six, seven, or eight months. The bitter cold of the northern latitudes, the changeable winds, the insufficient supply of water and food, the confined quarters, and the lack of hygiene caused outbreaks of diseases and great distress to both crew and passengers. After six months of travel, starvation and illnesses like scurvy or beriberi threatened all onboard. In 1629, a galleon lost 105 people; two years later 140 persons were buried at sea; 114 died on the ships of 1643. The *San José* was pulled out of the waters near Acapulco in 1657 one year after its departure from Cavite; it was drifting along the coast without a living soul onboard: "everyone had perished of pestilence or starvation, and when sighted the silent galleon with her freight of silks and cadavers was driving southward into the tropics." Father Cubero Sebastián wrote in his *Peregrinación del Mundo* (*Pilgrimage around the World*) that in 1680 he left Manila in the company of four hundred people. During a two-week stretch off the coast of California, he gave last rites to ninety-two persons; only 192 reached Acapulco.[46] In 1755, the *Santísima Trinidad*—later captured by the British—had a terrible crossing. The galleon sailed from Manila on July 23, and four days later the Marchioness of Obando gave birth to a son, while the chief steward's wife delivered a daughter soon after. These glad tidings were overshadowed by tragedy. The Marquis of Obando died on December 9, and two men delirious with fever killed themselves. On February 1, the Jesuits of Mission San José of Cabo San Lucas received two hundred sick passengers who arrived seeking medical care. Of the 435 people on the *Santísima Trinidad*, eighty-two had perished at sea, and those who survived were exhausted. When they reached Acapulco, only twenty-seven were able to stand on their feet.[47] Large numbers of fatalities were also a common misfortune in other navies. In 1609, Pyrard of Laval highly praised the Royal Hospital in Goa, where he was a patient—"all the plates, bowls, and dishes are of China porcelain"—but medical care was not successful. "In every year more than 1,500 corpses are removed from this hospital, while the number of sick admitted is infinite." The arrival of the Portuguese carracks usually brought more than three hundred ill persons to its wards.[48] In Batavia, mortality had been increasing since the last decade of the seventeenth century. Stavorinus commented that in the year 1768–1769, of all the sailors on the twenty-seven ships that arrived from Europe, one in six died. In 1782, on ten Indiamen carrying 2,653 men, 1,095 (43 percent) died before reaching the Cape of Good Hope, where 915 survivors entered the hospital. As soon as the East Indiamen anchored off Batavia, boats appeared to take the sick. During the 1780s the daily number of ill at the hospital included about one thousand patients, and every year two thousand Europeans died there.[49]

The main provisions loaded into galleons to feed the passengers and crew included biscuits, salted meat, and dried fish, in addition to live fowl, swine, and other animals. Twenty hogs, five hundred chickens, and large quantities of fruits from Albay were brought on Gemelli Careri's ship. Fruits and vegetables were eaten during the first weeks of the voyage. Obviously, the diet of high-rank and rich passengers was better than that of the common crew members, but even their provisions declined rapidly in quality with the passing of time. Prolonged crossings meant worsening deprivations for passengers who had no means to pay higher prices for better food and for sailors whose rations were already small. When the galleons departed from

Manila, they carried a supply of water in thousands of earthen jars and large bamboo vessels. Careri wrote, "It is the practice in this Voyage to carry the water in earthen jars to the number of two, three, or 4,000 proportionately to the number of people and bigness of the galleon." These vessels—Chinese jars and large bamboo containers—were placed at the bottom of the ship, above the ballast. As water was used during the voyage, seawater was poured into them to keep the ships' balance. Many of these jars were hung from the rigging, while the rest were stowed away. A few galleons had built-in cisterns. While passing through the rain belt of higher latitudes, galleon crews collected rainwater. In the eighteenth century, Lord Anson's chronicler reported on the galleons' method of replenishing supplies: "[They] take to sea with them a great number of mats, which, whenever the rain descends, they range slopingly against the gunwale from one end of the ship to the other, their lower edges resting on a large split bamboo; whence all the water which falls on the mats drain into the bamboo, and by this, as a trough, is conveyed into a jar."[50] Along the way to the Embocadero, the galleon could refill its water provision, and sailors cooked rice, "which apparently was a treat for them, as they were mostly consuming daily rations of biscuits, fried meat and fish and other staples such as beans."[51]

Passengers received their accommodations, cabins, or sleeping areas before leaving Cavite. Gemelli Careri wrote that the boatswain provided him with food during the voyage for 100 pesos, indicating, "It is usual to pay 500 or 600 pieces-of-eight for a cabin and diet, because the cabin costs more than the provisions."[52] Sailors were supposed to sleep where they could. Comfort depended on how much the voyager paid. The galleons' carpenters built cabins—on an average of five feet square—in the stern castle and on the upper and lower decks. Passengers were allowed to bring two trunks with their possessions, their own food, and a cot with a mattress and bed clothing. People with means brought a variety of victuals, including live hens and pigs, as well as servants to prepare their meals. Those less fortunate shared the same rations as the crew and paid a fee to the ship's master. On the way to the San Bernardino Strait, there was an abundance of fresh meat, fruits, and vegetables, but the further the galleon traveled from the island, the more monotonous the meals became and the faster the condiments disappeared. A typical meal while at sea might include fish cooked with only water and salt or buffalo meat that had been fried or boiled. The crew supplemented their fare with fish or any birds they were able to catch, which they sold to passengers. Careri was grateful for this: "Providence relieved us for a month with the sharks and *cachorretas*—tuna fish—the seaman caught which either boiled or broiled were some comfort."[53]

The captain, pilots, and ship's master had their own cabins in the stern castle. Their food was of higher quality because they brought their own supplies. Junior officers had smaller sleeping quarters, similar to those provided for passengers, in an enclosed partitioned area. Crew members were permitted to bring one sea chest with their belongings, which, during the voyage, they used as tables on which they could eat and play cards. In general, living conditions were appalling due to overcrowded quarters. In 1604, Pedro de Montes and his group of twenty Jesuits were assigned three ordinary cabins, ten feet long by eight feet wide—not much space for five men—and a fourth cabin that was slightly larger. Similar accommodations were given to Juan de Aguirre and his companions in 1625. The cabin was so small that the only way they could all fit inside when they went to bed was to lie with the feet of one resting on the head of another. They were more crowded because they had to keep their boxes of ship's biscuit in the cabin in order to have them handy. No one took off his clothes, "for the sake of holy modesty," and soon everyone suffered from vermin.[54] Gemelli Careri observed, "The ship swarms with little vermin the Spaniards call *gorgojos*, bred in the biscuit; so swift that they in a short time not only run over cabins, beds and the very dishes the men eat on, but insensibly fasten upon the body."[55] These creatures were not the sole source of discomfort; rats, mice, cockroaches, bedbugs, and lice all worked to torment the lives of everyone onboard. Bathing was out of the question during the voyage, and washing with seawater in a makeshift fashion was the only alternative. Doing laundry carried the same difficulties, and it was almost impossible to get rid of the lice. Crew rations swarmed with worms and maggots.[56] Careri remarked, "[An] abundance of flies fall into the dishes of broth, in which there also swim worms of several sorts."[57]

On February 27, 1767, Charles III ordered the expulsion of the Jesuits from his domains, including the Philippines, but typhoons interfered with His Majesty's decree. The *San Carlos* was the galleon assigned to transport the Jesuit fathers and brothers to Mexico and Spain. Horacio de la Costa quotes an anonymous diary of one Jesuit, who related the dreadful experience. There was a large amount of cargo in addition to four hundred passengers, and as a result, the sixty-two Jesuits were confined to accommodations fit for twenty people. After a few days at sea, twenty-five soldiers who "had been left out in the open without any place being assigned to them" joined the religious men. Their quarters were close to swine and other animals, which came to share the cabin with the Jesuits and soldiers on rainy days. "Thus, one of the fathers suddenly found himself with three pigs on his cot, and being unable to get them out, was forced to get out himself." He was somewhat fortunate because "another pig joined Father Provincial himself, and was of such generous proportions that if one of the ship's officers who happened to be passing by had not hauled it off the cot by main force, it would have smothered the Father." It was a common practice to carry live animals on the vessels of the European navies at the time.[58] On September 8, about one hundred leagues from the Mariana Islands, a typhoon assaulted the galleon, and in a few hours, it had lost all of its masts. The ship began to take on water, and some of the Jesuits helped the sailors working the pumps. There were four pilots onboard, among them one Dane and one Englishman. "All of them swore they had never in their lives experienced winds of equal fury." While they were turning back to the Philippines, another typhoon struck the *San Carlos*. The exhausted crew and passengers dropped anchor at Cavite on October 22. Two years later, in 1769, the same galleon took twenty-one of those travelers to Acapulco without any major incidents.[59]

A law of 1608 forbade carrying slave women on the galleon and mandated their confiscation in Acapulco. De los Ríos Coronel had written to the king regarding the disregard of this new ordinance, explaining that royal decrees and the penalty of excommunication by the archbishop were ineffectual: "Many sailors—and even others, who should furnish a good example—take slave women and keep them as concubines. He knew a certain prominent official who carried with him fifteen of these women; and some were delivered of children by him, while others were pregnant, which made a great scandal" upon arrival in Acapulco.[60] It seems that Portuguese ships followed the same custom. One historian comments, "Originally, the ships' officers seem to have been the chief offenders in bringing ladies of easy virtue to India." On the way to Portugal, slave girls were taken in the carracks, with the result that "some rather futile legislation was enacted against their being brought back to Lisbon."[61]

Like slave women, foreigners were forbidden to take passage on the galleons. The few who made the voyage were generally enrolled among the ship officers and served without salary. In this way the Italian merchant Antonio Carletti and his son Francesco embarked on the galleon in 1596, with Antonio serving as constable and Francesco as a guard. For a percentage, the captain kept their money in his cabin.[62] Another Italian, Gemelli Careri, traveled on the galleon a century later.

Entertainments like dancing, theatrics, and music were allowed, but all forms of gambling were forbidden. This prohibition had no effect on the galleon's officers, who participated in gambling and, in some instances, made handsome profits from their illicit activities. Domingo Navarrete commented that while traveling on a galleon under the command of Lorenzo de Ugalde, he had won more than 1,200 pieces of eight. It is likely that Ugalde had supplied the decks of cards and collected the customary gratuities.[63] Some people played chess or listened to readings from a novel or the lives of the saints. Less cultivated amusements included cockfights. Sailors, weather allowing, jumped into the ocean and swam, keeping an eye peeled for sharks. There were religious services to honor the saints' and other holy days. Priests on board comforted passengers in times of distress and danger and gave last rites when necessary.

The return voyage to Manila was safer and more pleasant, lasting between seventy-five and ninety days. As was done in Manila, prayers were offered in Mexico City for the success of the voyage. The galleon usually cleared Acapulco in February or March. Fernández Navarrete observed, "If the ships sail from Acapulco any time in February or even beginning of March, they will arrive in good time to put into Cavite, with safety."[64] Leaving Acapulco later in the spring could threaten the galleon with bad weather beyond the Mariana Islands and delay the voyage, adding to the danger of diseases. On the *Espíritu Santo* of 1606, forty passengers died, and the voyage of the *San Luis* in 1642 had eighty fatalities.

Westward across the Pacific, passengers suffered from heat as they sailed slowly down to the trade wind regions, but as soon as they reached 12 degrees north latitude they struck a cool, steady wind that blew them across a calm sea. Mariners called this stretch of the ocean *mar de damas*, the Ladies' Sea. After a stop at Guam for fresh water and food, the galleons resumed their course and made their first Philippine landfall early in July. The Dominican Domingo de Navarrete and his companions traveled to Manila in a small vessel, a *patache*, with a Portuguese pilot named Antunez. At the height of the Marianas, a native boat "made up to us; we lay by for it, to take in some refreshment it likely brought, which the natives of those islands exchange for nails and old iron," the latter indicating the natives' ongoing need for the strong metal.[65]

The galleons ordinarily entered or left the Philippines through San Bernardino Strait, between the southern extreme of Luzon and the northern coast of Samar. There were problems when the galleon arrived in the season of the southwest winds, or *vendavales*, in which case the ship waited until the wind changed. That was the case with Navarrete; the southwest wind drove the patache to sea. Finally, the ship approached a safe place, and "the plates—silver—and other goods belonging to his Majesty and private persons were secured." Missionaries and the rest of the passengers reached Manila by land.[66] If the galleons arrived at the Embocadero at the end of June, the monsoon could have set in, and "at such times to try to enter that labyrinth of islands and shoals with its swirling, shifting tides and currents was to court destruction."[67] The only option was to wait for a change in the wind or to spend the winter in the harbors of Palapag, Lampon, or some nearby refuge. The *San Antonio* of 1681 encountered heavy gales in the high latitudes, but the galleon returned to the islands without major damage. "It had not the good-fortune to come in as far as the point of Cavite (a piece of luck which seldom occurs), on account of the vendavales having set in steadily; and therefore it made port in Sorsogon." The *Buen Socorro* had a fortunate arrival at the harbor of Palapag in the province of Leyte, outside of the Embocadero. After mentioning the previous cases, Casimiro Díaz observed that "hardly a galleon built in these islands succeeds in making the entrance of the port of Cavite."[68] Governor Pedro Manuel de Arandía (1754–1759) ordered the galleons to winter at Sisiran in the Camarines coast if reaching Cavite was not feasible.[69] Once inside the Embocadero, the Manila galleon negotiated its way northwestward through the archipelago to Manila.[70]

A galleon's return laden with silver and new arrivals was a cause for great celebration in the colony. There was general joy in Manila, where the city streets were decorated and the church bells rang. In the cathedral and other churches, prayers were offered in thanksgiving for the safe arrival of the passengers and the fortunate outcome of business.

Officers and Sailors

The highest authority on the ship was the captain general; in the case of two galleons the captain sailed on the "*capitana*," and a second in command, the admiral, sailed on the "*almiranta*." Positions in the galleon's ranks were sold for a price. In fact, the most coveted gift a governor could bestow was the command of a galleon. The captain general was not a navigator, but he did possess the authority to appoint officers and sailing masters on his vessel. Le Gentil wrote in 1769 that the governor allocated 4,500 pesos to the captain general for the payment of the voyage's expenses. Usually, more officers were assigned than the voyage might require, giving employment and opportunity for enrichment to friends of the governor or the Mexican viceroy. Careri estimated that in 1636, a captain could receive from different venues a sum between 50,000 and 100,000 pesos. Merchants of Manila would give him gratuities; he collected 4 percent on the registered cargo and another percentage on the unregistered merchandise. Mexican and Peruvian merchants, as well as other officials, would give him commissions, which the captain would collect in addition to the returns from his private investments and irregular but frequent profits from gambling. Higher officers of the galleon amassed considerable sums, as well, and even the boatswain could end his voyage a rich man.

Other officers in the galleon's hierarchy were the captain of sea, who had a nautical background, as well as the ship's master, who was second in command, oversaw the daily routines of the vessel, and was expected to possess navigational skills. He received orders from the captain and the pilot, conveyed those commands to the crew, and was in charge of the manifold duties of the ship's administration. In Manila, the master took charge of supplying the vessel with equipment and provisions. He acted on behalf of the merchants who were shipping cargo on the galleon, supervised its loading onto the ship, and was in charge of the legal paperwork, in addition to collecting taxes and duties. Upon the galleon's arrival in Acapulco, he paid custom duties and other levies and was responsible for transferring the merchandise to its legitimate owners in Mexico. He took care of the galleon's maintenance and seaworthiness. On top of his many duties, he gave sailors the advance on their wages and paid the salary to the pilot.

A fourth naval officer, the boatswain (*segundo contramaestre*), was assisted by the steward (*guardian primero*), whose duties were keeping the ship clean, supervising the cooking fires and lights, and maintaining discipline among apprentices and pages. These pages, or cabin boys, entered into service at sea when they were between eight and ten years old. They were charged with keeping track of time by turning the sand clocks every half hour while reciting religious invocations, which were answered in chorus. They also chanted the "Good Day" each day, and before evening, they recited other prayers and the main tenets of the Christian faith, the *Credo*. They received orders from sailors and apprentices and gave help when needed. Apprentices were young sailors in training; their ages varied between seventeen and twenty years old.[71]

Other positions of responsibility on the galleon were the accountant and the overseer, who was in charge of the ship's register. Their main task was to ensure that all of the merchandise was properly registered. There was a notary on board to act as a legal witness for transactions and important events. The master of silver, *maestro de la plata*, was responsible for the bullion that was carried in payment for the goods shipped the previous year, as well as the situado funds. It was an expensive appointment to secure; he had to pay at least 3,000 pesos to be appointed. Obviously, those who occupied positions in the galleon were expecting their profits to exceed their own initial expenditures and financial outlay, which included payoffs to officials in Manila and Acapulco.

Navigation was under the authority of the *piloto mayor*, or leading navigational officer, but on many voyages there were other pilots onboard. Pilots were high-ranking government employees of high prestige.[72] Usually the official commander turned over the direction of the ship to the *piloto mayor*—"A few seasoned pilots were the mainstay of the navigation."[73] Their expertise was based on long personal experience. Because chronometers had not been invented yet, pilots had no way to ascertain longitude, which made maps of limited value—only in the 1780s did logbooks begin to record daily longitude readings using a chronometer. In stormy or cloudy weather the astrolabe was useless. To reach their destination, pilots used "dead reckoning," that is, calculating the ship's position based on its estimated speed, the direction sailed, the length of time since its last known position, and above all, the interpretation of the ocean's signs. Spanish and Portuguese pilots were highly regarded during these centuries. English admiral Richard Hawkins noted in 1622, "In this point of steeridge, the Spaniards and Portuguese do exceed all that I have seen, I mean for their care, which is chiefest in navigation. And I wish in this, and in all their works of discipline and reformation, we should follow their example."[74]

Recruiting sailors was difficult for all navies of the time, a problem aggravated by the high mortality on the Indian and Pacific voyages. Due to the lack of experienced seamen, foreigners found employment on the Manila galleons, with Danish, English, Irish, German, and French crewmen serving on many voyages. A good example was Geronimo Monteiro of Portugal, who had fourteen years of service when he was captured with the *Covandonga* in 1742.

Sailors had a bad reputation in the modern era and were considered to be at the bottom of the social scale in terms of prestige and rewards. The Spanish humanist Luis Vives (1493–1540) called them *fex maris* (dregs of the sea); the French memoirist Pyrard of Laval, after a long experience at sea, summarized his perspective: "All seamen while at sea are barbarous, cruel, and uncivil wretches, with no respect of persons, in short very devils incarnate";[75] Diogo do Couto, a Portuguese chronicler, wrote that sailors were "cruel and inhuman by nature." In the fleets of the Dutch East India Company crews had no better reputations, probably because "going into the service of the VOC was a desperate, last-ditch hope for those who hadn't been able to find any other employment."[76] A member of the company observed in 1677 that sailors "behave like wild boars; they rob and steal, drink and go whoring so shamelessly that it seems to be no disgrace with them." Apparently, they did not improve with the passage of time; in 1751, a passenger wrote, "For the sailors on board Indiamen, cursing, swearing, whoring, debauchery and murder are mere trifles."[77] Destitute and unemployed men in Europe filled out their countries' navies.

Harsh discipline was employed to control sailors. Violence and drunkenness were severely punished. Blasphemy was considered a high offense to

God, who could withdraw protection over the galleon and bring terrible consequences to all onboard. For the first offense, the blasphemer spent fifteen days gagged and in shackles with only bread and water to eat; the second blasphemy was punished by piercing the culprit's tongue with a burning iron.[78] Death sentences, keel-hauling, nailing the culprit's hand to the mast, flogging, and imprisonment in irons were common penalties in the navies of these centuries.

Galleons in the sixteenth and seventeenth centuries required a crew of about one hundred men; this number increased during the eighteenth century to a figure that varied between 150 and 250. Officers and skilled sailors came from Mexico or Spain, while the majority of the remaining crew members were Filipino, with the occasional Chinese sailor. There were usually five Filipinos to one Spaniard.[79] Some of the Spaniards who returned to Mexico enlisted as seamen to save the passage cost—1,000 pesos to Manila and 1,500 pesos to Acapulco. Filipinos from the interior of Luzon were unaccustomed to the ocean, but when there was a scarcity of available seamen, they were pressed into service. De los Ríos Coronel wrote to the king requesting that the Filipinos who served on the ships be natives from the coast, as they were good sailors. He noted that these men should be provided with clothes against the low temperatures of higher latitudes since so many of them died from the cold. "When each new dawn comes there are three or four dead men; besides, they are treated inhumanly and are not given the necessaries of life, but are killed with hunger and thirst."[80] One law of 1620 required that natives be clothed sufficiently, fed humanely, and treated well by the crew. Nonetheless, rations provided to Filipinos were about half what the Spanish sailors received. Toward the end of the voyage, when provisions became scarce and the quality of water was deplorable, Filipinos suffered the most. In the second half of the eighteenth century, another procurator, Leandro de Viana, extolled the Filipinos as agile in their maneuvers with the sails, quick to learn Spanish nautical terms, and knowledgeable in the use of the compass: "therefore on this trade route there are some very skillful dexterous helmsmen." As soldiers, they were spirited and courageous "when placed on a ship from which they cannot escape."[81] Poor treatment and meager payment justified a tendency among the Filipinos to desertion and a reluctance to fight unless under threat. Multiethnic crews were common in the modern era. In the Portuguese carracks sailing between Goa, Macao, and Nagasaki, the majority of the sailors were African slaves and Asians, save for the officers, soldiers, and gunners. In 1792, the VOC's return fleet to Europe arrived at the Cape of Good Hope with crews that had 233 Moorish, 101 Javanese, and 504 Chinese sailors, as well as 579 Europeans.[82]

Governor Santiago de Vera, writing to Philip II in 1589, indicated that the money for sailors' wages must be sent from Mexico, since "sometimes it is not brought, and at other times it is lost, thereby causing the sailors to die of starvation. Therefore the sailors serve half-heartedly, and desert."[83] Many Filipino sailors married Mexican women and lived in Mexico, settling in the state of Guerrero and nearby regions. For instance, out of seventy-five Filipinos who had left Manila on board the *Espíritu Santo* in 1618, only five made the return voyage. Once the galleon landed in Mexico, the Filipinos were hired by the natives to teach them to make palm wine (*tuba*), and within a short period of time the strong beverage became popular among Mexicans, competing with Spanish wines.

During the seventeenth century, crew members' salaries remained unpaid for as long as fifteen years. In other instances, sailors and soldiers received their pay in treasury warrants. Servants of high officials in Manila bought such vouchers for a fraction of their nominal value but would be reimbursed in full upon presenting them to the treasury. Royal officials in Acapulco did all they could to fleece the incoming sailors. Sebastián Hurtado de Corcuera proposed to the king in 1635 the following scale of payments:

> The Spanish common seamen who are employed anywhere shall receive pay of one hundred pesos per year, and the thirty *gantas* of rice per month [approximately 6.72 kg] on account of their pay. . . . The Indian common seamen who are employed anywhere shall receive forty-eight pesos per year, and fifteen *gantas* [3.36 kg] of cleaned rice per month on the account of their pay.[84]

Sixty years later, in 1697, Careri indicated that common Spanish seamen received 100 pesos or more, while a native's pay was 48 to 60 pesos. A monthly allotment of rice was added to supplement salaries, but natives always received a smaller amount than Spaniards.

Contingents of soldiers embarked on the galleons to provide protection. They were under the authority of the war captain, usually an infantry lieutenant also in charge of maintaining discipline onboard. Many soldiers were Filipino, but some Japanese also embarked in the same capacity during the seventeenth century. The master gunner, in charge of artillery, commanded a group of artillerymen. To keep the galleon in good condition during their voyage, the government employed a number of skilled workers, including the master carpenter, a sail master, a diver, caulkers, blacksmiths, and rope makers.

In addition to officers and sailors, the galleon carried slaves who had been purchased in Manila. Portuguese and Asian merchants continued the slave trade, bringing people from Africa, India, Timor, and other places in Southeast Asia. In 1672, Manila authorities banned the enslavement of Asians. However, the practice persisted; in eighteenth-century Veracruz, a group of Jesuits was required by the authorities to release twenty Asian servants.[85] The masters of these same slaves frequently sold them upon arrival in Acapulco. Careri sold an African slave for 400 pesos in Acapulco, where he observed the prevalence of a population of African origins.[86]

Acapulco

When signs of land appeared, there was a *Fiesta de las señas*, "*Te Deum* was sung and all persons congratulated one another with the sound of drums and trumpets, as if we had been in our port, whereas we were then 700 leagues from it."[87] Reports of the approaching galleon produced a degree of uncertainty, because it could be an enemy; nonetheless, prayers began in Mexico City when a messenger arrived, bringing letters from the coast. "The bells ring for joy; and this noise lasts, till a third express comes from Acapulco, who brings the viceroy advice of the galleon from China, being come to an anchor in the port." When the fleet arrived at Veracruz on the Atlantic side, the news was celebrated similarly.[88]

When the galleon entered the Acapulco harbor, it was tied to a robust tree by the shore. After the first port officials had made their initial inspection, the image of the Virgin was carried to the parish church, among the salvos of the galleon's guns and Fort San Diego's cannons. Gemelli Careri wrote in 1696, "Notwithstanding the dreadful sufferings in this prodigious voyage, yet the desire of gain prevails with many to venture through it, four, six, and some ten times." At the time of departure at Cavite, sailors had received only 75 pesos, and to collect the remaining wages they were required to sail back to Manila.

Careri calculated his galleon's proceeds. Merchant profits were between 150 and 200 percent. Representatives of merchants, called factors, received 9 percent of earnings, "which in 200,000 or 300,000 pieces-of-eight amounts to money." Galleon officers made handsome gains that further supplemented their salaries. "The master, his mate, and boatswain who may put aboard several bales of goods, may make themselves rich in one voyage." Captain Emanuel Arguelles cleared 25,000 to 30,000 pieces of eight in commissions, while a pilot made 20,000, and his mates each received 9,000 pesos. The kings' duties amounted to 80,000, "including the present to the Viceroy."[89]

When Gemelli Careri arrived, he was unimpressed by Acapulco and described it as a humble village of fishermen who lived in low adobe houses with straw roofs. He mentioned that at the port of El Marqués, southeast of Acapulco, ships from Peru landed to unload cacao and other merchandise forbidden by regulations. Acapulco's only advantage was its deep bay. The entrance was divided by the Isla de la Roqueta in two channels; the largest one, called the *Boca Grande*, was the passage by which galleons entered and left Acapulco. From 1615 to 1616, a Catholic Dutch engineer, Adrian Boot, constructed the fortress to protect the port; by 1618 Fort San Diego already had a garrison and artillery. The Spanish administration was under the authority of a *castellano*, or mayor, in charge of maintaining the fort, managing the town, collecting taxes, and supervising all of the operations related to the galleon, including the fair.

When the galleon made port, the mayor and treasury officials boarded it and reviewed the ship's registry, which indicated the quantities and nature of the merchandise and the number of slaves to be sold. Officials collected documents from royal functionaries in Manila, lists of crew and passengers, and the record of deaths during the voyage. After the inspection was completed, passengers disembarked from the galleons. Cargo was taken to royal warehouses, and the ship was inspected one more time for smuggled goods. Finally, shipwrights and carpenters repaired the galleon for its return to Manila.

Heat made the village quite unpleasant. Friar Domingo Navarrete wrote in the middle of the seventeenth century, "The temperature of the air is hellish . . . and therefore in the rainy season, which is the summer in Spain, all persons retire up the country for better air, excepting the blacks, some poor people and the soldiers." Foods and supplies came from a long distance, and everything was expensive. Navarrete, an experienced globetrotter, said, "I never saw a dearer country in all my travels." As an example, the parish priest drew an official salary, but in one year he earned 14,000 pieces of eight for performing Christian rituals; Careri gave the same figure and added that the priest's official salary was only 180 pesos. For the burial of the fort's commander, 500 pesos was demanded, and in 1696 the funeral of a rich merchant cost 1,000 pesos. Another example of Acapulco's high cost of living was the water business. Blacks controlled water provisions, and to carry onboard the necessary water for the trip to Manila, Navarrete paid 36 pesos: "the blacks monopolized this trade, and it must be as they please."[90] In 1696, they expected a daily salary of one peso.

After the galleon's arrival, "Acapulco was immediately transformed into an international center of trade."[91] The annual fair usually began in the middle of January and lasted until the end of February. A diverse throng attended the fair; the most relevant in economic terms were the merchants from Mexico City and Peru. The Mexicans arrived at the port using the unpaved mule train road known as "The China Road." Careri wrote about squalid accommodations, scarcity of food, and how hard it was to travel. He crossed the Papagayo River swimming; during winter, travelers floated across it on a raft supported by hollow pumpkins pulled by natives. Carletti, one hundred years earlier, described the procedure: "We placed ourselves on a mass of thick dry gourds, bound together with a netting of cane. On that we placed the saddle of our horse, which swam across. . . . Then four of those Indians one at each corner of the raft of bound gourds swam pushing it." Similar devices were used to cross the Mexicala River, or *Río de las Balsas*, further down the way.[92]

Manila merchants were sometimes forced to sell their remaining merchandise at lower prices when the date for the returning galleon to Manila was approaching. Knowing these circumstances, the Mexicans tried to delay bargaining to get goods as cheaply as possible. If Peruvian merchants were present with abundant silver, the merchants from Manila had an edge over the Mexicans. Another method was to purchase Asian goods in Manila instead of using a middleman in the Philippines, as when merchants from Mexico and Peru went to China in 1686 in an attempt to establish direct trade connections and left samples of fabrics as models for the Chinese silk weavers.[93] Careri witnessed the arrival of Peruvian merchants with 2 million pesos to buy Chinese goods. Mexican merchants arrived carrying pieces of eight, commodities from New Spain, and merchandise brought by the fleets to Veracruz and sold in Acapulco to merchants from Peru. A large part of the galleons' cargo was sold in Mexico; another portion was destined for markets in the Caribbean and South America; and finally, the fleets carried silks, cottons, and porcelains to Europe.

CHAPTER SIX

⟳

The Economy of the Line

China and Silver in the Modern Era

"The avidity of the Chinese for silver established a commercial epoch for the international economy." To illustrate his point, monetary historian Frank Spooner quotes a 1586 letter from a Florentine merchant: "Without this avidity the Spanish reals would not have raised so much in value as they now are. The Chinese among all the peoples of Asia are wild about silver as everywhere men are about gold."[1] Silver was the commodity that settled accounts on all continents and allowed European countries to trade in the extremely profitable Asian markets because, as Juan Grau y Monfalcón, procurator general of the Philippines, explained, "In Asia and the regions of the Orient, God created some things so precious in the estimation of men, and so peculiar to those provinces, that, as they are only found or manufactured therein, they are desired and sought by the rest of the world."[2] Spices, cotton, silk, tea, and porcelain were exchanged for bullion from the sixteenth century until the Industrial Revolution in England radically altered the basic structure of trade.[3]

During the sixteenth century, the market value of silver in the Ming Empire was double that in Europe. The relationship between the relative prices of silver and gold (bimetallic ratios) are striking: "From 1592 to the early seventeenth century gold was exchanged for silver in Canton at the rate of 1:5.5 to 1:7, while in Spain the exchange rate was 1:12.5 to 1:14, thus indicating that the value of silver was twice as high in China as in Spain."[4] In Persia the ratio was 1:10, and in India it was 1:8.[5] In theory, a merchant could use an ounce of gold to buy eleven ounces of silver in Amsterdam, then transport the silver to China and exchange the eleven ounces there for about two ounces of gold. Pedro de Baeza of Portugal, who served for three decades in the East Indies, actively promoted the trade of Chinese gold for silver from New Spain or Castile, stating in 1609 "that bringing gold from China means a gain of more than seventy-five or eighty per cent."[6] This price differential would continue for decades, until enough silver had accumulated in China for its value there to be equal to its value in the rest of the world.[7] In the words of Legarda, "If one were dealing with foreign exchange, these would represent broken cross-rates. The opportunities for arbitrage profits were staggering."[8]

Contemporaries were keenly aware of these opportunities, and the Manila galleons engaged in the bullion arbitrage trade. The vessels brought silver to purchase Chinese goods, but on their return voyage also carried a sizable quantity of gold to Acapulco. A good example is the cargo of the *Santa Ana*, captured by Thomas Cavendish in 1587. Guillaume Raynal, an eighteenth-century French traveler in the Philippines, wrote, "Cavendish found as much as 658,000 livres of [gold] upon the galleon that was sailing toward Mexico."[9] Thus, the Pacific route to China was Spain's exclusive means of direct access to the Chinese marketplace. Merchants in the American viceroyalties of New Spain and Peru avoided competing with European intermediaries by trading with merchants from Asia through Manila. Raynal pointed out the advantages involved in sending silver via the Pacific route: "Spaniards by sending it directly from America to the Philippines would save duties, time, and insurance; so that while they furnished the same sum as the rival nations, they would in reality make their purchases at a cheaper rate."[10]

Manila was the Pacific linchpin of this global commercial network. The initial reaction to the new settlement produced little enthusiasm in Mexico because the only spice on hand was cinnamon, and their native societies were considered a poor market for profitable trade. Notwithstanding, Juan Pablo Carrión, an officer who served under Legázpi, saw the future clearly: "No profit can be expected from the islands until trading connections can be opened with China and the rest of the Indies." The second governor of the colony, Guido de Lavezaris (1572–1575), wrote an upbeat report from Manila that concluded, "We are here stationed at the gateway of great kingdoms."[11] Time was to prove them right. Manila occupied a privileged position in the trade routes of China, Japan, India, and Southeast Asia. Gemelli Careri wrote at the end of the seventeenth century that "the Author of Nature placed Manila so equally between the wealthy kingdoms of the East and West, that it may be accounted one of the greatest places of trade in the world."[12]

A "relation of what was brought by the two ships which came from the Islands of the West" to Spain in 1573 provides a detailed account of the cargoes of silks, cotton, wax, cinnamon, gold, and "22,300 pieces of fine gilt china, and of other kinds of porcelain ware." In addition, "For their Majesties individually, are sent from those provinces many jewels and crowns of gold, with silks, porcelains, rich and large earthen jars, and other very excellent things which are sent by the chiefs in token of their allegiance."[13] It was fashionable among the European aristocracy to collect Chinese porcelain, and Philip II already possessed about three thousand pieces. To enlarge his collection, the king commissioned a number of vases in white and blue colors of classic Ming pottery. The kilns of Jingdezhen decorated the pieces with Castile and Leon's coats of arms, probably copied from an eight real coin.[14] The merchandise carried as cargo on the galleons was to continue practically unchanged until the end of the line.

The number of Chinese junks traveling to Manila at least doubled from six in 1574 to twelve or fifteen the following year. By 1576, trade was firmly established, and Chinese junks made Manila a customary port of call. Mexican merchants began to settle on the island, providing the knowledge and capital necessary to conduct business. The galleons' and junks' voyages determined economic life in the Philippines well into the eighteenth century. Never in the history of a country has a line of navigation—often a single vessel—had such a decisive impact. The galleon was practically the only means for colonial government officials, soldiers, friars, and merchants to reach Manila. Asian commodities, silver from Mexico and Peru, plants, germs, and ideas traveled the route across the Pacific. Casimiro Díaz described the galleon as "the artery that communicates the blood and the life for the preservation of these isolated islands—that is, the silver which, like a lodestone, attracts the most remote nations to the commerce and trade."[15]

Manila's role was to be an entrepôt in which colonial merchants acted as intermediaries between Asian producers and American viceroyalties. A Spanish officer noted that "the principal motive that leads the Spaniards to those islands is the profit from the trade with New Spain, for which they risk their lives and property in a long and painful voyage."[16] Despite the arduous journey, merchant life was quite relaxed. According to Antonio de Morga, who was in Manila from 1595 to 1598, the process of buying merchandise, completing all the required paperwork, and packing the bales and chests did not entail more than three months; two hundred years later, two months would suffice.[17] In an initial attempt to gain Manila a more active role in the Chinese market, Governor Francisco Tello allowed Juan Zamudio to sail to China in 1598 and negotiate the granting of a port to serve as a commercial outpost; Chinese officials assigned a place near Canton, called *El Pinal*, or "The Pine Tree." Morga, then president of the court of justice, supported the Spanish enclave because it would prevent large numbers of Chinese from settling in Manila and could facilitate price control and the dispatch of the annual galleon. The Portuguese in nearby Macao, however, were adamantly opposed, and the king, at the time ruler of both Spain and Portugal, was not supportive because it was necessary to foster unity between both halves of the empire against the Dutch.

Manila collected commodities from a multitude of places. From India came cottons, which in the eighteenth century were an important item of export, second only to Chinese silks. Earthen jars and a wide variety of porcelain arrived from China, alongside rugs from Persia and goods from Japan. Spices like clove, mace, pepper, and cinnamon were brought from the Moluccas, Java, and Ceylon, along with other eighteenth-century "drugs"— borax, camphor, minium, and musk—as well as tea and cigars. The galleon also carried gold, jewelry, precious stones, and uncut gems. Importing such items from Asia was illegal, but the law was commonly circumvented. In 1767, officials in Acapulco confiscated hundreds of rings and other jewelry set with diamonds and rubies, as well as rich crucifixes, reliquaries, and rosaries, including a cross decorated with eight brilliants. The same year, nine sailors' chests carried eighty thousand women's combs on the *San Carlos* galleon.[18] Fabrics from the Philippines—like *lampotes* or cotton gauze pieces from Cebu; cotton cloth, *mantas*, from Ilocos; and linen sheets, tablecloths, coverlets, cotton stockings, and hammocks manufactured throughout the islands—acquired great value at Mexican markets. Generally, in order to favor insular production, this locally produced merchandise was not taxed. However, "Silks in every stage of manufacture and of every variety of weave and pattern formed the most valuable part of their cargoes." The galleons carried Chinese silk for napkins and tablecloths or as fabric for making dresses and handkerchiefs. From California to Chile, rich liturgical vestments for parishes, missions, and convents were made of silk. Silk stockings were highly popular, and each galleon bore large quantities; in one case, a single ship carried more than fifty thousand pairs. Chinese merchants, recognizing how popular Asian products had become in New Spain, soon learned to accommodate the vagaries of the market and deftly copied the designs preferred by their customers. The Council of Mexico City inaugurated permanent facilities in its central plaza, the *Zócalo*, in 1703, establishing a market named the

Parian after the Chinese Parian in Manila. Stores in the Parian sold goods imported by the galleon, and the city government earned a substantial annual income renting out the shops.[19]

The church played a crucial role in the galleon trade through the *obras pias*. These associations, funded by merchants and churchmen and overseen by high-ranking laymen, supported charitable work in the Philippines. Their capital reserves amounted to millions of pesos. The most prominent of the obras pias was the Brotherhood of Mercy, or *Misericordia*, modeled on the confraternity founded by Queen Eleanor in 1498 in Lisbon. The *San Juan de Dios* and the Tertiary Order of San Francis confraternities belonged to the obras pias, as did less-prominent brotherhoods. In addition to their roles as charitable organizations, these confraternities transferred inheritances to distant heirs, acted as commercial banks and maritime insurance companies, and provided interest-free loans to the government when the *situado* failed to arrive or in times of emergency. Their funds were available to both wealthy merchants and minor traders. Loans fluctuated between 20 and 50 percent for the Acapulco trade, between 12 and 18 percent for the China trade, and between 16 and 22 percent for ventures to India.[20] Calculating investment risks depended on the merchant's creditworthiness, the economic prospects of the fair at Acapulco, the chance of a shipwreck, and the possibility of an enemy capture. The demand for Asian products increased if Mexico had plentiful harvests or a boost in silver production, or if Peruvian ships landed at Acapulco. Merchants usually borrowed a sum from the obras that was twice what they intended to invest on the galleon; this ensured that the merchant would have enough reserves to pay the interest on the capital in case he could not pay the principal for another year. To compensate for shipwrecks and losses, a merchant would try to invest any remaining funds in the next galleon to pay his debt to the obras and to continue trading. Failing one's financial obligations implied loss of access to credit and banishment from the galleon enterprise. Some investors were able to borrow money in Mexico at 25 percent to pay debts to the obras in Manila, contracted at 40 or 50 percent.[21]

The Chinese were adept at packing silks efficiently to maximize space. Bales were tightly wrapped, protecting their contents from seawater and insects, with cheaper goods on the outside to deceive zealous officials as to their value. On the way out to the open Pacific, illegal goods joined the cargo. Each galleon's hold was full to maximum capacity, and additional chests and bales obstructed passages, cabins, and decks. Bundles of merchandise occupied spaces reserved for necessary supplies and filled in the powder magazine. Guns were stored in the hold, a short-sighted solution that created space for cargo but also meant that weapons were not readily at hand during encounters with the enemy; for instance, the *Santísima Trinidad*, a sixty-gun ship, had only ten in position when the British captured it. Occasionally, the galleon towed rafts carrying waterproof bundles. Often, galleons took to sea lacking the extra sails and spars required for difficult navigation or the amounts of water and food necessary for a voyage that could take up to seven months. Several times galleons had to turn back to Manila to unload the excess weight; in other cases, the ships were lost. The viceroy of Mexico, the Count of Monterrey, attributed the loss of the *Santa Margarita* and *San Gerónimo* in 1600 to overloading.

During the first years of the galleon trade, Manila charged no levies on the cargoes. Governor Diego Ronquillo established a rate of 3 percent, charged to imports. The duty increased to 6 percent in 1606 and 8 percent in 1714. After 1760, rates were reduced. Gómez Pérez Dasmariñas imposed a tax on exports in order to pay for the construction of the city walls, but the tax was discontinued by royal order after the walls' completion. During the wars with the Dutch, the Spanish government collected an export duty that returned more than 7,500 pesos a year. The majority of the taxes on the trade, called *almojarifazgo*, were collected in Mexico. In the first decades of the galleon line, vessels paid 12 pesos for each ton of merchandise that landed at Acapulco. In 1586, the amount rose to 45 pesos. Five years later, a royal decree established a duty of 10 percent over the value of the merchandise. Viceroy Marquis de la Laguna (1680–1686) substituted a flat tax of 74,000 pesos instead of the previous value-based tax; a general law in 1720 reorganized the trade and increased this sum to 100,000 pesos. The regulations of 1734 reverted the earlier increases to an *ad valorem* tax at a rate of approximately 16 percent. In 1776, the rate on legal merchandise was reduced to 9 percent. Surprisingly, merchandise over the legal limit was taxed at 16 percent, indicating how common it was to ignore the *permiso*. There were other fees levied in Acapulco, like the *averia* (a tax for the defense of the galleons) and a small duty called the admiralty tax, or *almirantazgo*. The *alcabala* (a sales tax of 6 percent of the goods' value) was paid on merchandise from Acapulco when it arrived in Mexico City. Earnings from the almojarifazgo returned to the Manila treasury to support Spain's administration of the islands. All of these figures illustrate Vera Valdés Lakowsky's assertion that the taxes charged on the galleon trade were always substantial, another indication that the Philippines was a stream of revenue and not a losing proposition for the Crown.[22]

Two galleons typically crossed the Pacific each year during the first half century of the line, but a single vessel became customary after those initial years, with few exceptions. The greater cost of building and maintaining two ships was overly high, and the prevailing practice of sending only one galleon is reflected in the regulations of 1726 and 1734, which only mention a single vessel.

Upon leaving the Philippines, the galleons faced a precarious predicament should they encounter an enemy, since their guns were usually stored in the hold. To provide protection in times of war, armed vessels escorted the galleons along the coast of New Spain. In the Philippines, ships frequently met the incoming galleon to accompany it through the San Bernardino Strait, up to the port of Cavite. In the second half of the seventeenth century, the Jesuit Francisco Colín implemented a system of bonfires to signal the presence of enemy ships to the approaching galleons; on the coast of Mexico, beacons from the mainland and from Cedros Island performed the same function.

Upon arriving at Acapulco, the galleon was repaired and readied to receive passengers and cargo. The most important article carried by the returning galleon was the silver from the sales at the fair, which was held under the surveillance of the master of silver, whose duty was to guard the chests containing the pesos and present the documents showing the outstanding amount owed to each shipper in Manila. In addition to silver, the merchandise typically consisted of cacao from Guayaquil (today the main port of Ecuador); cochineal, a dye pigment from Oaxaca; oil from Spain; wines; and other goods in smaller quantities. There were always more passengers on the galleon's voyage to Acapulco than there were on its eastward crossing: royal officials, the new governor, his family and retinue, friars and merchants from Mexico and Peru, convicts from New Spain, and banished persons. Contingents of soldiers also sailed on the galleon. Veteran infantry accompanied Governors Gómez Pérez Dasmariñas in 1590 and Pedro Bravo de Acuña in 1602, during the war with the Dutch. However, the majority of soldiers were not volunteers, and authorities had difficulty gathering the forces required for the Philippines. Many recruits were afraid of the climate and would desert before reaching Acapulco; others took drastic measures, like the desperate soldiers who organized a mutiny to gain control of the *Concepción* in 1667. Ten years later, in 1677, all criminals willing to enlist were offered a pardon and a salary of 125 pesos a year. Despite these enticements, only a small number of convicts volunteered. The colonial historian Casimiro Díaz made the significant observation that in 1678, the Governor Juan de Vargas sailed on the *San Antonio* and "brought one of the best and most copious reënforcements of soldiers that had been received here; for they numbered more than three hundred Europeans, and came from Nueva España, without the stigma of being convicts or men taken from the jails."[23]

In addition to the hazards of navigation, the galleon faced enemy ships. The English captured four galleons in battle. In 1587, Thomas Cavendish took the *Santa Ana*; Woodes Rogers captured the *Encarnación* in 1709; Commodore Anson took the *Covadonga* in 1743, followed by Admiral Cornish's seizure of the *Santísima Trinidad*. The *Santa Ana*'s capture vividly exemplifies the customary galleon trade. The ship, not expecting any attack, had no cannons on board. Because of their great disparity in size, the English ships *Content* and *Desire* could only carry a portion of the goods from the much larger *Santa Ana*; they made additional room by leaving the crew of more than 190 Spaniards and Filipinos on a beach, but this still did not create enough space for the *Santa Ana*'s entire cargo. Cavendish retained two Japanese sailors, three boys from Manila, a Portuguese traveler familiar with China, and a Spanish pilot from the *Santa Ana*'s crew. They loaded all of the gold (about 122,000 pesos' worth) and an assorted load of silks, spices, wines, and various stores. The English burned the galleon, along with all that they could not carry away. In a "Letter from the Manila Audiencia to Felipe II" of 1588, the judges observed, "this was one of the greatest misfortunes that could happen to this land; because it is estimated from the investments made, and the treasure and gold carried, that the cargo of the said vessel would have been worth in Mexico two millions [of pesos]."[24]

A Spanish diplomat forwarded a report from England to Philip II, dated 1569, about the events surrounding Cavendish's arrival in England. The victorious ship, *Desire*, sailed before the Court at Greenwich. "Every sailor had a gold chain round his neck, and the sails of the ship were of blue damask, the standard of cloth of gold and blue silk." The effect of the sudden arrival of such an amount of bullion on London's money market was considerable: "Cavendish must have brought great riches, for they are coining new broadangels, and gold is cheaper here than ever it was. Spanish pistolets, which four months ago were worth 12 reals 11 maravedis, will not now pass for 11 reals 24 maravedis, in consequence of the great abundance of them here."[25]

Textiles and the Galleons

The lower price of Chinese textiles, when compared to those carried by the fleets, was the source of high returns in the American market. The Spanish in the Philippines required the natives to cover their bodies as they had done in the New World, which meant that indigenous peoples dressed in affordable garments of silk and cotton. Authorities wrote to the king complaining that "from these islands before the Chinese took away for clothing 30,000 pesos, now given the natives' disorder and excess they take 200,000 pesos from his Majesty's kingdoms."[26] If such were the consequences on the islands, the same policies in America created a much higher demand, reflected in the transformation of New Spain silk manufacturing. After 1579, large quantities of silk reached Acapulco; Mexican silk culture consequently began to decline. Meanwhile, the arrival of large supplies of Chinese yarn benefited local silk manufacturers in Mexico City, Puebla, and Oaxaca, which altogether employed more than fourteen thousand people.[27] A substantial portion of Mexico's finished silk products headed for Peru. A 1594 letter from a Spanish official in Lima to Philip II explains the rationale: "A man can clothe his wife in Chinese silks for two hundred reals, whereas he could not provide her clothing of Spanish silks with two hundred pesos."[28] A royal officer compared the prices of silk goods in Manila and Lima, capital of the Viceroyalty of Peru, and calculated the profit to be approximately 200 percent in 1620 to 1621. For instance, the price of a picul of raw silk—about 60.47 kilograms, or 133 pounds—was 200 pesos in Manila; in Lima, the same quantity fetched 1,950 pesos, while a picul of Canton satin was worth 5 pesos on the islands and 50 pesos in Lima.[29] When in 1718 the Crown forbade galleons from carrying silks, Baltasar de Zúñiga, viceroy of New Spain and future president of the Council of Indies, simply refused to implement the decree, alleging that Chinese textiles were cheaper than fabrics coming from Spain and adding that the majority of the people in Mexico preferred products from the Manila Galleon, the *Nao de China*.[30]

The Crown reiterated the decree of 1604 forbidding trade between Acapulco and Lima in 1609, 1620, 1634, 1636, and 1706, indicating the degree of observance, or lack thereof, regarding such regulations. The decree of 1634 was nonetheless partially successful in blocking Mexican silk products, but this measure encouraged the flow of finished Chinese silk to Peru, thereby leading to the destruction of New Spain's powerful silk manufacturers.[31] Smuggling and fraud between Mexico and Peru "became far more lucrative and took place on a scale that can be described as gigantic."[32] On Lima's Street of Merchants, forty shops sold luxuries from Europe and Asia; some of the owners had over 1 million pesos in capital. A viceroy in 1602 described Lima and its inhabitants to the king: "All wear silk, and of the most fine and costly quality. The gala dresses and clothes of the women are so many and so excessive that in no other kingdom of the world are found such." Woodes Rogers of England wrote in 1712, "The ladies, who are extravagant in their apparel, impoverish the country by purchasing the richest silks." These trends continued well into the eighteenth century, when in 1735 two Spanish navy officers, Jorge Juan y Santacilla and Antonio de Ulloa, saw Chinese porcelain for sale in the shops of Lima and observed Chinese silks sent from Chile to Panama.[33]

Contraband in the Pacific Ocean trade was well established. In 1602 the City Council of Mexico City (*cabildo*) wrote to the king that the galleons carried 5 million pesos annually.[34] Francisco de Vitoria Baraona, a merchant of Puebla, claimed in 1634 that the value of the smuggled merchandise was between 3 and 4 million pesos and blamed the galleon for the decline of Atlantic commerce. One later historian agrees with the estimate, writing that between 1635 and 1638 the "short-lived Atlantic advance was no more than a reaction, a change in the pattern of investment due to the closing down of the Mexico-Peru trade during these years."[35]

Exact figures on the silver sent to Manila are not available. Numbers from New Spain and Peru are estimates because official reports could not take into account fraud and smuggling, which greatly increased in periods of economic crisis. Schurz estimates "that the average for the most prosperous periods was about 2,000,000 pesos . . . even more were quite possible, though not common." He indicates that during the war with the Dutch, the value of the silver cargo could have fallen under 1 million pesos.[36] Later historians give higher numbers. According to Pierre Chaunu, between 1570 and 1780, two-thirds of Mexican silver was exported from Acapulco; Louisa S. Hoberman estimates that during the seventeenth century, the Philippines received between 29 and 35 percent of New Spain's production.[37] Chuan Han-Sheng calculates that silver exports via Acapulco maintained a consistent level of 2 million pesos annually—the equivalent of 55 metric tons of silver—during the seventeenth century. Hoberman gives somewhat higher estimates, at least until 1634. She calculates that the totals were closer to 4 million pesos in 1630, 6 million in 1637, and another 4 million in 1638. Mariano A. Bonialian adds that from the end of the seventeenth century through the first four decades of the eighteenth century, the average was 2 million pesos, with a peak value of 4 million.[38] Such figures are plausible, given that for the last twenty-five years of the seventeenth century until the first decades of the eighteenth century, large quantities of Peruvian-coined silver were in use alongside Mexican pesos without being included in Acapulco's official accounts.[39] Bonialian's figures are consistent with those of Jerónimo de Uztáriz—a knowledgeable Spanish administrator—who estimated in 1724 an annual shipment from Acapulco of 3 million pieces of eight.[40]

Galleon Line Regulations

Over the course of two and a half centuries, the Spanish Crown issued decree after decree establishing detailed legislation covering all aspects of the line in Manila and Acapulco. Enforcing such laws was a different matter. In

Manila the whole citizenry from top to bottom, including the church, was united on ignoring regulations. Governors in the Philippines and viceroys in New Spain actively participated in the galleon trade. It was customary to retire as a viceroy or from the governorship with considerable earnings. The Dominican Thomas Gage mentioned that Rodrigo Pacheco y Osorio, Marquis of Cerralvo and viceroy of New Spain from 1624 to 1635, used to receive 1 million pesos a year as a monopolist of salt, from his involvement in trade with Spain and Manila, and from numerous gifts. "He governed ten years, and in this time he sent to the King of Spain a popinjay worth half a million, and in one year more he sent the worth of a million to the Count of Olivares, and other courtiers to obtain a prorogation for five years more."[41] Another viceroy, the Marquis de la Laguna (1680–1686), invested 50,000 pesos a year in the galleon. Galleon officers were usually agents of the Mexican viceroy. When Gemelli Careri landed in Acapulco in 1696, he wrote in his diary that the treasurer of the new viceroy of Peru was at the port, borrowing 100,000 pesos from Peruvian merchants to pay a debt of 300,000 pesos he had contracted buying the vice regal position and transporting his family to America.[42] Obviously, he was not in a hurry to antagonize his creditors by enforcing trade regulations.

The Manila galleon regulations illustrated the equilibrium that the Crown tried to maintain among competing interests and business groups. The legal framework that administered galleon commerce was codified in the "Laws of the Indies," a body of legislation issued by the Spanish Crown for its American and Asian possessions. Governors in the eighteenth century introduced some alterations and reforms by the 1734 decrees that settled the dispute between Manila and Cadiz, followed in 1769 by the *Supplementary Regulations*, which organized trade until 1815. Peninsular merchants complained that textiles shipped from Spain could not compete with Chinese fabrics. They and the Crown bemoaned that the silver leaving by the Pacific route was out of reach of royal officials and merchant houses in Seville.

Initially, the galleon trade was open to the viceroyalties of New Spain and Peru by a 1579 decree. Soon after, in 1581 and 1582, Governor Gonzalo Ronquillo greatly profited by sending ships to Peru. Almost immediately, in 1582 and reiterated in 1591, authorities forbade direct traffic between Manila and Peru. Governor Luis Pérez Dasmariñas's 1596 attempt to restore commerce with Peru and Governor Diego Fajardo's 1620 scheme to send a ship to Panama were not welcomed and did not change royal policy. In fact, Acapulco was the only legal port of call for trade across the Pacific until the last decades of the eighteenth century. Only after 1779 was a direct link established between Manila and Peru. Trade among ports in the Pacific was also interdicted; the first decree, issued in 1592, was reiterated a number of times in the sixteenth and seventeenth centuries, which indicates its limited success. Peruvian merchants engaged in trade with Acapulco to avoid taxes, to take advantage of cheap prices compared to the Portobelo fairs, to profit from the availability of Chinese textiles that were legally forbidden, and to exercise a degree of control over the flow of goods to the viceroyalty. Peruvian ships visited Acapulco and ports in the vicinity like El Marqués, Huatulco, or Zihuatanejo.[43]

To control the amount of merchandise, a limit called the *permiso* was established. In 1593, the permiso value of the cargo at Manila was 250,000 pesos; the Crown reiterated the same legal limits in 1604 and 1619. This figure increased to 300,000 pesos in 1702, to 500,000 pesos in 1734, and to 750,000 pesos in 1776. Legally, Mexico could always send an amount of silver that doubled the value of legal merchandise, indicating that authorities considered a profit of 100 percent to be customary.

The Crown considered the galleon to be for the support of the colonizers, and every Spanish citizen of Manila shared in the galleons' revenues through shares, or *boletas*. The idea was that each Spaniard received an allotted space on the galleon to ship merchandise to Acapulco. The galleon's hold was divided into equal parts of uniform size called a bale, or *fardo*. Each bale corresponded to four *piezas*, and each pieza was represented by a *boleta*. According to regulations, the boleta's value was 125 pesos. However, not all citizens had the capital required to engage in trade, and as a result a market for boletas came into being, with boletas bought and sold at a price higher than their legal value. The majority of Manila citizens were dependent on this boleta market. In 1620, the king, with the customary degree of success, issued a law against speculation in boletas, reiterated by decrees in 1638, 1734, and 1776. In addition to citizens and government officials, the cathedral chapter, regular orders, and obras pias received boletas. Individual ecclesiastics participated in the boleta market through laypeople, despite legal prohibitions. Schurz describes the boleta system as "a dignified form of dole, with a high market value in itself, the sale of which would provide the funds for the support of the original recipient until the drawing of the next year."[44] Such procedures support Oskar H. K. Spate's characterization of the galleon's trade as a joint-stock company whose social seat was located in Luzon.[45]

Galleon tonnage regularly exceeded the legal capacity, and limits on quantities of silver and other merchandise were consistently evaded through subterfuge by authorities, merchants, and anybody else involved in the galleon's operations. A glaring example was the position of Acapulco's *alcalde*, or mayor, which in the first half of the eighteenth century was controlled by the Gallo y Pardiñas and the Linage families. Mexican merchants usually gave them large bribes when the galleon arrived, and they received a return of approximately 5 to 10 percent on the value of all silver leaving the port. In addition, they exacted one silver real from each person in charge of the mules that transported bullion to Acapulco and sold supplies to soldiers from their own shops.[46] Institutional incentives, as well, contributed to evasion of laws. Local and viceregal governments were eager to increase customs revenue, which required larger quantities of goods than was legally allowed; additional encouragement was provided by the 10 percent divided among the viceroy and officials at Acapulco on any merchandise above the permiso.[47] The underlying reality was that the Spanish Crown could exercise little power over American commerce because the consulados of Seville, Mexico, and Lima had managed trade in exchange for periodic contributions to finance wars since 1600. Merchants from New Spain and Lima were able to control the export and import of goods, as well as the bullion leaving the continent. The Lima consulate received permission to use the western ports of El Realejo and Sonsonate in today's Central America, which anticipated their gradual abandonment of the Portobelo fairs on the Atlantic side and implied a powerful impulse to import Asian textiles via Acapulco.

In the words of Guillermina del Valle Pavón, "The regulations were flagrantly and systematically violated due to the collusion between merchants and vice-regal authorities."[48] Corruption and disregard for regulations were not exclusive to the Spanish; other Europeans abroad behaved in the same fashion. Afonso de Albuquerque of Portugal wrote to King Manuel in 1510, "The people in India have rather elastic consciences, and they think they are going on a pilgrimage to Jerusalem when they steal."[49] English and Dutch employees followed the Portuguese example. In the words of Holden Furber, "Operations of East India Companies overseas were shot through and through with practices not in accord with the aims of those who chartered them as national monopolies."[50] However, when the central government decided to enforce the law, they had means at their disposal. The events of Pedro de Quiroga's years in Acapulco provide a good illustration of the galleons' procedures and their reverberations in New Spain and the Philippines.

A Royal Inspector's Visit

In the middle decades of the seventeenth century, New Spain suffered a concatenation of disasters. In 1629, a terrible flood inundated Mexico City, with the water line reaching a height of 6.56 feet and submerging the shops of the Zócalo.[51] A disease named *cocoliztli* spread death among the people between

1629 and 1631, contributing to the viceroyalty's demographic decline. In the Central Valley of Mexico, the population fell from 325,000 in 1570 to 60,000 in the 1640s.[52] Silver production began to slow down in the middle of the decade in parallel to declines in the amount of mercury Almadén was yielding and Huancavelica was sending to New Spain. Mining output grew until the 1630s and then underwent a period of contraction. Along with the greatly reduced supply of indigenous labor, the miners were facing increasing costs for mercury and other supplies, as well as expensive drainage operations. The general economy followed the vicissitudes of the silver industry. When mining suffered, agricultural production (which depended on supplying Zacatecas and San Luis Potosí) contracted, as well. A similar negative trend affected the ranches of Nueva Vizcaya and the textile manufacturers of Puebla, Mexico, and Tlaxcala.[53] In the meantime, the official fleet system from Seville to America was in deep crisis. American entrepreneur capital was invested in local ventures while remittances of bullion to Spain followed a downward trend due to growing military expenditures and diminished silver production.

The arrival of the new viceroy, the Marquis of Cadereita (1635–1640), coincided with disasters for the Spanish Empire in general and for the American colonies in particular. The Dutch had attacked Honduras and taken Curaçao in 1633. The cocoliztli was still raging, and mining was in decline. The viceroy observed in 1638: "Just to think what is being lost in these vice-royalties pains me, and all the more so when I consider that the Almighty blessed this land with so many silver mines. All could be saved if we had more mercury and more labour." War with France began in 1635, and the viceroy proceeded to confiscate French merchants' capital. In 1637, the outgoing fleet to Spain "was carrying 1,230,000 pesos of silver for the crown," according to Cadereita, which "was more than 500,000 pesos above the average remittance of previous years." These actions produced general discontent, and the viceroy, writing to Madrid in 1639, indicated "that there might occur 'a popular commotion.'"[54] His letter was a serious warning in light of a violent insurrection in 1624 that had deposed the Marquis de Gelves from his position. This was the first time in the history of the Americas that a viceroy had been removed from office due to a local rebellion. "The dangerous riot of 1624 was provoked to some extent by Gelves's seizure of Philippine contraband and rigorous tax collection."[55] In the middle of such a critical situation, Philip IV sent Pedro de Quiroga y Moya, the royal inspector or *visitador*, to the port of Acapulco in 1635 to inquire about the Manila-Acapulco galleon business. Well aware of merchants' behavior and suffering from acute financial distress, the Spanish Crown decided to act. The visitador discovered that the registered value of the arriving galleons' merchandise was only 800,000 pesos, when its true worth was in the neighborhood of 4 million pesos.[56] Quiroga responded by revaluing merchandise and accordingly collecting legal duties. In Schurz's words, "he laid an embargo on the line," required a fine of 600,000 pesos to raise it, "and then interfered with the return of what proceeds remained from the sale of the cargo."[57] The situation became worse in 1636, when the king reiterated the 1634 decree prohibiting all commerce between Mexico and Peru. Merchants in the Philippines reacted forcefully to such events by refusing to dispatch another galleon until the previous state of affairs was restored. During 1636 and 1637, two years of interrupted trade, only one small patache crossed the Pacific with 150,000 pesos of cargo, property of Conde-Duque de Olivares, Philip IV's powerful first minister.[58] The following year Sebastián Hurtado de Corcuera, the governor of the Philippines, wrote to the king, informing him that, as a protest against Quiroga's procedures, the galleon *Nuestra Señora de la Concepción* would not carry a freight list. It became an empty gesture when the galleon was lost in a wreck. This calamity was followed by another disaster in the spring of 1639, when the incoming galleon from Acapulco foundered off the east coast of Luzon. This was not the end of sorrows; a galleon returning to Mexico in the summer of the same year sank near Japan.

The case of *Nuestra Señora de la Concepción* is a good example of how the galleon trade was managed. The ship displaced two thousand tons, and its cargo was valued at 4 million pesos. Among its treasures were the ill-gotten gains of Governor Sebastián Hurtado de Corcuera, including "a solid gold plate and ewer set, thought to be a gift from the King of Spain to the Emperor of Japan." Officials in Manila accused the governor of misappropriating the objects and sending them back to Spain as personal property.[59] In charge of the galleon was the governor's nephew, a young man in his twenties, "of little age or experience in military or naval matters. For this reason . . . the officers of the *Concepción* lost respect and obedience for him, each one seeking to give orders and be obeyed, splitting into factions and attacking each other, in which mutiny men were killed and wounded." The wind broke the masts, rendering the ship uncontrollable.[60] On September 20, 1638, the galleon perished on the reefs of Saipan, in the Northern Mariana Islands.

Imperial authorities preferred small revenues to a total absence of taxes and, given the social tensions in Mexico, they decided to change policies. Juan de Palafox y Mendoza, a new general visitador to the viceroyalty, was more accommodating, and things returned to their fraudulent routine. Reverberations from Quiroga's activities and the wreck of the galleons would last far longer in Manila. The immediate deadly consequence was a Chinese uprising from November 1639 to March 1640.

Chinese Merchants: The Sangleys

Chinese merchant communities in Malacca, Penang, Singapore, and Manila connected the Ming and Qing empires with global networks of trade. Chinese profits from maritime trade were quite high. However, according to Gang Deng, returns declined over time during the Ming dynasty (1368–1644). "The average profit from the Sino-South Asian trade was only 150 percent." During this same period, profits from high-quality silk exports fell from 200 to 140 percent. "In spite of this tendency, the high yield from maritime trade was an economic fact."[61]

The Chinese had several advantages that allowed them to profit more from trade than Europeans. First, Chinese merchants operated on the principle of decentralized small households-cum-firms that responded efficiently to market trends. Second, historical and cultural links between China and other Asian countries provided merchants with institutional and personal connections to those areas.[62] Spanish admiral Gerónimo Bañuelos y Carrillo recalled the visitador activities and in exaggerated terms described the silver taken by the sangleys: "The king of China could build a palace with the silver bars from Peru which have been carried to his country because of that traffic, without their having been registered, and without the king of Spain having been paid his duties, as has been well shown by Pedro de Quiroga y Moya."[63]

Chinese merchants with small capital borrowed money at high interest rates, leaving their wives and children with the lender as security. Usually, a junk was hired by a wealthy merchant, who rented space in the hold for others at a rate of 20 percent of the gross sales. Merchandise was stored below deck in watertight compartments, in which merchants slept atop their cargo during the ten-day voyage to Manila, 650 miles from their ports of origin. The junk trade was dependent on a number of variables: information received about silver on the Manila market, pirate activities, and disturbances in the empire or in the coastal provinces.

Timothy Brook remarks, "Adapting to Spanish tastes in design allowed Chinese silks to dominate the world silk markets by the turn of the seventeenth century. Similarly, the porcelain makers of Ching-te-chen, especially as imperial orders declined after 1620, turned to producing porcelains in Japanese and European styles."[64] Export activity had a profound influence on Chinese coastal areas. In 1639, a native of Fujian "outlined his reasons for supporting maritime trade: 1) silk and silk textiles from China often sold for double the domestic price in the Philippines and Southeast Asia; 2) porcelain and other Chinese products were also highly priced overseas; and 3) large numbers of unemployed artisans from China had found work in the Philippines."[65]

When junks arrived in Manila, Chinese agents were waiting for them. These intermediaries knew how much silver the galleon had brought and the prices that merchants could quote to the Spaniards and had connections with colonial inspectors to distribute the required bribes. These brokers charged between 20 and 30 percent of the sales price. After these previous deliberations, customs officers inspected the incoming junks and collected taxes.

As was the case with other Southeast Asian destinations, trade to the Philippines required large junks of about 350 tons, with a crew and passengers that numbered between two and four hundred men.[66] Chinese captains transported immigrants, dropping them in safe places before reaching Manila. It seems that some of the larger junks could carry up to five hundred people.[67] A large number of these Chinese immigrants remained in the Philippines. The Chinese—*sangleys* in colonial documents from the Amoy dialect "sang li," which means trade—were officially relegated to the Parian neighborhood under the range of Spanish artillery. The number of junks varied notably. At the end of the sixteenth century, thirty or forty were arriving yearly. In 1616 only seven arrived, but fifty came in 1631, and thirty made the voyage in 1636.[68]

By 1573, two years after Manila's founding, Governor Guido de Lavezares wrote to Philip II, "The Chinese have come here on trading expeditions, since our arrival, for we have always tried to treat them well. . . . They have come in greater numbers each year and with more ships; and they come earlier than they used to, so that their trade is assured to us." As early as 1589, these emigrants had acquired landed property in the vicinity of Manila, and Spanish landowners would give them money to work their land; the Chinese would repay the advances in a very short time at a profit to all parties. Chinese vegetable growers became an integral part of the capital for centuries. From early on, the Spaniards realized that the Chinese were indispensable to the life of the colony. In 1583, Bishop Salazar wrote to Philip II about the Parian in enthusiastic terms: "In it is carried on the whole commerce of China, involving every sort of merchandise"; he continued in this vein by enumerating the number of craftsmen, marveling at the cheapness of their work in construction, and praising the many services provided by such an industrious people.[69] In 1638 Bañuelos y Carrillo described the sangleys' neighborhood, inhabited at the time by twenty thousand merchants:

Every kind of merchandise has its own separate quarter, and those goods are so rare and curious that they merit the admiration of the most civilized nations. . . . There is no Spanish house where nine or ten of these merchants cannot be seen every morning, which take their merchandise there; for all the traffic passes through their hands, even all that is used for the sustenance of the Spaniards. . . . These people have a subtle and universal intelligence. They imitate whatever one presents to them, and they make the article as well as do those who invented it.[70]

Spanish bureaucrats made a highly lucrative business of selling residence certificates to the Chinese who remained in Manila after the annual junk fleet had departed. A Chinese non-Christian paid eight pesos for such a license in addition to five reals as tribute and twelve reals in house tax. In one decree regarding this practice, the king admonished, "The Chinese have been allowed to increase in numbers, because of greed for the eight pesos which each one of them pays for his license." Some of the officials exacted the eight pesos several times during the year, on the pretext that a renewal of the license was required.[71] In the seventeenth century, many Chinese were living outside the Parian, some having settled in the surrounding provinces or on other islands, where they engaged in trade with smaller junks and sampans. Chinese Manilans who were Christian or had married Christians resided in the Binondo and Tondo quarters of the city. These people did not pay the customary tribute for ten years after their conversion, and afterward they paid a lower rate than natives.

The Chinese Rebellion of 1603

"To the poor Chinese from Fujian, Manila was the Gold Mountain," comments Brook. A Chinese official named Zhou Qiyuan wrote regarding them: "These petty traders view the huge waves under the open sky as though they were standing at their ease on a high mound . . . and look upon foreign chieftains and warrior princes as though they were dealing with minor officials." Such notions and attitudes had deadly consequences.

In 1603, Gao Cai, a eunuch responsible for collecting custom duties in Fujian and a personal appointee of the emperor, charged "with raising as much silver as he could for the emperor's private purse," decided to send a delegation to Manila to find out the truth about their storied gold.[72] Such a course of action had its origins in Beijing, when a captain of the imperial guard sent a memorandum to emperor Wan Li with the information that a cabinetmaker called Tiongeng told him that there was a mountain of gold and silver without a known occupant or owner in the proximity of Manila. He promised to bring back to the imperial treasury 100,000 taels of gold and 300,000 of silver from this marvelous place. How Chinese authorities could have given credit to such hearsay is hard to fathom. Nonetheless, mandarins were dispatched with the cabinetmaker to Manila.[73] Bartolomé Leonardo de Argensola, charged by the president of the Council of Indies to write about the Philippines and the Moluccas, referred to these events and the following uprising: "In the foregoing March, a Chinese ship came into the Bay of Manila, in which, as the guards gave the account, there came three great mandarins, with suitable pomp and retinue." The governor received them, and they explained "that their king had sent them . . . that they might with their own eyes see a golden island called Cavite, near Manila." The Spanish governor allowed the dignitaries to visit the port of Cavite to see by "their own eyes" the absence of gold. The disabused mandarins returned to China empty-handed, except for 30,000 pieces of eight collected from the sangleys. Spanish authorities could not believe the mandarins' story; suspicions were aroused, and the archbishop F. Miguel de Benavides proclaimed in sermons that an armada from China was coming to take the city with support from the local sangleys.

The governor sprang to action. He ordered the razing of the Parian's buildings close to the city walls, expanded the moat, and had a conference with the Japanese community, asking them to join the Spaniards against their traditional enemies. For their part, the Chinese were fearful of the general massacre the preparations portended. Artisans and small merchants left the Parian and joined the truck gardeners, fishermen, salt workers, stone-masons, charcoal makers, carpenters, and other Chinese workers who lived on the north bank of the Pasig River. "The Japanese were swaggering about boasting that they had been asked to take part in slaughtering every Sangley in the land. Tagalog hoodlums joined them . . . calling them traitorous dogs."[74] In this state of ominous anxiety, rich sangleys requested permission from the governor to move inside the walls with their possessions. Fearing a conspiracy of these sangleys with black slaves, their request was denied; notwithstanding, some of their property was moved into the walled city.

On a Sunday morning on October 5, the feared rebellion broke out. Spanish and Japanese soldiers confronted the Chinese with additional help from members of religious orders and irregular groups of natives, including the Aetas of the hills. The Japanese and natives supplemented the work of the Spanish artillery against the rebels, "for they killed many of them, and particularly such as had been wounded by the small shot and brass guns on the wall." The Chinese attackers were desperate, their "brutal courage" the result of having taken "their anfion, that is, a composition of opium," wrote Leonardo de Argensola. The leader of the Cambodia expedition (1599), Luis Pérez Dasmariñas, rashly confronted an overwhelming force of sangleys, proclaiming that "twenty five soldiers were enough to deal with all China . . . Don Luis was killed there by the same people that had slain his father."[75]

The Spanish response to the revolt was merciless. In the Pampanga, Fernando de Avalos, the highest authority of the province, captured four hundred sangleys "who being carried to a creek in the river bound two and two, and delivered to the Japanese they slew them all." Carnage continued over the following days. Martín de Herrera, captain of the Governor's Guard, attacked a body of one thousand Chinese: "only one was taken alive, though the governor would have had many saved to serve in the galleys; but the Japanese and natives are so bloody, that neither his orders, nor Major Azcueta or other commanders could curb them." According to the *Mingshi* (*History of the Ming*), twenty-five thousand sangleys were massacred; the total is calculated at twenty-three thousand in some Spanish sources and fifteen thousand according to Archbishop Benavides. Governor Corcuera, in a letter to Chinese authorities, said, "30,000 were not killed, nor even half that number."[76] Argensola concludes: "Some affirm the number of the Sangleys slain was greater, but that the magistrates concealed it, for fear notice should be taken of their fault in admitting so many to live in the country contrary to the King's prohibitions."[77] The magistrate Téllez de Almazán wrote that the suspicions of the archbishop regarding an incoming Ming armada were unfounded, but the mandarins' arrival providentially allowed the authorities to get rid of thousands of Chinese.[78] The governor returned 70,000 pesos' worth of merchandise deposited in the walled city to the few surviving merchants, and the troops received the remaining 360,000 pesos in unclaimed goods.[79]

The Spaniards were fearful of news about the slaughter reaching China. The governor sent two ambassadors to Macao and requested that the Portuguese report any military preparations against the Philippines. The envoys also carried letters to Chinese authorities pleading for the junks to return, the situation in Manila having become critical due to the absence of craftsmen, truck gardeners, and food supplies. Following the arrival of thirteen junks to Manila, the governor wrote to King Philip III, "This country has been greatly consoled at seeing that the Chinese have chosen to continue their commerce, of which we were much in doubt."[80] Already in 1605, two years after the events, six thousand Chinese were living in the Parian. The *Mingshi* recalls, "After that time the Chinese gradually returned to Manila; and the savages, seeing profit in the commerce with China, did not oppose them. For a long time they continued to gather again in the city."[81] By 1621 there were approximately twenty-two thousand Chinese living in Manila.

The Rebellion of 1640

Clearly, Pedro de Quiroga's visit was detrimental to merchants' interests and to church finances in the Philippines and dealt a blow to the sangleys and to the economy of southern China. If all of these misfortunes were not enough, before crossing the Pacific, Governor Hurtado de Corcuera increased the damage done to the Chinese. Fray Juan de la Concepción wrote:

> In passing through Mexico Señor Corcuera found so much cloth from this [Chinese] commerce stored in the warehouses that, in consideration of the interests of the merchants, he thought it best not to send a ship [to Acapulco] that year; as a result, in this year of 1638 the Chinese found less silver [in the Philippines] than their business required. It also contributed [to their discontent] that, since the royal treasury was unable to meet the great expenses of so many armed fleets and wars, the contributions [levied] on the Chinese were greater and more exacting—not only in actual money, but in other necessary supplies.[82]

In 1639, heavy clouds were gathering over the colony. Muslim raids reached terrifying proportions, and the sangleys were restless due to the authorities' heavy exactions. In order to allow sangleys to remain in Manila after the junks' departure, officials collected 25 pesos per head; in 1603 this illegal charge had been just 6 pesos. On August 4, two large junks out of the five returning to China were pushed ashore by the wind, and six hundred Chinese drowned. "On account of the lack of succour in these two years, many were returning, leaving their houses and shops deserted." Three days later, news of the arrival to the Luzon coast of the *almiranta* of the previous year and the patache of two years prior were celebrated "with the utmost joy, and all the bells were rung." Wives wearing mourning garments for their husbands took them off, and "the Chinese, who learned the news on board their ships, disembarked, and returned to their shops and their trading."[83] Such rejoicing was interrupted by a message announcing that both ships were wrecked at Nueva Segovia and that 150 persons had died. The situado was rescued, but its value was not enough to ameliorate the situation. The procurator-general Monfalcón added a crucial detail about Chinese commercial practices: "besides selling the merchandise for very suitable prices, they gave credit for them until they came back again." This financial arrangement allowed merchants without ready funds to profit from the trade.[84] However, silver shipments to Manila during previous years were not enough to settle debts to the sangleys and Portuguese.[85] If trade was suffering, measures taken by Governor Corcuera ostensibly did nothing to improve the mood among the Chinese. He decided to send more than six thousand sangleys to grow rice in Calamba, south of Manila. Exploiting this land would "produce there the rice sufficient to the *presidios*"—military outposts—"of these islands, by which his Majesty would be spared a great expense."[86] The sangleys were placed under the abusive authority of the alcalde mayor Luis Arias de Mora, a particularly greedy bureaucrat. Many of them fell sick, and more than three hundred died due to the unhealthy climate.

An anonymous report published in 1642 indicated that the sangleys of Manila wrote to the Chinese pirate Yquan Sanglus to encourage him to assault the galleons coming from Acapulco. Christmas Day of 1639 was the agreed-upon date for the sangley uprising, but the Chinese in Calamba precipitated events by killing Arias de Mora. The assassination signaled the beginning of a widespread insurrection all over Luzon.[87] The Spaniards counted on the collaboration of a company of Filipinos from Pampanga, along with Japanese and Moros—"who had come with the ambassador of Sanguyl." A Jesuit noticed that in Cavite the Chinese were "peaceable" and that "they very willingly dragged out some pieces of artillery" to defend the port. Other groups evinced a state of mind similar to those exhibited during the 1603 insurrection. Another Jesuit wrote, "The Japanese, blacks, and Indians are full of courage, whatever is the outcome; I believe that they will rejoice, if the opportunity arises, to satiate themselves for once with killing Chinese."[88] The narrative of the following events comes from the contemporary document "Relation of the Insurrection of the Chinese." Forces were highly unequal, if the writer is to be credited. While the Spanish army amounted to three hundred Spaniards and eight thousand native troops, the number of Chinese was thirty-five thousand in Manila and its environs, with ten thousand more waiting in the provinces. Losses on the Spanish side totaled about forty-five Spaniards and three hundred natives. Chinese deaths were counted in the thousands. "Thus is made very evident, by the unequal and disproportionate number [of deaths] on both sides, the Special protection of our Lord over our army."[89] The sangleys' armament, "javelins and Japanese catanas fastened to poles . . . sickles and pruning-hooks, also fastened to poles; iron tridents; and bamboos with sharp points hardened in fire"[90] and few firearms could not defeat a well-disciplined colonial army provided with harquebuses and artillery. The terrified Spaniards treated the Chinese without mercy, as shown by the events in Manila and Cavite:

> Fire was set to the Parián; it immediately began to burn. . . . Many persons who had concealed themselves were burned to death; others, who thought it a less evil to be the object of our men's harshness than to become the prey of the flames, rushing from the building, threw themselves upon the sharp swords. . . . [In Cavite] while the Ave Maria was ringing, the warden went to all the religious orders, requesting that priests should go to baptize the infidels and hear the confessions of the Christians, since all of them must die. . . . The number of those who died in the port of Cavite reached one thousand three hundred.[91]

The extermination order also applied to the city of Manila and the provinces. In the capital, after a general massacre—"through all the streets the Sangleys were seen lying dead"[92]—only two hundred merchants, who came out of their hiding places, were spared and taken into custody. A Jesuit priest who spoke fluent Chinese served as an intermediary between the rebels and the authorities.[93] The revolt ended with a treaty signed by the governor and the Chinese. On February 4, 1641, 7,793 sangleys surrendered to Corcuera and were taken to Manila into custody, where they were to be deported to China.

All groups participated in the slaughter of the Chinese: "ranchmen and mulattoes"; the Pampango infantry, one of whose commanding officers was the friar Juan de Sosa; the Zambal archers, under another friar, Antonio de las Misas; natives from the Cagayan province; islanders from Ternate in the Moluccas; and Tagalogs. Students from the University of Santo Tomás, commanded by the Dominicans, and the scholars of San José, under the Jesuits, followed the call to arms. "The religious hastened to take arms and defend the walls on the day of the attack."[94] A historian of the Philippines, Joaquín Martínez de Zúñiga, wrote in 1803, "Very few of our people were killed, but Manila was reduced to great distress by the loss of so many of its useful class of citizens, as unquestionably the Chinese were." Speculating about the reasons behind native support, he observed, "The Indians fortunately had remained perfectly tranquil, which was rather to be attributed to their fixed hatred of the Chinese than their attachment to the Spaniards."[95]

Historians give the figure of Chinese killed at about twenty thousand, and contemporary documents suggest it to have been twenty-two or twenty-four thousand. The exact number is unknown, and it is plausible that the number of victims was considerably lower but in sufficient number to justify Casimiro Díaz's observation that "for more than six months, it was impossible to drink the water in the rivers, they were so corrupted by the dead bodies; nor did the people eat fish in a circuit of many leguas, since all these were fattened on human flesh."[96]

Like his predecessor in 1603, the governor was mindful of the consequences and immediately sent a Chinese junk to the empire explaining that the war had finished and that the insurrectionists were the culprits but that Chinese merchants were welcome and could arrive safely as always. Five junks soon sailed from China with merchandise and took two thousand sangleys back with them.[97] Despite the Spaniards' fears, the sangleys were essential to the economic life of the colony and, after every massacre, European authorities followed the same three steps: "(1) apologies to the Empire from the Europeans, (2) renewal of trade relationships with China, and (3) speedy restoration of the Chinese population in those colonies."[98] In a few years the Parian shops had been rebuilt, and the Spaniards collected taxes and rents from the sangley merchants once more. Notwithstanding regulations forbidding the Chinese to live in the provinces, "the peddlers' barges were once again on the move, bringing up to the fall line of the rivers the myriad products of Chinese ingenuity, from crowbars to combs, from pistols to porcelain."[99]

The fall of the Ming dynasty in 1644 and the War of the Three Feudatories (1673–1681) opened up a period of turmoil in China with serious reverberations in the Philippines. In 1662, the Ming loyalist Koxinga, who had taken Taiwan from the Dutch, sent an Italian Dominican friar, Victorio Ricci, to request the tribute payment from Governor Sabiniano Manrique de Lara (1653–1663). Afraid of a coalition between an invading force and the sangleys, the governor disarmed the non-Christian Chinese and recalled the garrisons from Zamboanga and the Moluccas. Given these ominous preparations, many Chinese left the colony, but about two thousand rose in revolt. Spanish and Pampango troops defeated them, and afterward a number of non-Christian Chinese were expelled. Koxinga died in Taiwan, and threats from that quarter disappeared. After 1662, only two thousand sangleys were living in the Parian.[100]

The last seventeenth-century incident with the Chinese took place in 1686 when fugitives from Chinese law under the leadership of an ex-convict planned to overpower Spanish troops in Manila, plunder churches and stores, and sail away with their booty. They were defeated by local troops.

Estimates of the number of Chinese living in the Philippines during these centuries are not accurate; the figures are based on tax records, which are not always reliable. Nonetheless, historians and bureaucrats from colonial times were extremely impressed by these violent confrontations and recorded those events with great attention to detail. The underlying reason for such hostilities was the fear generated by Chinese numbers in a small Spanish population. Both groups were caught in a symbiotic dependence from which they could not break free. The natives and other subaltern groups resented the economic role played by the sangleys and joined the colonizers against them. Unfortunately, the Manila events were not isolated phenomena in Southeast Asia. About fifty years later, the Dutch "free burghers" of Batavia were in economic dire straits: the price of spices had fallen, and the market for Java coffee was in crisis. "On top of all of this unfounded rumours swept through the European community that the Chinese were about to attack them. In October 1740, the Europeans and Eurasians rose and massacred the Chinese."[101]

CHAPTER SEVEN

The Eighteenth Century and the Galleon Line

A New Ecological Regime

Widespread diseases, wars, and economic crises affect societies up to the present, but the eighteenth century was a turning point in the history of humanity in terms of continuous population growth and economic productivity made possible by new plants and a different regime of diseases, followed by the Industrial Revolution.

The Columbian and Magellan Exchanges encompassed the arrival of American plants in Africa, Asia, and Europe and the simultaneous exportation of vegetable and animal species from the Old World to America. In China, peanuts appeared on the lists of local products in Chang-shu County in the Yangtze delta by 1538, and sweet potatoes were cultivated in Fukien and Yunnan by the middle of the sixteenth century. Most plants from the New Continent arrived first in Fujian, probably via Chinese settlers in the Philippines and other southern archipelagos. Portuguese Macao and Burma contributed as well to the spread of these cultivars. Corn, sweet potatoes, and peanuts grew well in the poor, hilly, or sandy soil that characterized areas of previously marginal productivity.[1] There was a downside, though; cultivation of these previously lightly settled areas led to deforestation, soil erosion, and floods.

Tobacco, too, became an important plant, building on the centuries-long use of opium for medicinal purposes in China. The leaf arrived in the Philippines in the 1570s and in Fujian between 1573 and 1619. Soon its use expanded through the empire, and tobacco became a valuable cash crop.

The new plant reached Java in 1601. Local Chinese began buying and sell-ing opium and tobacco mixtures in Dutch Batavia around 1671. Jonathan D. Spence writes, "The smoking of *madak* or of tobacco dipped in opium solution can be seen as the connecting point between tobacco and opium proper."[2] In the last quarter of the eighteenth century, raw opium supplanted the use of madak.

American plants made possible the Qing dynasty's economic and social developments during the eighteenth century. "When rice culture was gradu-ally reaching its limit and beginning to suffer from the law of diminishing re-turns, the various dry land food crops introduced from America contributed most to the increase in national food production and made possible a con-tinual growth of population."[3] These new foods, which required much less labor than rice and other cereals, made possible massive increases in Chinese exports and freed up workers and land to produce silk, tea, sugar, and pottery for the world market.[4] John King Fairbank has enumerated three eighteenth-century processes that determined the course of Chinese and world history: the European presence in coastal China, the doubling of the territorial size of the Chinese Empire, and the doubling of the Han Chinese population.[5] Scholars argue about the timing, but significant Chinese population growth under the Qing dynasty is indisputable.

American plants were not the single source of portentous transformations. Since the fifteenth century, a crucial biological process homogenized the world's disease pools; distant populations suffered the same kind of infec-tions and acquired a similar range of antibodies, which inhibited the spread of epidemics.[6] Global transformations in the ecologies of crops and diseases enabled a fundamentally different demographic rhythm, the taking off of very rapid population growth.[7] China is a good example of these historical trends: there was a long period in the empire of prevailing social peace, free from warfare. Following a process that William H. McNeill named "the vital revolution," epidemics caused less demographic damage, since the survivors of some childhood diseases developed a lifelong immunity to the correspond-ing pathogens; consequently, lower adult mortality contributed to larger families and more offspring. The Chinese population had reached more than 400 million people by 1800.[8] "China's circumstances, in other words, gave full scope to the new possibilities inherent in the changed disease regime, crop distribution, and military technology resulting from the opening of the oceans to human movement."[9] This population surge involved interregional migration on a grand scale to Sichuan, the Yangtze highlands, the Han River region, and other lightly populated areas. The Qing dynasty conquered Taiwan, extended its hegemony over Tibet, and incorporated territories of the Asian heartland into the empire. In the last decades of the eighteenth century, Russia and China divided Central Eurasia, signaling the end of the steppe peoples' political power. Peter C. Perdue explains the interdependence between monetary issues, merchants, and Qing expansion: the dynasty encouraged merchant capital into new occupied territories by providing the necessary infrastructure and security, while the imperial administration used the merchants and their logistics to relieve food shortages and promote trade. Taxes, paid in silver, required that officials provide support to the markets in which farmers sold their goods and acquired bullion. "Although the bulk of its tax revenue came from the land, that revenue itself depended on an extensively monetized agrarian economy, which relied on extensive cooperation with the merchant class."[10]

The Mexican Silver Cycle

Demographic and market growth in China heightened demand for bullion; this demand-side pressure increased silver's value within China to 50 percent above its price in the rest of the world. Spanish American mines produced more silver in the eighteenth century than in the sixteenth and seventeenth centuries combined.[11] Peru's production in the eighteenth century more than tripled and surpassed even its seventeenth-century maximum, while Mexico's output was well over double Peru's for most of the 1700s.[12]

In the first half of the eighteenth century the gold-to-silver ratio in China remained at 1:10, while in Europe this ratio was 1:15.[13] Much of this bullion was again destined for China, with India as a transit route. Once again, arbitrage profits entered merchants' calculations. Isaac Newton, Master of the Mint in London, wrote in his *Minute* of 1717, "In China and Japan one pound weight of fine gold is worth but nine or ten pounds weight of fine silver, and in East India it may be worth twelve. And this low price of gold in proportion to silver carries away the silver from all Europe." John Conduitt, who succeeded Newton as Master of the Mint, added with further precision in 1730, "The importation of gold into Europe has been much increased, by the discovery of the new mines in Brasil, and, consequently, it is less valuable; and the real intrinsic value of silver is much enhanced, by the great demand of silver for the several East India Companies set up in Europe."[14] In the 1720s and 1730s, captains and East India Company (EIC) officers tried to take advantage of the difference between the gold-to-silver ratios in China and Europe. In India after 1741, the company minted quantities of a new gold coin, the "star" pagoda, using the metal brought to Madras by the growing trade with China and Manila. Francisco Martínez de la Costa, a Spaniard living in Manila in 1743, estimated that Filipinos bartered with foreigners 2 million pesos of gold.[15] The presence of country traders and the EIC at Canton by the end of the seventeenth century—China and other Southeast Asian countries were gold producers—implied that the gold in the East India trade resulted in greater profits for the English than for traders from continental Europe. Bullion arbitrage contributed to English supremacy in Asia.[16]

During the eighteenth century, silver flowed to Asia mainly in the form of Mexican pieces of eight known as *dos mundos* and *bustos* according to their symbols. The mints manufactured half a billion dos mundos between 1732 and 1772 and nearly 900 million bustos between 1772 and 1822.[17] The prevalence of Mexican coinage all over the world was evident. In southern China, Mexican pieces of eight circulated in larger amounts than in Mexico, and pesos were present throughout the Pacific Islands and from Siberia to Mumbai. Colonists in North America accepted only pieces of eight as payment, and American businessmen with these pesos purchased slaves on the west coast of Africa and brought tea from China to the United States.[18]

Since the Crown's mint normally collected one peso in eight in the form of seigniorage fees, in addition to the myriad taxes based upon the silver trade, distant Chinese demand for these coins enhanced Spanish finances appreciably. Asian-European trade flourished anew during the first half of the eighteenth century. Importation of hundreds of millions of pesos in silver eventually saturated the Chinese marketplace, as before, to the extent that from 1750 onward the gold-to-silver ratio in China was above 1:15, while in Europe the ratio declined to between 1:14.5 and 1:14.8.[19] The Qing Empire continued to import silver pesos during the second half of the eighteenth century, but the profit rate per unit of silver was modest compared with the heights reached during the upward trends of the Potosi/Japan or Mexico cycles. Ordinary profit margins continued while Mexican mines kept producing large quantities of silver until the end of the century. Fluctuations in the bullion market explain why Commodore Anson brought silver from the Acapulco galleon to London. In the year 1700, a similar haul would have been destined for China because the price of silver fetched a 50 percent premium vis-à-vis Europe.[20]

The Tea and Opium Cycle

The Qing government confined trade with Europeans to the port of Canton and placed it under the supervision of a group of prominent merchants organized into a cartel called the *Co-Hong*. This cartel fixed prices, collected duties, and bore responsibility for the behavior of their European correspondents. European traders' residences were restricted to the Wampoa dock and the waterfront known as Thirteen Factory Street.

Silver's purchasing power diminished as British commercial activities became increasingly influential in the global marketplace. The Battle of Plassey in 1757 led to British control of Bengal, which in turn initiated a fundamental change in Asia's trade patterns. "After the conquest of Bengal, the wealth which the British acquired and the control which they won over some of Bengal's commodities, such as opium, enabled them to begin to carve out routes of their own."[21] Since the 1750s, Britain had steadily solidified its hegemonic position in the east, whereas French and Dutch influence waned. The independence of the American colonies in 1781 turned British efforts toward Asia, where India became the center of its empire.

The EIC managed to gain control of a new, rapidly growing market involving the importation of Bengali opium into China in exchange, in part, for Chinese tea exports. "The point is not that silver discontinued its journey into China during the second half of the eighteenth century—it did not— but rather that opium and tea became the high-profit markets, with silver playing a complementary role in terms of profitability."[22] According to Louis Dermigny, silver constituted 90 percent of the value of British exports to Canton during the first half of the eighteenth century, whereas for the period from 1775 to 1795, 35 percent of British exports to Canton were in the form of merchandise and only 65 percent were in silver. He refers to a "cycle of tea" in describing British trade in Canton since 1760.[23] Behind the opium exports and the "cycle of tea" was Britain's demand for the Chinese plant. London tea imports reached 2.5 million pounds by 1760, 9 million pounds by 1769–1770, 14 million pounds in 1785–1786, and 23 million pounds by the end of the century.[24] Conversely, opium traffic grew more than twentyfold between 1729 and 1800, which contributed to diminishing the flow of bullion from London to China.[25] The British earned a clear profit of at least 100 percent on their sales of opium to the Dutch in Calcutta, and opium business constituted nearly 20 percent of the Indian government's annual revenue.[26]

The tea-and-opium connection itself was part of a complex web of trade and new ways of organizing the production of agricultural commodities at a global level during the century. For instance, English people consumed sugar with tea, which required the importation of prodigious quantities of slave-produced sugar from the Americas. Sugar came from expanding plantation economies dedicated to growing cash crops like sugar, coffee, and cotton.

The Molucca and Banda Islands that had been of such economic importance during the sixteenth and seventeenth centuries lost their relevance as valuable spices began to be grown elsewhere. There were sustained efforts to cultivate them in Brazil, East Africa, and some tropical islands. Pierre Poivre, a Frenchman, decided to naturalize nutmeg and clove in the Mauritius and Reunion Islands in the Indian Ocean, recently acquired by France. In 1770, he brought untreated nutmeg and clove seedlings from the Moluccas (the Dutch used to sterilize the nuts with lime before exporting them). In twenty years, both plants had spread to Madagascar and Zanzibar in Africa and to Martinique and Grenada in the Caribbean. The Dutch monopoly finally ended.[27]

The War of Jenkins' Ear and the Manila Galleon

In 1738, Captain Robert Jenkins told a distressing story before the House of Commons in London. It seems that in 1731 the Spaniards boarded his ship and confiscated its cargo, while Jenkins had been bound to the mast, whereupon the boarders had cut off his ear. He showed the House a jar with his ear preserved in brandy and stated that in this dire circumstance "he committed his soul to God and his cause to his country." Captain Jenkins lost his cargo and ear because of sustained Spanish activities against foreign vessels in American waters. To counter smuggling, the Spanish Crown had given licenses to ships called *guardacostas*, which allowed them to capture vessels engaged in illegal trade. "Between 1713 and 1731 more than 180 English trading ships had been illegally confiscated or robbed by guardacostas, according to the British government."[28] The prime minister, Sir Robert Walpole, was willing to allow these indignities in order to avoid war, explaining in a speech to Parliament the real nature of Spanish commerce: "At present there is scarce any nation in Europe who has not a larger property in her plate ships and galleons than Spain herself has. . . . Spain herself is no more than the canal through which all these treasures are conveyed all over the rest of Europe."[29] Walpole was right. Foreign vessels accounted for three-quarters of all the shipping engaged in the American trade, which supposedly should have been under the monopolistic control of the House of Trade in Andalusia. The majority of merchandise sold in the New World was foreign because merchant houses located on the peninsula simply transshipped manufactured products from abroad, and European manufactures and slaves "informally, illegally, and uncontainably" arrived in American territories from Dutch, English, and French Caribbean islands occupied since 1650.[30] As one historian summarizes, "The incapacity of the official Spanish trade system to minister to the needs of the empire was both flagrant and notorious. Without smuggling the Spanish colonies would have collapsed."[31] Despite these economic realities, war began between Britain and Spain. A fleet sailed to the Pacific commanded by Admiral Vernon with the intent to attack Spain's American ports—"It was a naval campaign with confused objectives."[32] A small squadron under Commodore George Anson received the order "to look out for the Acapulco ship, which sails from that place to Manila at a certain time of the year."[33] In May 1743, Anson's *Centurion* captured the Manila galleon *Covandonga*, dealing a serious blow to commerce. "By 1744, every trader in the China Sea was feeling the effects of the suspension of silver shipments from Mexico," which explains why in 1746 two ships from Batavia with crews of English merchants arrived on the coast of New Spain willing to exchange bullion for Asian goods. Their presence in Mexico coincided with the arrival in Manila of a galleon carrying silver, which eased the situation.[34]

In addition to wars and the galleon line's interruptions, the price of Asian commodities was increasing due to competition in the markets of origin between the Dutch and British companies. Between 1734 and 1770, the price of Chinese goods increased an average of 147 percent, and Indian merchandise increased 165 percent. Prices all over the world had hit an upward trend.[35] In the meantime, competing with the galleons' textiles were similar products brought to American markets by European merchants, including cotton goods from Cataluña, designed to imitate Indian fabrics and appropriately called *Indianas*. Demand in the Acapulco market declined significantly, and there was a substantial withdrawal of Mexican capital from the galleon trade. This tendency became acutely apparent after the capture of the *Covandonga* demonstrated that large sums could disappear in a single event. In the Viceroyalty of Peru, the capture of Portobelo by the British Admiral Edward Vernon accelerated the disappearance of the Spanish fleets—*galeones*—and fairs, replaced by British ships that arrived in Buenos Aires and Peru by the Cape Horn route.[36]

The War of the Austrian Succession (1740–1748) and the Seven Years' War between France and Great Britain (1756–1763) were fought primarily for control of North America, the West Indies, and Africa. Given the diplomatic landscape of the period, the Spanish Empire sided with Bourbon France. Another crucially important theater of war was the Moghul Empire. During the Seven Years' War, the British captured French Pondicherry in 1761. Prior to this conflict, Robert Clive had defeated Bengali resistance at the Battle of Plassey in 1757, and the Afghans won a victory over the Marathas near Delhi in 1761. These events had the combined effect of leaving the British in such a position that those Indian rulers could not successfully challenge their power.[37]

Until opium became available as an export substitute, silver was the unavoidable medium of exchange for China trade, and Manila was a nearby source of bullion. By 1700, individual Englishmen—from Governor Elihu Yale, who owned four country ships, to mates and boatswains—participated in the Manila trade.[38] EIC commercial operations depended on Manila's silver. Any disruption of the galleon sailing implied severe damage to trade, such as in 1712, when the EIC in Madras was unable to trade with China, Malaysia, and Indonesia; in 1715 and 1727, company administrators complained that they were in jeopardy for want of Manila's silver business. The arrival of the white metal from the Red Sea and the Philippines and demand in Bengal and China determined the price of silver in southern India.[39] British merchants, Armenians, and later the French gathered textiles in Asian markets and contributed considerably to the galleon's cargo. French vessels were trading between Peru and Manila around 1713 given France and Spain's political alliance, but the Crown soon discontinued these voyages.

In 1742, to avoid being isolated if hostilities between the British and French erupted during the War of the Austrian Succession, the governor opened up Manila to Danish ships such as the *Dansborg*, which received a warm reception. British captains saw in the concession to the Danes a new loophole to increasing participation in the Manila trade.[40] Roughly 45 percent of the silver circulating in Madras came via Manila. In 1740, London and the Philippines sent to the EIC in India almost the same amount: 54,223 pounds from Britain, 54,425 pounds from Manila.[41] However, a crucial factor was the arbitrage trade in silver. "If the premium difference outweighed the profit realizable from local reinvestment the silver may be reshipped to China even after arriving back in India." For instance, in 1786 Madras investors sent silver to Canton to profit from the higher price of silver there.[42] During the first half of the eighteenth century, in exchange for silver, Indian cotton pieces arrived in Manila with a value between 150,000 and 300,000 pesos.[43]

The Seven Years' War in the Philippines

During the 1750s, the Philippines were in crisis on many levels. Muslim raids were devastating, and in 1755 the Chinese again received an order of expulsion, although hundreds avoided it by converting to Christianity; the islands had no governor, and the bishop of Cebu filled the post ad interim from 1759 to 1761, waiting for the next governor, Archbishop Manuel Rojo del Río of Manila.

In 1761, Charles III signed the so-called Family Pact (*Pacto de Familia*) with the Bourbons of France. The consequent rupture of relations between Spain and Great Britain was followed by a declaration of war in January of

1762. In the same year, the British conquered Havana in Cuba and Manila in the Philippines. Because communications between the Philippines and Spain took one and a half years either way, authorities in Manila were ignorant of all of these diplomatic and military developments. It is true that Armenian merchants from Madras indicated to the archbishop that a fleet was getting ready to conquer Manila; also, a priest received a letter with the same information and a missive, arriving via Canton, containing news about the war between Spain and Britain. However, the British fleet was approaching a city unprepared to confront the oncoming enemy. In the minds of the Spaniards, supernatural omens mitigated the lack of military preparation. At the time there was a community of women dedicated to the religious life under the direction of a holy woman called Mother Paula. In a conversation with the attorney general of the colony, she told him "that Manila would not be taken, that the English had all come to the city to be converted to Catholicism," and he transmitted the news to the governor. Mother Paula was proven wrong when, on September 22, a fleet of thirteen vessels with more than six thousand men on board entered Manila Bay under the command of Admiral Samuel Cornish and Brigadier General William Draper. The first encounter with the Spaniards took place on September 24, and the defenders withdrew inside the walls. The British forces requested the surrender of the city, but a Council of War on September 25 decided to defend Manila "to the last extremity." The friars communicated to the archbishop another encouraging message from Mother Paula that "Saint Francis was going to work a miracle on behalf of the Manilans; that he would be seen on the walls, with his cord in his hand, defending the city and repulsing the assault."[44] Despite omens and proclamations, the Spaniards capitulated ten days after the Council of War's first meeting. The British required the cession of the whole archipelago and 4 million pesos. Both requests went unfulfilled. In the words of a Spanish historian, "the pusillanimous Governor" only collected 546,000 from contributions of merchants, the obras pias funds, silver from churches, and his own silverware.[45]

While the British could count on such an accommodating governor-archbishop, a member of the High Court of the Island, Simón de Anda, organized a spirited resistance against the invading forces. He established his residence at Bacolor, the capital of Pampanga and most loyal territory of Luzon. He soon organized an army of Spaniards, French troops from Pondicherry that had deserted the British forces, and native Pampango soldiers. At that time, the galleon *Filipino* was due from Acapulco. The British captured the pilot the captain had requested, thus becoming aware of the galleon's approach. Meanwhile, Anda ordered the galleon's captain to run the ship into Palapag harbor. The British search party was unable to find the 3 million pesos the galleon was carrying. Under the direction of a Franciscan friar, the money went by sea to Santor, a small village on the Pampanga coast, thus providing much-needed funds to Anda's campaign. A different fate awaited the two-thousand-ton galleon *Santísima Trinidad*. The galleon had left for its voyage to Acapulco, but a storm broke its masts, and it headed back to the islands. When the galleon reached the San Bernardino Strait, two British frigates attacked and captured it. The admiral seized the cargo of 1,048 bales of textiles, plus boxes and other valuables that Cornish placed at auction, disregarding the claims made by the archbishop.[46]

A large number of Chinese were living in the Philippines at the time. In the words of Martínez de Zúñiga, "Although the Señor Arandía—the previous governor—had sent away all the pagan Chinese, others replaced them after his death, and the augmentation of their numbers which took place in three years was incredible."[47] The British hoped that tensions between colonizers and locals would help them achieve their goals of conquering Manila and occupying an island in the Sulu archipelago. The invading force counted on the support of the Filipinos and Chinese because "the animosity of the natives against the Spaniards" and the Chinese, "especially those who by the zeal of the Spanish clergy have been lately banished from Manila, will immediately resort for protection and security in all they want."[48] The British attained their aim in Sulu. The sultanates of the southern Philippines had achieved such a degree of stability that the Spanish, Dutch, and British would negotiate with the sultans as sovereign rulers. Alimudin, the Sultan of Sulu, ceded Balambangan Island to the British East India Company in 1762 to establish an alliance that would protect the sultanate from the Spaniards.

The British assessment proved right, and the Chinese joined the British troops hoping that the invasion would improve their situation. As soon as the British "took possession of Manila, these Chinese gave them every aid, and accompanied them in all their expeditions."[49] In fact, after a British attack against a convent in Bulacan, the invading troops delivered to the Chinese an Augustinian friar and "all the Indians found in the place . . . who murdered them in cold blood, in revenge for the death of their countrymen" who had perished in the engagement.[50] The Chinese of Guagua in Pampanga, along with others from the Manila area, numbering in total more than five thousand, had plotted to rise in arms the night of December 24, 1762, when all Spaniards and Filipinos would be at Christmas midnight Mass. A Chinese man revealed the plot to his fiancé, and she gave the alarming news to the parish priest. Anda sent an envoy to the insurgents to propose an agreement, but they refused it. "Our people then advanced, seeing they must have recourse to arms, and made an immense carnage among them."[51] The 130 survivors of this uprising were condemned to death. The acting governor issued a decree "that all the Chinese in the islands should be hanged, which orders were put in execution very generally, but where the order had been disregarded, he readily overlooked the omission."[52] This time, the native Filipino population did not join the Spaniards in killing the Chinese. In the *History of the Father Dominicans*, the author calls the people of Guagua "imbecilic" because they did not take an active part in the fight and remained unmoved by the events taking place.[53] Things could have been worse, as they were when the Filipinos and Chinese joined forces in a minor revolt in San Pablo de los Montes in the province of Laguna.[54] The number of Chinese casualties as a consequence of Anda's decree was about six thousand. A Filipino historian writes that "because of the stream of human blood that flowed over Philippine soil during that yuletide season, the event had been aptly recorded by historians as the 'Red Christmas of 1762.'"[55]

The apathy of the natives, the Chinese revolt, and the British occupation were only a few of the many challenges that confronted the Spaniards. "A profound demoralization took hold of the Manila Filipinos as soon as they witnessed the Spanish defeat, for they had been treated only to spectacles celebrating the victories of Spanish arms."[56] Rejection of tribute and labor services and grievances against abusive Spanish authorities led to Filipino uprisings like the Iloko rebellion of Diego Silang and disturbances in Cagayan, Laguna, Batangas, Tayabas, Cavite, Samar, Panay, Cebu, and Zamboanga. Natives expelled or killed Spanish officials and friars.[57] Particularly difficult to control was the revolt of Juan de la Cruz Palaris, which began in 1762. In the words of Martínez de Zúñiga, "The most obstinate rebellion of the Indians was in the province of Pangasinan." The insurgents were able to resist until March of 1765, but the consequences were devastating. Ten thousand natives were killed, others perished of hunger, "and the first enumeration that was made of the province after the rebellion, it was found that twenty-six thousand nine hundred and twenty-seven persons were deficient of the proper number, composing nearly half the population."[58] The war between Spain and Great Britain ended with the Treaty of Paris in 1763.[59]

The Chinese in Eighteenth-Century Philippines

China was, in many respects, the fastest-growing empire of the eighteenth century, and Chinese immigrants continued arriving in the islands.[60] Pierre de Pagés, a traveler who visited the Philippines in 1768, described Chinese activities in Luzon by noting, "At present they amount to more than 20,000 who, after engrossing the whole of the manufactures and the principal part of the trade of Manila, begin to turn their attention to agriculture."

Nevertheless, not all of the Chinese in Luzon were merchants. A number of them had worked in agriculture long before the eighteenth century. In the environs of Manila, they were truck gardeners providing the city with produce as early as 1589. In addition to these independent agriculturalists, the Chinese worked for Spanish landowners and in the Augustinian and Jesuit states because they were considered better farmers than the Filipinos.

Hostility against the Chinese in Manila led these merchants to establish small sangley enclaves elsewhere called *pariancillos*, after the Parian in Manila. Sangleys provided the small capital and entrepreneurship for the provinces.[61] Regulations forbade the Chinese from moving outside Manila and trading with the natives. Sangley converts to Christianity could freely engage in commerce and were exempt from tribute for ten years after their conversion. Many of them married Filipino women and lived in their wives' villages. Chinese non-Christians were allowed to go to the provinces after buying a permit; such transactions were a source of illicit income for Spanish officials, who usually demanded more than the legal payment. They bribed the local authority, the alcalde mayor, with a substantial initial sum, followed by regular donations. "The Chinese then set about making themselves indispensable to the economy of the town. One of the chief methods they used was to give credit to the natives on rice and tuba purchases and take a lien on the next rice crop as payment. Often a local farmer found himself owing the whole of his next season's crop to the Chinese."[62]

By the mid-eighteenth century, groups of Chinese spread from Luzon to the islands of Panay, Cebu, and Zamboanga.[63] The provincials of the religious orders, in a document of 1701, complained that the ban on sangleys in the provinces had been disregarded, noting that "this prohibition is neither obeyed nor respected."[64] The Chinese, in addition to the "Moors, Armenians, and other barbarians, have settled without the walls of Manila, and in various provinces," and the interactions among these infidels and the recently converted Christian Filipinos had disastrous consequences because:

> Religion is considered, by the said Christians, as intolerable, although it is not such, whether in itself, in its effects, or in the obligations which they assume by becoming Christians—which, in the feeble light of their understanding, is the same as being reduced only to subjection to the ecclesiastical minister, the alcalde-mayor, and the burdens of tributes and repartimientos.[65]

There were two attitudes with respect to the Chinese: The officials who sold residence and trading permits, the people engaged in the galleon trade, and the friars tended to welcome more Chinese residents because the Chinese paid higher taxes than the Filipinos. The annual tax consisted of eight pesos for a residence permit, five reals per head, a contribution to a "community chest" of twelve reals, and payment for religious instruction, in addition to frequent special levies.[66] In contrast, the newly arrived governors, "whose interests were not yet corrupted by Chinese bribes," and the imperial authorities in Spain, who worried about colonial security, had the opposite point of view and were in favor of a minimal foreign population.[67] Such was the case in 1709 with Governor Martín de Ursúa y Arismendi, Count of Lizarraga. In the words of Martínez de Zúñiga:

> His first care was to send out of the islands all those Chinese who had been hitherto in the habit of remaining annually after the departure of the junks, to the great prejudice of the Spaniards. . . . All were expelled except those who were mechanics, or in the service of the public. The indulgence granted to these, was ascribed to the advantage the Governor derived from the licenses he issued for that purpose.

Moreover, he continues disparaging the commercial practices of the sangleys:

> They adulterated the weights and measures, as well as the different articles of sugar, wax, and almost every other commodity, so as not to be easily discovered. They were all monopolizers, watching narrowly the wants of the inhabitants, and the demand for different articles of consumption, which they kept back until they rose to their price. All this they had long practised with impunity, as, by virtue of presents duly applied, they were able to secure powerful protectors; and although sometimes they were fined, they took care that, even on the very day the fine was exacted; they should be reimbursed by the advanced price they fixed on the very goods in question.[68]

It seems that there was some truth to his observations. A French visitor writing in 1840 described monopolistic commercial practices that corresponded with Zúñiga's account. "They would buy up all the available goods, divide them up among the Chinese retailers, they offered a solid front against any would-be rival."[69] The "competitive edge" of family ties implied that the Chinese progressed in status from itinerant peddlers to owners of several shops. "Fortified by family and clan relationships, they established a vast network of retail outlets. . . . One family group frequently owned all the shops dealing in certain goods throughout the Manila area." Such trade networks allowed Chinese control over the islands' economy to branch widely.[70] The Spaniards were not the only ones affected by Chinese commerce. The British had secured a base on the Sulu archipelago, and the Chinese bought the produce of the islands at a higher price than was profitable to the British, squeezing them out of the market. These sangleys traded in a variety of commodities like cotton cloth, iron and other hardware goods, earthenware, silks, copper, and sea products, including tortoiseshell, mother of pearl, sea slugs, birds' nests, shark fins, and so on. Because they had been dealing with the people and datus of the islands for centuries, they had overwhelming advantages. They considered the required bribes and extortions as regular commercial practices included in prices as transaction costs.[71]

Reforms in the Philippines

The Jesuit Juan J. Delgado wrote in 1749 that Manila was suffering great penury because there had been no galleons from Mexico in three years. He continued, "without exaggeration," that the Chinese in the city numbered more than forty thousand, their total population in the archipelago double that figure. They had come in large numbers "due to the great famine that that Empire had suffered in those years."[72]

Affluent merchants from Mexico City dominated trade with Acapulco. From 1710 to 1760, they arrived in Manila frequently, registering as citizens to receive landing space on the galleon; afterward, agents took care of their business. Such practices excluded the majority of Spanish citizens in Manila from the business of the line, and when as an alternative they attempted to participate in local markets, they discovered that the Chinese had monopolized the trade and retail business of the colony.

Upon his arrival in 1754, the new governor, Pedro Manuel de Arandía, took measures to align the colony with new imperial policies. He reorganized the infantry, established a corps of artillery, provided adequate salaries to the troops, and reformed the arsenal at Cavite.[73] Furthermore, he was the first Spanish official to bring an economic development perspective to the Philippines, trying a different approach toward the Chinese. First, he ordered the construction of a new quarter, the *alcaicería*, or silk market of San Fernando, where the incoming sangleys were required to dwell until the junks' departure. Father de la Concepción wrote that the purpose of such buildings was to provide a place "in which trade might be carried on; the heathen merchants to return immediately to their own country, without going inland from Manila or having any dealings with the natives."[74] Arandía's second initiative was to form a trading company under official protection: membership was offered to Spaniards, natives, and mestizos of Chinese descent. The amount of capital raised was 76,500 pesos divided in shares of 500 pesos each. The clear purpose of this trading company was to wrest control from the Chinese over the wholesale and retail business of the islands.[75] Among the goals of the project were to raise the employment rate among natives, teach them useful skills, prevent the outflow of silver, and provide a market for native products. These lofty aims were accompanied by a series of incentives: the company was exempt from levies on manufactured cotton goods for ten years, and it was permitted to import merchandise from other countries without paying taxes. In addition, the company was allowed to take charge of funds from the obras pias in "order to invest them at five percent in its business; and be secure from financial exaction by the governors."[76] Soon the company found out that the capital raised was not enough. The governor demanded 100,000 pesos from the Misericordia, the richest of the obras pias, and 30,000 pesos from the Third Order of San Francisco. Clipped silver coins used for trade in the archipelago were given as payment for the company's merchandise but were not accepted in foreign markets, which implied serious losses. In Spain, authorities opposed the company, and it dissolved within a year of its establishment. Retail trade therefore remained in the sangleys' hands.[77]

The third measure taken by the governor was to expel Chinese merchants. Ships were ready for this task on June 30, 1755. With the help of the religious orders, hundreds of Chinese people received baptism on the same day in order to avoid deportation. It seems that Chinese conversions had not been very sincere, given that when the Chinese who sided with the British were expelled, the Spaniards lamented that "they threw off from their necks the Rosary and rid themselves of all the signs of Catholics."[78] The banished Chinese relocated in the Sulu archipelago and Mindanao, where they engaged in trade financed by the Moro datus.[79] It was not a free arrangement. The datus advanced money and more often forced it on them, at a high annual interest rate of 25 or 30 percent.[80] However, in 1778, under Governor José Basco y Vargas, the Chinese were allowed to return to Manila. Entry permits favored agricultural laborers. "The connection between the return of the Chinese in this guise and the new cash-crop economy became apparent seventy to eighty years later."[81]

Since the middle of the eighteenth century, the local economy was being transformed due to Spanish attempts to produce exportable crops like sugar, indigo, cotton, abaca, and tobacco. This new agriculture was accompanied by "the most important social phenomenon of the century 1750–1850 . . . the rise of the Chinese mestizos to a position of economic and social prominence." Taking advantage of Chinese expulsions of 1755 and 1766, the descendants of Filipino and Chinese couples took over retail trade and crafts, controlled the provision of the Manila market, leased property from religious orders, and took over land from the natives. The mestizos cultivated tobacco and other cash crops, becoming the agents of the economic transformation. In the eighteenth century, as soon as mestizos constituted a substantial group, they were classified as such, and their taxation regime changed. They were charged three pesos, about double the amount paid by native Filipinos.[82]

The Moro Wars in the Eighteenth Century

Moro raids became highly destructive in the decades between 1752 and 1773. These incursions were large undertakings; in an attack on Palompon on the island of Leyte, one thousand men arrived in "twenty-five boats which gives an idea of the size of these vessels. Each one could carry from forty to fifty warriors with their weapons and *lantakas*—bronze cannons—and still leave room for captives and the booty that they captured."[83]

Hostilities between the Spanish and the Dutch in the seventeenth century had allowed for the consolidation of Muslim power; subsequently, the eighteenth century witnessed an increase in raid activity by the sultanates, motivated by an increasing demand for slaves in the Jolo and Mindanao markets. The Moros took slaves to the Dutch East Indies in exchange for money and guns. One of the consequences of these aggressions was the depopulation of the Visayas and Mindanao territories under colonial authority, which meant a loss of tribute for the Crown. In Kalibo (Panay Island) from 1750 to 1757, the number of tributaries went from 1,174 to 549; in Butuan (northern Mindanao), the number dropped from 800 to 130. Northern Mindanao suffered terrible depopulation: in these years, three hundred persons were captured from Butuan, two thousand from Caraga, and sixteen hundred from Siargao; the gold mines of Surigao were abandoned.[84] The government in Manila was slow to assist the threatened communities, and economic interest compounded their apathy. A missionary complained: "At times while the pirates were devastating one island, in the next island the leaders of the squadron sent to pursue them were peacefully exhibiting their merchandise for sale."[85]

A new wave of raids followed the British invasion of 1762 in response to Chinese market demand. During the eighteenth century, the British East India Company and "country traders" incorporated the Sulu zone into their area of operations, contributing to an increase in slave raiding. The British brought textiles, arms, and ammunition to the Jolo Indians to barter for pearls, sea slugs, and birds' nests and took the goods to Canton in exchange for tea. Forced labor was required to collect forest and marine products, and soon Jolo became an entrepôt that attracted merchants, seagoing peddlers, and Chinese traders. The sultanate prospered from market profits, control of internal and external trade, and the financing of maritime expeditions. To consolidate political power, sultans shared slaves and firearms with subordinate datus.[86] On top of the many Filipinos killed or enslaved and the severe disruptions to local economies and social life that resulted, the colonial government's requirements for labor, provisions for garrisons, and punitive expeditions made the plight of the Filipinos much worse. During raiding season, trade between the islands was dangerous, colonial adminis-tration was unable to function, and ruinous Treasury disbursements went to confront the tenacious raiders.[87]

Changes in Spanish Imperial Policy

During the reigns of Fernando VI (1746–1759) and Carlos III (1759–1788), there were significant changes in imperial policies. The economic strategy was to transform the Spanish economy along mercantilist lines, similar to the economies of the English, French, or Dutch. In order to succeed, it was nec-essary to develop the peninsula's agriculture and manufactures and to sell its products in American markets, thereby excluding European and Asian com-petitors and better exploiting colonial resources. Fundamental pieces of the plan were dismantling the monopolistic trade system, implementing admin-istrative reforms, and establishing a more efficient tax collection system to support the metropoles' finances. Politically, the reforms tried to concentrate the power exercised at the time by the church and the Merchant Guilds, or *Consulados*, in the hands of the Mexican and Peruvian governments.[88]

In the Philippines, three years after the British invasion, Audiencia mem-ber Francisco Leandro de Viana wrote a 1765 memorandum detailing plans for developing the local economy and changing the galleon's monopolistic operations, a set of proposals parallel to the Crown's new political orienta-tion. Among other suggestions, he emphasized the advantage of conducting trade with Spain through the Cape of Good Hope, and to make his point, he described the profitable business of European ships trading at Canton: "In most years there come to the port of Canton, in the empire of China, twenty-four, twenty-eight, or thirty ships—English, French, Dutch, Swedish, and Danish; they carry our pesos fuertes (which is the money most valued in China and throughout India) . . . cochineal [grana] from our own America, and the opium of India, are also two main lines of this commerce."

The ships returned to Europe "with *chá* or tea, and with some porcelain . . . and, finally, they carry a great amount of silk, both raw and in fabrics, which is their principal lading." Agents of these nations gave designs for fabrics to the Chinese, "which are every year invented, and they weave the stuffs of the same width as those of Europa. Afterward they sell these, as coming from Francia, Inglaterra, and other European countries." The consequences were detrimental to the Acapulco trade because

> A large portion of the said fabrics or stuffs come to Nueva España in our trading-fleets, and, although they are of the same quality as those which the galleons carry from here to Acapulco—with only the difference that the latter are wider and somewhat more lustrous than the former—there is a very great difference in the prices; for the mere name of "French" or "English" confers value and estimation on the said fabrics throughout the kingdom of Mexico, and the mere name of their being "Chinese" renders those which go by way of Acapulco of little value.[89]

In a document of 1729 addressed to Cardinal Fleury, a minister of France, a representative voiced the concerns of French merchants in Cadiz complaining that the Chinese were imitating French silks and selling them 50 percent cheaper. Meanwhile, the galleon was bringing more and more cotton fabrics, and French silks suffered.[90] Meanwhile, a large amount of textiles of Asian origin arrived on the Mexican market from the Atlantic side, dealing a considerable blow to the galleon economy.

In addition, Viana proposed the creation of a commercial company, to grow cotton, cacao, and sugar—"the province of Pampanga alone is capable of producing more sugar than can be consumed in China"—the development of iron and gold mining, and other profitable enterprises. Viana believed that the company would put a stop to foreigners taking advantage of American treasure:

> All the silver that is coined in the dominions of España comes to a halt in foreign kingdoms, among our greatest enemies. The treasures of the Indias pass through the aqueduct of Cadiz, without leaving even a trace on the conduits of the Spanish merchants, as can be demonstrated by [comparing] the riches that the Indias have produced, and the poverty of the Spaniards.[91]

Optimistically, he envisioned the idea of a means of travel between the Pacific and the Atlantic Oceans—a forerunner of the Panama Canal—financed by the company.

> If the prosperity of the said company will be as great as the circumstances here set forth promise, we ought to expect that, in order to facilitate its commerce and save transportation, some part of its gains will be employed in the improvement of the Panama route—in making the Chagre River more navigable, and perhaps in seeking the easiest mode of joining the two seas, or in finding other means for conveying the goods by water from one port to the other.[92]

Viana's memorandum was part of several schemes that aimed to expand the island group's trade, diversify its economy, and exploit its natural resources. In 1753, José Calvo, a Jesuit, projected the formation of a company to exploit the agricultural and mineral possibilities of the Philippines and trade directly with the peninsula.[93] Nicholas Norton had a project authorized by the Spanish Crown around 1760 to establish a direct line between Manila and Cadiz and to exploit cinnamon, pepper, and other spices in the islands. English merchants like Raymundo and Bernardo O'Kelly and Vicente O'Kenneri, who occupied positions on the galleons like master of silver, or pilots went to New Spain as agents of merchandise loaded in Manila.[94]

Irish pilot Richard Bagge suggested exporting goods like cacao, sea slugs, camphor, pearls, and gold from the islands to China in exchange for silk and porcelain in 1764. Such developments implied adjustments in other areas of the state. The Marques de la Ensenada, a minister of Fernando VI who shared these new ideas, wrote, "as long as Spain lacks a competent navy, its closest rivals, France and England, will not respect it."[95] The downside was that any improvement of colonial administration implied a substantial development of its defensive system and, consequently, war with Britain.[96]

Nonetheless, plans to change the Filipino economy were under way. Attempts to trade from Cadiz with Asia via the Cape of Good Hope were taking shape. In 1732, the British ambassador informed London that the Spanish king had authorized a single voyage to Manila via the Cape, financed with funds from Britain, and that other businessmen were pushing the same idea. Both the British and Dutch governments complained about the violation of their companies' charts, and the king yielded to pressure.[97] Nonetheless, the route came back to the fore when in 1765, the frigate *Buen Consejo* arrived from Spain following the Cape of Good Hope route with European merchandise to exchange for Asian goods on the account of Manila's merchants. There were fourteen voyages in total until 1784. Due to the small cargo space of the frigates, the volume of trade during those years was unimportant. However, profits were not the reason for the voyages; it was part of a government strategy to try to remove Mexican merchants from the Asian textile market.[98]

After October 12, 1778, with the law of free trade between Spain and America, there had been a dramatic reorganization of colonial commerce. Restrictions on intercolonial trade were removed, and taxes were reduced to facilitate exchanges among American territories. The system of fleets from Spain to America was discontinued, and the House of Trade in Cadiz closed its doors in 1790. After such reforms, there was at least a fourfold increase in the value of exchanges between Spain and its empire; however, the war with

Britain in 1796 soon interrupted this upward trend.[99] Free trade excluded foreign vessels from participating legally in American commerce. Similarly, the British government issued the 1786 Navigation Act to restrict the transportation of colonial merchandise to British ships. European empires did not plan to abandon control of colonial trade. Nonetheless, there were changes in the patterns of control.[100] This atmosphere of liberalized regulations encouraged private traders to engage in colonial ventures. A company formed by the five major guilds of Madrid, *gremios mayores*, sent a cargo of goods to the Philippines in 1778, accompanied by commissioners who moved their residence to Canton in the following year. However, by 1783, the company was loading substantial quantities of goods aboard the galleon, indicating that the Acapulco trade was more profitable than direct trade to Spain.[101]

In the Philippines, the appointment of Governor José Basco y Vargas (1778–1787) was a turning point in the public administration of the colony. He aimed to establish fiscal independence from the Mexican situado and to establish trade based on domestic production by connecting the economies of Spain, the Philippines, and the American territories. He encouraged the cultivation of indigo, pepper, and hemp, as well as the manufacture of silk and cotton textiles. On March 1, 1782, the tobacco monopoly, *estanco*, was established in the islands. The government controlled all steps of tobacco cultivation and harvesting, as well as the marketing of cigars from state factories. In the last third of the eighteenth century, in addition to the tobacco estanco and the galleon's taxes, Filipino tributes contributed substantially to colonial budgets. From 1782 to 1795, the Philippines sent 1,971,696 pesos to the Spanish Treasury, a complete reversal of the earlier pattern in the flow of funds between the central government and that of the islands.[102] In 1811, the Mexico situado was officially discontinued.

Competition with the galleon line appeared in the form of the Royal Philippine Company, *Real Compañía de Filipinas*, in 1785. Before this year, there was a series of projects to establish companies; for instance, in 1766 the concern of Aguirre, Del Arco, and Albuquerque tried to establish a line from Spain to the islands. The Royal Philippine Company was an attempt to connect the Americas, the Philippines, and Spain, with the aim of developing the Philippines's resources. In addition to direct trade between Cadiz and Manila, company ships were permitted to trade directly with Canton, Calcutta, and Lima. The company appointed resident factors in Asian ports, and itinerant agents traveled among these markets to buy commodities for the company. However, the world economy had changed. Lacking strict oversight and in some cases enticed by the large profits of opium commerce, agents and other officials neglected their work for the company and engaged in private business.[103]

Merchants in Manila, afraid of losing their monopoly on the Acapulco galleons, opposed the competition the company's arrival in the market introduced, just as they had opposed the frigates' voyages. Nonetheless, the company petitioned the Crown to participate in the galleon trade, showing where the real profits remained.[104] After 1789, the Royal Philippine Company's activities began to decline.

During those years, the company was involved in ongoing efforts to commercialize the islands' products, like indigo, sugar, Ilocos cotton, and so on. One of the unintended side effects was the establishment in the Philippines of foreign commercial agents from France, the United States, and Britain. The decrees of 1785 and 1787 legally opened up the port to Asian ships, Portuguese and Indian vessels whose presence was already customary. A decree of 1789 allowing European vessels to land at Manila made the city a *de facto* free port.

The End of the Galleon Trade

In the last decades of the seventeenth century, merchants of Mexico City organized in the Consulado controlled the marketing of the fleet's merchandise coming via Veracruz and the galleon's goods from Acapulco. The Consulado organized associations of merchants to distribute Asian textiles in New Spain, Guatemala, Havana, Ecuador, and Peru, and occasionally to send them to Spain by the returning fleet.[105] They were the financiers of the viceroyalty's internal commerce, advancing funds for mining operations, textile manufacture, and agricultural development as well as exercising absolute control over retail trade. "The galleon traffic made it possible for merchants in New Spain to liberate themselves from metropolitan commerce and allowed them an autonomous commercial policy in tune with the interests of the colony instead of those of the metropolis."[106] Due to the absence of European intermediaries, the line provided an alternative outlet to import textiles and spices at better prices than the same goods brought by the fleets.[107]

During the second half of the eighteenth century, the liberalization of Spanish regulations facilitated the arrival of Asian goods on the Atlantic side. Meanwhile, the upper classes in Mexico began to consume European imported silk, and on the galleons, Indian cotton goods gradually supplanted Chinese fabrics. The foundation of the Royal Philippine Company and above all the implementation of "free trade" measures put an end to the Mexican

Consulado's control over transatlantic and transpacific exchanges.[108] The change was apparent when the British at the port of San Blas in New Spain were exchanging cotton for silver. By 1810, American merchants and ships were trading in Californian ports like Monterrey and San Francisco; two Spanish frigates captured the American ship *Mercury*, confiscating its sea otter pelts and taking them to Canton.[109]

After the company's foundation in 1785, there was a steep decline in the galleon trade. From 1778 to 1786, three galleons and two small vessels lost their cargoes, valued at 3.5 million pesos. Twelve years later, the *San Andrés* sank with all its hands, and the *Magallanes* lost its passage. There were no ships from Manila in 1788, 1790, 1792, 1802, 1803, 1805, and 1812, and impoverished investors could only partially stock the holds of several galleons. In 1786, the galleon had to sell its merchandise at a loss due to competition with contraband goods. The arrival in Acapulco of three vessels from Manila in 1800 and four in 1801 ruined the Acapulco market for almost a decade. In 1811, the galleon was discontinued for four years during the Napoleonic War in Spain. In China, the exportation of tea and importation of cotton and opium carried by Europeans at Canton implied the decline of the junk trade. Oversupply in the American markets became prevalent due to the smuggling of European and Indian goods and legal merchandise from the Royal Philippine Company. The last galleon returned to Manila in 1815. From this date until 1821, smaller ships from Manila sailed not to Acapulco but to other Mexican ports, such as San Blas, Tepic, Sonsonate Guyamas, and Mazatlan. The American wars of independence resulted in the final collapse of the system based on the extraction of silver and the supply of Asian textiles.[110]

The expansion of the opium trade received additional support from the capital of private Spanish merchants who were previously engaged in the galleon trade. Laruleta & Company and its successor, Mendieta, Uriarte & Company, were based in Calcutta. The leading names in Canton were Yrisari & Company and Lorenzo Calvo & Company. After 1826, there was a collapse of American silver supplies in the Canton market, which required resorting to credit and bills of exchange. "The fall of the Spanish American colonies in depriving the Canton trade of silver led to the modification of the Canton financial methods."[111]

The End of the Line

The Acapulco-Manila galleons navigated the waters of the Pacific Ocean for about 250 years. When compared to the commercial organization of today's large container ships or oil tankers, it was not a smooth operation.

Wars, shipwrecks—more than thirty galleons were lost at sea—and a variety of other misfortunes frequently disrupted the line. The British captured four ships, thousands of people died crossing the oceans, and property losses were considerable. However, the large vessels kept sailing, supported by Filipino labor and resources, the work of miners in Peru and New Spain, and the ongoing exchange of American silver for Asian textiles. Ecological exchanges of gigantic importance, as well as the movement of Americans, Asians, and Spaniards on both sides of the largest ocean on earth were related to the sailing of the ships. The manifold aspects of this line were linked to its lucrative operations. Considering the high profits accrued by participants in the trade, from an actuarial point of view "total losses were comparatively few and the percentages of missing and captured crew men would have caused no great concern to modern underwriters."[112] These galleons originated the first planetary economy, the intercontinental market from which emerges the globalized world in which we live.

Notes

Introduction

1. Clarence H. Haring, *Trade and Navigation between Spain and the Indies in the Time of the Hapsburgs* (Gloucester, MA: Peter Smith, 1964), 146.

2. Kirti N. Chaudhuri, *The Trading World of Asia and the English East India Company, 1660–1760* (Cambridge: Cambridge University Press, 1978), 10.

3. Henry Kamen, *Empire: How Spain Became a World Power, 1492–1763* (New York: HarperCollins, 2003), 506.

4. Kamen, *Empire*, 508.

Chapter 1. The Philippines before the Spaniards

1. Pedro Chirino, "Relation of the Filipinas Islands and of What Has There Been Accomplished by the Fathers of the Society of Jesus," in *Philippine Islands 1493–1898*, ed. Emma Helen Blair and James Alexander Robertson, vol. 12, *1601–1604* (Cleveland, OH: A. H. Clark Company, 1904), 183.

2. James Francis Warren, "Weather, History and Empire: The Typhoon Factor and the Manila Galleon Trade, 1565–1815," in *Anthony Reid and the Study of the Southeast Asian Past*, ed. Geoff Wade and Li Tana (Singapore: Institute of Southeast Asian Studies), 190.

3. François Pyrard, *The Voyage of François Pyrard of Laval to the East Indies*, vol. 2 (London: Hakluyt Society, 1887–1888), 169.

4. Laura Lee Junker, *Raiding, Trading, and Feasting: The Political Economy of Philippine Chiefdoms* (Honolulu: University of Hawaii Press, 1999), 16, 61.

5. William Henry Scott, *The Discovery of the Igorots: Spanish Contacts with the Pagans of Northern Luzon* (Quezon City: New Day Publishers, 1974), 52–53.

6. José S. Arcilla, *An Introduction to Philippine History* (Manila: Ateneo de Manila University Press, 1998), 155–56; Miguel Selga, *Charts of Remarkable Typhoons in the Philippines, 1902–1934: Catalogue of Typhoons, 1348–1934* (Manila: Bureau of Printing, 1935), 42.

7. Horacio de la Costa, *The Jesuits in the Philippines, 1581–1768* (Cambridge, MA: Harvard University Press, 1961), 405.

8. Pedro Cubero Sebastián, *Peregrinación del mundo* (Madrid: Ediciones Polifemo, 1993), 21–22.

9. Frederick L. Wernstedt and J. E. Spencer, *The Philippine Island World: A Physical, Cultural, and Regional Geography* (Berkeley: University of California Press, 1967), 83.

10. Anthony Reid, *Southeast Asia in the Age of Commerce, 1450–1680*, vol. 1, *The Lands below the Winds* (New Haven: Yale University Press, 1988), 2–3.

11. Reid, *Southeast Asia*, vol. 1, 45.

12. Onofre D. Corpuz, *The Roots of the Filipino Nation* (Quezon City: University of the Philippines Press, 2005), 618; Linda A. Newson, *Conquest and Pestilence in the Early Spanish Philippines* (Honolulu: University of Hawaii Press, 2009), 251.

13. Gómez Pérez Dasmariñas, "The Manners, Customs, and Beliefs of the Philippine Inhabitants of Long Ago, Being Chapters of a Late 16th Century Manila Manuscript," trans. Carlos Quirino and Mauro Garcia, *Philippine Journal of Science* 87, no. 4 (1958): 413.

14. Francisco Ignacio Alzina, *Una etnografía de los indios visayas del siglo XVII* (Madrid: Consejo Superior de Investigaciones Científicas, 1996).

15. Newson, *Conquest and Pestilence*, 252–53.

16. Newson, *Conquest and Pestilence*, 21.

17. Reid, *Southeast Asia*, vol. 1.

18. Chirino, "Relation of the Filipinas Islands," 212–13.

19. Antonio de Morga, *Sucesos de las Islas Filipinas*, ed. J. S. Cummins (Cambridge: Cambridge University Press, 1971), 249.

20. Alzina, *Una etnografía*, 144; Reid, *Southeast Asia*, vol. 1, 50.

21. Sheldon Watts, *Epidemics and History: Disease, Power, and Imperialism* (New Haven: Yale University Press, 1997), 137.

22. Morga, *Sucesos* (1971), 249–50n1.

23. Francesca Bray, *Science and Civilization in China*, vol. 6, *Biology and Biological Technology Part II: Agriculture*, ed. Joseph Needham (Cambridge: Cambridge University Press, 1984), xiii.

24. Gregorio F. Zaide, *Philippine Political and Cultural History*, vol. 1 (Manila: Philippine Education Company, 1972), 10.

25. Bray, *Science and Civilization*, 13–15.

26. Reid, *Southeast Asia*, vol. 1, 22.

27. Reid, *Southeast Asia*, vol. 1, 20–22.

28. Diego de Artieda, "Relation of the Western Islands Called Filipinas," in *Philippine Islands 1493–1803*, ed. Emma Helen Blair and James Alexander Robertson, vol. 3, *1569–1576* (Cleveland, OH: A. H. Clark Company, 1903), 202.

29. Artieda, "Relation of the Western Islands," 202.

30. William Henry Scott, *Barangay: Sixteenth-Century Philippine Culture and Society* (Quezon City: Ateneo de Manila University Press, 1994), 35.

31. John L. Phelan, *The Hispanization of the Philippines: Spanish Aims and Filipino Responses 1565–1700* (Madison: The University of Wisconsin Press, 1959), 111.

32. Reid, *Southeast Asia*, vol. 1, 50.

33. Morga, *Sucesos* (1971), 252–53; Antonio de Morga, *Sucesos de las Islas Filipinas* (Madrid: Ediciones Polifemo, 1997), 268n424.

34. Quoted in Scott, *Barangay*, 63, 126.

35. Mark Elvin, *The Pattern of the Chinese Past* (Stanford: Stanford University Press, 1973), 138.

36. Reid, *Southeast Asia*, vol. 1, 2.

37. Junker, *Raiding, Trading, and Feasting*, 63.

38. Phelan, *Hispanization of the Philippines*, 16.

39. Scott, *Barangay*, 60–61.

40. Juan de Plasencia, "Customs of the Tagalogs," in *Philippine Islands 1493–1898*, ed. Emma Helen Blair and James Alexander Robertson, vol. 7, *1588–1591* (Cleveland, OH: A. H. Clark Company, 1903), 173–74.

41. Scott, *Barangay*, 50.

42. Junker, *Raiding, Trading, and Feasting*, 345; Morga, *Sucesos* (1971), 252; Plasencia, "Customs of the Tagalogs," 180; Scott, *Barangay*, 3.

43. William Henry Scott, *Cracks in the Parchment Curtain and Other Essays in Philippine History* (Quezon City: New Day, 1985), 22.

44. Anthony Reid, *Southeast Asia in the Age of Commerce*, vol. 2, *Expansion and Crisis* (New Haven: Yale University Press, 1993), 12.

45. Juan de Plasencia, quoted in Junker, *Raiding, Trading, and Feasting*, 345–46.

46. Morga, *Sucesos* (1971), 252.

47. Junker, *Raiding, Trading, and Feasting*, 123–24, 302, 333.

48. Scott, *Barangay*, 131.

49. Phelan, *Hispanization of the Philippines*, 15, 20.

50. Scott, *Barangay*, 6–7.

51. Melchor Dávalos, "Letter to Felipe II," in *Philippine Islands 1493–1898*, ed. Emma Helen Blair and James Alexander Robertson, vol. 6, *1583–1588* (Cleveland, OH: A. H. Clark Company, 1903), 61.

52. Morga, *Sucesos* (1971), 274; see also Phelan, *Hispanization of the Philippines*, 20; Scott, *Barangay*, 13.

53. *Colección de documentos inéditos para la historia de España*, vol. 3 (Madrid: Academia de la Historia, 1886), 126–27.

54. Guido de Lavezaris, "Slavery Among the Natives," in *Philippine Islands 1493–1803*, ed. Emma Helen Blair and James Alexander Robertson, vol. 3, *1569–1576* (Cleveland, OH: A. H. Clark Company, 1903), 260.

55. Morga, *Sucesos* (1971), 276.

56. Arcilla, *Introduction to Philippine History*, 41.

57. Alzina, *Una etnografía*, 205.

58. Chirino, "Relation of the Filipinas Islands," 310.

59. Corpuz, *Roots of the Filipino Nation*, 22.

60. Morga, *Sucesos* (1971), 269.

61. Alzina, *Una etnografía*, 9.

62. Junker, *Raiding, Trading, and Feasting*, 221.

63. Cubero Sebastián, *Peregrinación*, 24.

64. "Description of the Philippinas Islands," in *Philippine Islands 1493–1898*, ed. Emma Helen Blair and James Alexander Robertson, vol. 18, *1617–1620* (Cleveland, OH: A. H. Clark Company, 1904), 97–98.

65. Junker, *Raiding, Trading, and Feasting*, 235.

66. Alzina, *Una etnografía*, 25; Morga, *Sucesos* (1971), 249; Scott, *Barangay*, 180.

67. Alzina, *Una etnografía*, 371; Charles Mann, *1493: Uncovering the New World Columbus Created* (New York: Random House, 2011), 21.

68. Scott, *Barangay*, 182–84.

69. Quoted in Scott, *Barangay*, 153.

70. Morga, *Sucesos* (1971), 261.

71. Morga, *Sucesos* (1971), 261.

72. Noel Perrin, *Giving Up the Gun: Japan's Reversion to the Sword, 1543–1879* (Boston: D. R. Godine, 1994), 18.

73. Quoted in Scott, *Barangay*, 69.

74. Guillaume Le Gentil, *A Voyage to the Indian Seas* (Manila: Filipiniana Book Guild, 1964).

75. Scott, *Cracks in the Parchment Curtain*, 10.

76. Phelan, *Hispanization of the Philippines*, 141, 144.

77. Juan Pacheco Maldonado, "Letter to Felipe II," in *Philippine Islands 1493–1803*, ed. Emma Helen Blair and James Alexander Robertson, vol. 3, *1569–1576* (Cleveland, OH: A. H. Clark Company, 1903), 298.

78. Alzina, *Una etnografía*, 270.

79. Morga, *Sucesos* (1971), 248.

80. Morga, *Sucesos* (1971), 261.

81. Alzina, *Una etnografía*, 25.

82. Alzina, *Una etnografía*, 270.

83. Gemelli G. Careri, *A Voyage to the Philippines: And an Appendix of the Chapters on the Philippines in the Travels of Fray Sebastián Manrique* (Manila: Filipiniana Book Guild, 1963), 57.

84. Morga, *Sucesos* (1971), 262.

85. Anthony Reid, "Economic and Social Change, c. 1400–1800," in *The Cambridge History of Southeast Asia*, vol. 1, *From Early Times to c. 1800*, ed. Nicholas Tarling (Singapore: Cambridge University Press, 1992), 468.

86. William Henry Scott, *Looking for the Prehispanic Filipino and Other Essays in Philippine History* (Quezon City: New Day Publishers, 1992), 24–39.

87. Gaspar Corrêa, *The Three Voyages of Vasco da Gama and his Viceroyalty* (London: Hakluyt, 1869), 159–64.

88. Corrêa, *Three Voyages*, 247.

89. Lewis Hanke, *Cuerpo de documentos de siglo XVI: Sobre los derechos de España in las Indias y las Filipinas* (México: Fondo de Cultura Económica, 1943), 72; Scott, *Barangay*, 24–39.

90. Pyrard, *Voyage of François Pyrard*, 284.

91. Francesca Trivellato, *The Familiarity of Strangers: The Sephardic Diaspora, Livorno, and Cross-Cultural Trade in the Early Modern Period* (New Haven: Yale University Press, 2009), 240–41.

92. Morga, *Sucesos* (1971), 323n2.

93. Reid, "Economic and Social Change," 481.

94. Scott, *Barangay*, 30–31.

95. Fernão Mendes Pinto, *The Travels of Mendes Pinto*, ed. Rebecca D. Catz (Chicago: University of Chicago Press, 1989), 46–49.

96. Zaide, *Philippine Political*, 42.

97. Morga, *Sucesos* (1971), 280.

98. Reid, *Southeast Asia*, vol. 2, 160.

99. Reid, "Economic and Social Change," 494.

100. Zaide, *Philippine Political*, 39.

101. Junker, *Raiding, Trading, and Feasting*, 219.

102. Junker, *Raiding, Trading, and Feasting*, 219–20.

103. Junker, *Raiding, Trading, and Feasting*, 219–20.

104. Benito J. Legarda, *After the Galleons: Foreign Trade, Economic Change and Entrepreneurship in Nineteenth-Century Philippines* (Madison: Center for Asian Studies, University of Wisconsin–Madison, 1999), 10.

105. Junker, *Raiding, Trading, and Feasting*, 211–12, 260.

106. Legarda, *After the Galleons*, 10.

107. Junker, *Raiding, Trading, and Feasting*, 6, 379.

108. Reid, *Southeast Asia*, vol. 1, 105.

109. Junker, *Raiding, Trading, and Feasting*, 201–3.

110. Legarda, *After the Galleons*, 8.

Chapter 2. The Origins of Spanish Settlement in the Philippines

1. Matt K. Matsuda, *Pacific Worlds: A History of Seas, Peoples, and Cultures* (New York: Cambridge University Press), 171.

2. Sanjay Subrahmanyam, *The Portuguese Empire in Asia, 1500–1700: A Political and Economic History* (London: Longman, 1993), 276.

3. Adam Smith, *An Inquiry into the Nature and Causes of the Wealth of Nations* (New York: Random House, 1937), 238.

4. John Maynard Keynes, *A Treatise on Money*, vol. 2 (London: Macmillan, 1950), 156n1.

5. Keynes, *Treatise on Money*, vol. 2, 150n4, 156n1.

6. Keynes, *Treatise on Money*, vol. 2, 156–57.

7. Smith, *Inquiry*, 675–76.

8. Harry E. Cross, "South American Bullion Production and Export, 1550–1750," in *Precious Metals in the Later Medieval and Early Modern Worlds*, ed. J. F. Richards (Durham, NC: Carolina Academic Press, 1983), 397.

9. Fernand Braudel, *The Mediterranean and the Mediterranean World in the Age of Philip II*, vol. 1 (New York: Harper & Row, 1976), 517.

10. Henry Kamen, "The Decline of Spain: A Historical Myth?" *Past and Present* 81, no. 1 (1978): 41.

11. Quoted in Ian Morris, *Why the West Rules—For Now: The Patterns of History and What They Reveal about the Future* (New York: Farrar, Straus, and Giroux, 2010), 460.

12. Thomas Mun, "England's Treasure by Forraign Trade: or, The Ballance of our Forraign Trade is the Rule of our Treasure," in *A Select Collection of Early English Tracts on Commerce, from the Originals of Mun, Roberts, North, and Others*, ed. John Ramsay McCulloch (London: Political Economy Club, 1856), 143.

13. Ward Barret, "World Bullion Flows, 1450–1800," in *The Rise of Merchant Empires: Long-Distance Trade in the Early Modern World, 1350–1750*, ed. James D. Tracy (Cambridge: Cambridge University Press, 1990), 225.

14. Luis de Camões, *Os Lusíadas*, verse 131.

15. Charles R. Boxer, *The Portuguese Seaborne Empire, 1415–1825* (New York: Alfred A. Knopf, 1969), 111.

16. Geoffrey Parker, *Europa en crisis 1598–1648* (Madrid: Siglo XXI, 3 a. ed, 1986), 82.

17. Keynes, *Treatise*, vol. 2, 159.

18. Clarence H. Haring, *Trade and Navigation between Spain and the Indies in the Time of the Hapsburgs* (Gloucester, MA: Peter Smith, 1964), 32.

19. Mun, "England's Treasure," 144.

20. G. Céspedes del Castillo, "Las Indias durante los siglos XVI y XVII," in *Historia de España y América social y económica*, vol. 3, *Los Austrias: El imperio español en América*, ed. J. Vicens-Vives (Barcelona: Vicens-Vives, 1972), 506.

21. François Pyrard, *The Voyage of François Pyrard of Laval to the East Indies*, vol. 2 (London: Hakluyt Society, 1887–88), 219–20.

22. Mark Elvin, *The Pattern of the Chinese Past* (Stanford: Stanford University Press, 1973), 222.

23. Gang Deng, *Chinese Maritime Activities and Socioeconomic Development c. 2100 B.C.–1900 A.D.* (Westport, CT: Greenwood Press, 1997), 131.

24. Takeshi Hamashita, "The Tribute System and Modern Asia," in *Memoirs of the Research Department of the Tokyo Bunko* (N. 46, Tokyo, 1988), 97.

25. Subrahmanyam, *Portuguese Empire*, 9.

26. F. W. Mote, *Imperial China 900–1800* (Cambridge, MA: Harvard University Press, 1999), 743.

27. Mote, *Imperial China*, 745.

28. Quoted in Richard Von Glahn, *Fountain of Fortune: Money and Monetary Policy in China, 1000–1700* (Berkeley: University of California Press, 1996), 127.

29. William S. Atwell, "Ming China and the Emerging World Economy, c. 1470–1650," in *The Cambridge History of China*, vol. 8, part 2, *The Ming Dynasty, 1368–1644* (Cambridge: Cambridge University Press, 1998), 393–94, 401–2.

30. Kirti N. Chaudhuri, *The Trading World of Asia and the English East India Company, 1660–1760* (Cambridge: Cambridge University Press, 1978), 409.

31. Boxer, *Portuguese Seaborne Empire*, 174–75; Deng, *Chinese Maritime Activities*, 119.

32. Deng, *Chinese Maritime Activities*, 131.

33. Anthony Reid, *Southeast Asia in the Age of Commerce*, vol. 2, *Expansion and Crisis* (New Haven: Yale University Press, 1993), 7.

34. Reid, *Southeast Asia*, vol. 2, 7.

35. Carlo M. Cipolla, *Guns, Sails and Empires: Technological Innovations and the Early Phases of European Expansion 1400–1700* (New York: Pantheon Books, 1965), 81.

36. Daniel R. Headrick, *The Tools of Empire: Technology and European Imperialism in the Nineteenth Century* (New York: Oxford University Press, 1981), 3.

37. J. R. McNeill and William H. McNeill, *The Human Web: A Bird's-Eye View of World History* (New York: W. W. Norton & Company, 2003), 194–95.

38. Reid, *Southeast Asia*, 219–33.

39. Cipolla, *Guns, Sails and Empires*, 128.

40. María Lourdes Díaz-Trechuelo, *Arquitectura española en Filipinas, 1565–1800* (Sevilla: Escuela de Estudios Hispano-Americanos [Consejo Superior de Investigaciones Científicas], 1959), 58.

41. Onofre D. Corpuz, *The Roots of the Filipino Nation* (Quezon City: University of the Philippines Press, 2005), 148.

42. Gregorio F. Zaide, *Philippine Political and Cultural History*, vol. 1 (Manila: Philippine Education Company, 1972), 366.

43. Chaudhuri, *Trading World*, 114.

44. Charles R. Boxer, *The Dutch Seaborne Empire: 1600–1800* (New York: Alfred A. Knopf, 1965), 95–96.

45. Subrahmanyam, *Portuguese Empire*, 214–15.

46. Subrahmanyam, *Portuguese Empire*, 213.

47. Gaspar Corrêa, *The Three Voyages of Vasco da Gama and His Viceroyalty* (London: Hakluyt, 1869), 240–41.

48. Quoted in Subrahmanyam, *Portuguese Empire*, 59.

49. K. M. Panikkar, *Asia and Western Dominance* (New York: Collier Books, 1969), 13.

50. Reid, *Southeast Asia*, vol. 2, 271.

51. Corrêa, *Three Voyages*, 318n1.

52. Corrêa, *Three Voyages*, 275.

53. Corrêa, *Three Voyages*, 276, 281.

54. Corrêa, *Three Voyages*, 330.

55. Corrêa, *Three Voyages*, 331.

56. Corrêa, *Three Voyages*, 333.

57. Corrêa, *Three Voyages*, 331–33.

58. John Keay, *The Spice Route: A History* (Berkeley: University of California Press, 2006), 174.

59. Chaudhuri, *Trading World*, 115.

60. Reid, *Southeast Asia*, 20.

61. Panikkar, *Asia and Western Dominance*, 35.

62. Boxer, *Portuguese Seaborne Empire*, 42.

63. Vitorino Magalhaes Godinho, *Mito e mercadoria, utopía e prática de navegar, séculos XIII–XVIII* (Lisboa: Difusao Editorial, 1990), 331.

64. Keay, *Spice Route*, 201.

65. William Henry Scott, *Looking for the Prehispanic Filipino and Other Essays in Philippine History* (Quezon City: New Day Publishers, 1992), 43.

66. Donald F. Lach, *Asia in the Making of Europe*, vol. 1, bk. 1 (Chicago: Chicago University Press, 1965), 115.

67. Antonio Pigafetta, "Account of Magellan's Voyage," in *The First Voyage Round: The World by Magellan Translated from Pigafetta and Other Contemporary Writers*, ed. Lord Stanley Alderly (London: Hakluyt Society, 1874), 127.

68. Oskar H. K. Spate, *The Spanish Lake* (Minneapolis: University of Minnesota Press, 1979), 41; Pablo E. Pérez-Mallaína, *Spain's Men of the Sea: Daily Life on the Indies Fleets in the Sixteenth Century* (Baltimore: The Johns Hopkins University Press, 1998), 55.

69. Pérez-Mallaína, *Spain's Men*, 171–72.

70. Samuel Eliot Morison, *The European Discovery of America: The Southern Voyages, A.D. 1492–1616* (New York: Oxford University Press, 1974), 361.

71. Pigafetta, "Account of Magellan's Voyage," 65.

72. Pigafetta, "Account of Magellan's Voyage," 64–65.

73. Pigafetta, "Account of Magellan's Voyage," 65.

74. Pigafetta, "Account of Magellan's Voyage," 68.

75. Pigafetta, "Account of Magellan's Voyage," 71.

76. Pigafetta, "Account of Magellan's Voyage," 71.

77. Morison, *European Discovery*, 420.

78. William Henry Scott, *Barangay: Sixteenth-Century Philippine Culture and Society* (Quezon City: Ateneo de Manila University Press, 1994), 71.

79. Pigafetta, "Account of Magellan's Voyage," 79.

80. Pigafetta, "Account of Magellan's Voyage," 91.

81. Pigafetta, "Account of Magellan's Voyage," 91.

82. "Letter from Charles I. Barcelona April 19, 1519," in Pigafetta, "Account of Magellan's Voyage," xxxiv.

83. Pigafetta, "Account of Magellan's Voyage."

84. Pigafetta, "Account of Magellan's Voyage," 116.

85. Pigafetta, "Account of Magellan's Voyage," 111.

86. Pigafetta, "Account of Magellan's Voyage," 117.

87. Pigafetta, "Account of Magellan's Voyage," 124.

88. Pigafetta, "Account of Magellan's Voyage," 139.

89. Pigafetta, "Account of Magellan's Voyage," 143.

90. "Life and Voyages of Fernão de Magalhães," in *Philippine Islands 1493–1803*, ed. Emma Helen Blair and James Alexander Robertson, vol. 1, *1493–1529* (Cleveland, OH: A. H. Clark Company, 1903), 247–48.

91. Pigafetta, "Account of Magellan's Voyage," 162.

92. Spate, *The Spanish Lake*, 57.

93. Ramón Carande, *Charles V y sus banqueros*, vol. 3 (Barcelona: Crítica, 1990), 40.

94. Herrera, quoted in Pigafetta, "Account of Magellan's Voyage," 175–76.

95. Mairin Mitchell, *Friar Andres de Urdaneta, O.S.A.* (London: MacDonald and Evans, 1964), 37.

96. Morison, *European Discovery*, 498.

97. In Zaide, *Philippine Political and Cultural History*, 132.

98. Zaide, *Philippine Political and Cultural History*, 133.

99. Mitchell, *Friar Andres de Urdaneta*, 74.

100. Mitchell, *Friar Andres de Urdaneta*, 74.

101. Scott, *Barangay*, 170–73.

102. Scott, *Barangay*, 170–73.

103. "The Expedition of Ruy Lopez de Villalobos, 1541–46," in *Philippine Islands 1493–1803*, ed. Emma Helen Blair and James Alexander Robertson, vol. 2, *1521–1569* (Cleveland, OH: A. H. Clark Company, 1903), 65.

104. Mitchell, *Friar Andres de Urdaneta*, 86–87.

105. Earl J. Hamilton, *El Tesoro americano y la revolución de los precios en España, 1501–1650* (Barcelona: Ariel, 1975), 247–48.

106. "Resume of Contemporaneous Documents, 1559–68," in *Philippine Islands 1493–1803*, ed. Emma Helen Blair and James Alexander Robertson, vol. 2, *1521–1569* (Cleveland, OH: A. H. Clark Company, 1903), 80–81.

107. Edward McCarthy, *Spanish Beginnings in the Philippines, 1564–1572* (Washington: The Catholic University of America Press, 1943), 22.

108. José Toribio Medina,. *Historia del tribunal de la Inquisición de Lima: 1569–1820*, tomo 2 (Santiago de Chile: Fondo Histórico y Bibliográfico José Toribio Medina, 1956), 16.

109. McCarthy, *Spanish Beginnings*, 27.

110. McCarthy, *Spanish Beginnings*.

111. Zaide, *Philippine Political and Cultural History*, 140–41.

112. Pérez-Mallaína, *Spain's Men*, 40–41.

113. José Montero y Vidal, *Historia general de Filipinas*, tomo 1 (Madrid: Imprenta y Fundición de Manuel Tello, 1887), 68.

114. Nicholas P. Cushner, "Legazpi, 1564–1572," *Philippine Studies* 13, no. 2 (1965): 176–77.

115. Cushner, "Legazpi," 177.

116. Miguel Lopez de Legázpi, "Relation of the Voyage to the Philippine Islands, 1565," in *Philippine Islands 1493–1803*, ed. Emma Helen Blair and James Alexander Robertson, vol. 2, *1521–1569* (Cleveland, OH: A. H. Clark Company, 1903), 210.

117. Cushner, "Legazpi," 181.

118. Mitchell, *Friar Andres de Urdaneta*, 139.

119. "Copy of a Letter Sent from Sevilla to Miguel Salvador of Valencia," in *Philippine Islands 1493–1803*, ed. Emma Helen Blair and James Alexander Robertson, vol. 2, *1521–1569* (Cleveland, OH: A. H. Clark Company, 1903), 231.

120. Miguel Lopez de Legázpi, "Letters to Felipe II of Spain, 1567–68," in *Philippine Islands 1493–1803*, ed. Emma Helen Blair and James Alexander Robertson, vol. 2, *1521–1569* (Cleveland, OH: A. H. Clark Company, 1903), 238.

121. William Henry Scott, *Cracks in the Parchment Curtain and Other Essays in Philippine History* (Quezon City: New Day, 1985), 47.

122. Luis Alonso Alvarez, *El costo del imperio Asiático: La formación colonial de las islas Filipinas bajo dominio español, 1565–1800* (La Coruña: Universidade da Coruña, 2009), 92.

123. McCarthy, *Spanish Beginnings*, 88.

124. W. E. Retana, *Relación de la conquista de la Isla de Luzón* (Madrid: Viuda de M. Minuesa de los Ríos, 1898), 21.

125. Retana, *Relación de la conquista*, 21.

126. Quoted in Alonso Alvarez, *El costo del imperio Asiático*, 88.

127. Antonio Morga, *Sucesos de las Islas Filipinas* (Madrid: Ediciones Polifemo, 1997), 281.

128. Scott, *Barangay*, 244.

129. Retana, *Relación de la conquista*, 25.

130. Corpuz, *Roots*, 154.

131. Horacio de la Costa, *The Jesuits in the Philippines, 1581–1768* (Cambridge, MA: Harvard University Press, 1967), 315.

132. Quoted in Alonso Alvarez, *El costo del imperio Asiático*, 78.

133. Alonso Alvarez, *El costo del imperio Asiático*, 79.

134. Ana M. Prieto Lucena, *El contacto hispano-indígena en Filipinas según la historiografía de los siglos XVI y XVII* (Córdoba: Servicio de Publicaciones Universidad de Cordoba, 1993), 153.

Chapter 3. Spanish Settlement in the Philippines

1. Victor Lieberman, *Strange Parallels: Southeast Asia in Global Context, c. 800–1830*, vol. 2, *Mainland Mirrors: Europe, Japan, China, South Asia, and the Islands* (Cambridge: Cambridge University Press, 2009), 33.

2. John L. Phelan, *The Hispanization of the Philippines: Spanish Aims and Filipino Responses 1565–1700* (Madison: The University of Wisconsin Press, 1959), 8.

3. Luis Alonso Alvarez, *El costo del imperio Asiático: La formación colonial de las islas Filipinas bajo dominio español, 1565–1800* (La Coruña: Universidade da Coruña, 2009), 31.

4. Henry Kamen, *Empire: How Spain Became a World Power, 1492–1763* (New York: HarperCollins, 2003), 225.

5. Manel Ollé, *La empresa de China: De la armada invencible al galeón de Manila* (Barcelona: El Acantilado, 2002), 72.

6. Lewis Hanke, "Dos cartas al rey contra los moros de las Filipinas por el Lic. Melchor de Avalos (1585)," in *Cuerpo de documentos del siglo XVI: Sobre los derechos de España en las Indias y las Filipinas* (Mexico: Fondo de Cultura Económica, 1943), 72.

7. Santiago de Vera (1587), in Francisco Colín, *Labor evangélica, ministerios apostólicos de los obreros de la Compañia de Jesús*, vol. 2, ed. Pablo Pastells (Barcelona: Imprenta y Litografía de Henrich y Compañía, 1900), 354.

8. Colín, *Labor evangélica*, vol. 2, 356.

9. Colín, *Labor evangélica*, vol. 2, 354–56.

10. Colín, *Labor evangélica*, vol. 2, 444.

11. Colín, *Labor evangélica*, vol. 2, 438–44.

12. Horacio de la Costa, *The Jesuits in the Philippines, 1581–1768* (Cambridge, MA: Harvard University Press, 1961), 128.

13. José S. Arcilla, *An Introduction to Philippine History* (Manila: Ateneo de Manila University Press, 1998), 139–40.

14. Hernando de los Ríos Coronel, "Memorial on Navigation and Conquest," in *Philippine Islands 1493–1898*, ed. Emma Helen Blair and James Alexander Robertson, vol. 9, *1593–1597* (Cleveland, OH: A. H. Clark Company, 1904), 303.

15. Sanjay Subrahmanyam, *The Portuguese Empire in Asia, 1500–1700: A Political and Economic History* (London: Longman, 1993), 124–25.

16. Charles R. Boxer, *The Portuguese Seaborne Empire 1415–1825* (New York: Alfred A. Knopf, 1969), 261.

17. Gregorio F. Zaide, *Philippine Political and Cultural History*, vol. 1 (Manila: Philippine Education Company, 1972), 234–38.

18. In William L. Schurz, *The Manila Galleon* (New York: E. P. Dutton, 1959), 68.

19. Guido de Lavezaris, "Affairs in the Philippines after the Death of Legazpi," in *Philippine Islands 1493–1898*, ed. Emma Helen Blair and James Alexander Robertson, vol. 9, *1593–1597* (Cleveland, OH: A. H. Clark Company, 1909), 184.

20. Antonio Morga, *Sucesos de las Islas Filipinas*, ed. J. S. Cummins (Cambridge: Cambridge University Press, 1971), 254.

21. Pedro Chirino, "Relation of the Filipinas Islands and of What has There Been Accomplished by the Fathers of the Society of Jesus," in *Philippine Islands, 1493–1898*, ed. Emma Helen Blair and James Alexander Robertson, vol. 12, *1601–1604* (Cleveland, OH: A. H. Clark Company, 1904), 230.

22. Francisco Javier Campos y Fernandez Sevilla, "Las órdenes mendicantes en Filipinas: agustinos, franciscanos, dominicos y recoletos," in *España y el Pacífico: Legázpi*, ed. Leoncio Cabrero, vol. 2 (Madrid: Sociedad Estatal de Conmemoraciones Culturales, 2004), 271.

23. de la Costa, *Jesuits in the Philippines*, 558.

24. Benito J. Legarda, *After the Galleons: Foreign Trade, Economic Change and Entrepreneurship in Nineteenth-Century Philippines* (Madison: Center for Asian Studies University of Wisconsin-Madison, 1999), 34.

25. Peter Boomgaard, *Southeast Asia: An Environmental History* (Santa Barbara: ABC Clio, 2007), 121; Chirino, "Relation of the Filipinas Islands," 208.

26. Linda A. Newson, *Conquest and Pestilence in the Early Spanish Philippines* (Honolulu: University of Hawaii Press, 2009), 21.

27. Chirino, "Relation of the Filipinas Islands," 297.

28. Newson, *Conquest and Pestilence*, 22.

29. In Colín, *Labor evangélica*, vol. 2, 511.

30. Boomgaard, *Southeast Asia*, 121–22.

31. Newson, *Conquest and Pestilence*, 255, 258.

32. Newson, *Conquest and Pestilence*, 239.

33. William Henry Scott, *Barangay: Sixteenth-Century Philippine Culture and Society* (Quezon City: Ateneo de Manila University Press, 1994), 140.

34. Chirino, "Relation of the Filipinas Islands," 186.

35. Morga, *Sucesos* (1971), 263.

36. Morga, *Sucesos* (1971), 297–98.

37. Luis Angel Sánchez Gómez, "Las élites nativas y la construcción colonial de Filipinas (1565–1789)," in *España y el Pacífico: Legázpi*, vol. 2, ed. Leoncio Cabrero (Madrid: Sociedad Estatal de Conmemoraciones Culturales, 2004), 44.

38. Francisco Ignacio Alzina, *Una etnografía de los indios bisayas del siglo XVII*, bk. 3, ed. Victoria Yepes (Madrid: Consejo Superior de Investigaciones Científicas, 1996), 88; Scott, *Barangay*, 60.

39. Onofre D. Corpuz, *The Roots of the Filipino Nation*, vol. 1 (Quezon City: University of the Philippines Press, 2005), 17.

40. Alonso Alvarez, *El costo del imperio Asiático*, 36.

41. Phelan, *Hispanization*, 110.

42. Diego Aduarte, "Historia de la Provincia del Sancto Rosario de la Orden de Predicadores, Manila, 1640," in *Philippine Islands 1493–1898*, ed. Emma Helen Blair and James Alexander Robertson, vol. 32, *1640* (Cleveland, OH: A. H. Clark Company, 1905), 273.

43. Phelan, *Hispanization*, 46–49.

44. Aduarte, "Historia de la Provincia," 42–44.

45. Corpuz, *Roots*, 121.

46. Alonso Alvarez, *El costo del imperio Asiático*, 145–77.

47. Phelan, *Hispanization*, 33, 64.

48. Phelan, *Hispanization*, 33.

49. Thomas Gage, *Travels in the New World* (Norman: University of Oklahoma Press, 1958), 7.

50. Pedro Borges Morán, "Aspectos característicos de la evangelización en Filipinas (1521–1650)," in *España y el Pacífico: Legázpi*, vol. 2, ed. Leoncio Cabrero (Madrid: Sociedad Estatal de Conmemoraciones Culturales, 2004), 304.

51. Horacio de la Costa, "The Development of the Native Clergy in the Philippines," in *Studies in Philippine Church History*, ed. Gerald Anderson (Ithaca: Cornell University Press, 1969), 87.

52. Gage, *Travels*, 58.

53. Domingo Navarrete, *The Travels and Controversies of Friar Domingo Navarrete 1618–1686*, vol. 1 (Cambridge: Cambridge University Press, 1962), 38.

54. Gage, *Travels*, 107.

55. In de la Costa, *Jesuits in the Philippines*, 228–29.

56. Phelan, *Hispanization*, 43.

57. de la Costa, *Jesuits in the Philippines*, 232.

58. Phelan, *Hispanization*, 98, 104.

59. Fernando Palanco, "Resistencia y rebelión indígena durante los primeros cien años de soberanía Fernando española," in *España y el Pacífico: Legázpi*, vol. 2, ed. Leoncio Cabrero (Madrid: Sociedad Estatal de Conmemoraciones Culturales, 2004), 82.

60. de la Costa, *Jesuits in the Philippines*, 479, 480.

61. de la Costa, *Jesuits in the Philippines*, 250.

62. Guillaume Le Gentil, *A Voyage to the Indian Seas* (Manila: Filipiniana Book Guild, 1964), 50.

63. Antonio García-Abásolo, "Llegada de los españoles al Extremo Oriente," in *Gran historia universal*, vol. 27, *Descubrimiento y conquista de América* (Madrid: Club Internacional del Libro, 1986), 166.

64. Corpuz, *Roots*, 219.

65. Victor Lieberman, *Strange Parallels*, vol. 2, 834–36; Anthony Reid, *Southeast Asia in the Age of Commerce*, vol. 2, *Expansion and Crisis* (New Haven: Yale University Press, 1993), 157–61.

66. Alonso Alvarez, *El costo del imperio Asiático*, 170.

67. Alonso Alvarez, *El costo del imperio Asiático*, 192–201.

68. Navarrete, *Travels*, vol. 1, 92.

69. Navarrete, *Travels*, vol. 1, 123.

70. Leslie Bauzon, "Deficit Government: Mexico and the Philippine Situado (1606–1804)," unpublished PhD diss. (Duke University, 1970), 129.

71. Navarrete, *Travels*, vol. 2, 391.

72. Juan Grau y Monfalcón, "Informatory Memorial Addressed to the King, Madrid, 1637," in *Philippine Islands 1493–1898*, ed. Emma Helen Blair and James Alexander Robertson, vol. 27, *1636–1637* (Cleveland, OH: A. H. Clark Company, 1905), 139.

73. Bauzon, "Deficit Government," 158–59.

74. Bauzon, "Deficit Government," 193.

75. Bauzon, "Deficit Government," 92–93.

76. Jonathan I. Israel, *The Dutch Republic and the Hispanic World 1606–1661* (Oxford: Oxford University Press, 1982), 294–95.

77. García-Abásolo, "Llegada," 175; John L. Phelan, *The Kingdom of Quito in the Seventeenth Century: Bureaucratic Politics in the Spanish Empire* (Madison: The University of Wisconsin Press, 1967), 112.

78. Dennis Flynn and Arturo Giraldez, "Spanish Profitability in the Pacific: The Philippines in the Sixteenth and Seventeenth Centuries," in *Pacific Centuries: Pacific and Pacific Rim Histories Since the Sixteenth Century*, ed. Dennis Flynn, Lionel Frost, and A. J. H. Latham (New York: Routledge Press, 1999), 32.

79. Charles R. Boxer, *The Tragic History of the Sea 1589–1622* (Cambridge: Cambridge University Press, 1959), 17.

80. Jan De Vries, "Connecting Europe and Asia: A Quantitative Analysis of the Cape-route Trade, 1497–1795," in *Global Connections and Monetary History, 1470–1800*, ed. Flynn, Dennis, Arturo Giraldez, and Richard Von Glahn (Aldershot, UK: Ashgate, 2003), 42, 72, 76.

81. Holden Furber, *Rival Empires of Trade in the Orient 1600–1800* (Minneapolis: University of Minnesota Press, 1976), 300–1; Phelan, *Hispanization*, 98.

82. Boxer, *Portuguese Seaborne*, 19–20; Fernand Braudel, *The Perspective of the World*, vol. 3 (Berkeley: University of California Press, 1993), 488; Reid, *Southeast Asia*, 73; Subrahmanyam, *Portuguese Empire*, 222.

83. Kirti N. Chaudhuri, *The Trading World of Asia and the English East India Company, 1660–1760* (Cambridge: Cambridge University Press, 1978), 200.

84. de la Costa, *Jesuits in the Philippines*, 661.

85. Bartholomé de Letona, "Description of Filipinas Islands, 1662," in *Philippine Islands, 1493–1898*, ed. Emma Helen Blair and James Alexander Robertson, vol. 36, *1649–1666* (Cleveland, OH: A. H. Clark Company, 1906), 205.

86. Robert R. Reed, "The Colonial Origins of Manila and Batavia: Desultory Notes on Nascent Metropolitan Primacy and Urban Systems in Southeast Asia," *Asian Studies* 5, no. 3 (1967): 561.

87. Corpuz, *Roots*, 208.

88. Corpuz, *Roots*, 91.

89. de la Costa, *Jesuits in the Philippines*, 533.

90. Corpuz, *Roots*, 219.

91. Phelan, *Hispanization*, 102, 151.

Chapter 4. The Seventeenth Century

1. Brian Fagan, *The Little Ice Age: How Climate Made History 1300–1850* (New York: Basic Books, 2000), 105.

2. Victor Lieberman, *Strange Parallels: Southeast Asia in Global Context, c. 800–1830*, vol. 1, *Integration on the Mainland* (Cambridge: Cambridge University Press, 2003), 102.

3. Brian Fagan, *Little Ice Age*, 49. "Other authorities restrict the term 'Little Ice Age' to a period of much cooler conditions over much of the world between the late seventeenth century and mid-nineteenth centuries" (Fagan, *Little Ice Age*, 49–50).

4. David D. Zhang, Jane Zhang, Harry F. Lee, and Yuan-qing He, "Climate Change and War Frequency in Eastern China over the Last Millennium," *Human Ecology* 35, no. 4 (2007): 411, 414.

5. Zhang et al., "Climate Change and War Frequency."

6. Charles Mann, *1493: Uncovering the New World Columbus Created* (New York: Random House, 2011), 172.

7. Anthony Reid, "The Seventeenth-Century Crisis in Southeast Asia," *Modern Asian Studies* 24, no. 4 (1990): 654–57.

8. Casimiro Díaz, "The Augustinians in the Philippines, 1670–1694," in *Philippine Islands 1493–1898*, ed. Emma Helen Blair and James Alexander Robertson, vol. 42, *1670–1700* (Cleveland, OH: A. H. Clark Company, 1906), 234.

9. J. P. Geiss, "Peking under the Ming, 1368–1644" (PhD dissertation, Princeton University, 1979), 165.

10. Adam Smith, *An Inquiry into the Nature and Causes of the Wealth of Nations* (New York: Random House, 1937), 192.

11. Reid, "Seventeenth-Century Crisis," 657.

12. Geoffrey Parker, *Europe in Crisis: 1598–1648* (Oxford: Wiley-Blackwell, 1979), 188.

13. Charles R. Boxer, *The Portuguese Seaborne Empire 1415–1825* (New York: Alfred A. Knopf, 1969), 107.

14. Jonathan I. Israel, *The Dutch Republic: Its Rise, Greatness, and Fall 1477–1806* (Oxford: Oxford University Press, 1998), 315–17.

15. John Lynch, *Spain under the Habsburgs*, vol. 2, *Spain and America 1598–1700* (New York: Oxford University Press, 1969), 69.

16. Engel Sluiter, quoted in John L. Phelan, *The Kingdom of Quito in the Seventeenth Century: Bureaucratic Politics in the Spanish Empire* (Madison: The University of Wisconsin Press, 1967), 89.

17. In Henry Kamen, *Empire: How Spain Became a World Power, 1492–1763* (New York: HarperCollins, 2003), 286; John Mun, "England's Treasure by Forraign Trade: or, The Ballance of our Forraign Trade is the Rule of our Treasure," in *A Select Collection of Early English Tracts on Commerce, from the Originals of Mun, Roberts, North, and Other*, ed. John Ramsay McCulloch (London: Political Economy Club, 1856).

18. M. A. P. Meilink-Roelofsz, *Asian Trade and European Influence in the Indonesian Archipelago between 1500 and about 1630* (The Hague: Martinus Nijhoff, 1962), 263.

19. In William L. Schurz, *The Manila Galleon* (New York: E. P. Dutton, 1959), 351.

20. Meilink-Roelofsz, *Asian Trade*, 268.

21. Berthold Laufer, "The Relations of the Chinese to the Philippine Islands," *Smithsonian Institution, Miscellaneous Collections* 50, no. 13 (1907): 278n1.

22. J. H. Elliott, *The Count-Duke of Olivares: The Statesman in an Age of Decline* (New Haven: Yale University Press, 1986), 301, 303.

23. Sebastián de Pineda, "Philippine Ships and Shipbuilding," in *Philippine Islands, 1493–1898*, ed. Emma Helen Blair and James Alexander Robertson, vol. 18, *1617–1620* (Cleveland, OH: A. H. Clark Company, 1904), 174–75.

24. Pineda, "Philippine Ships."

25. Francisco Colín, *Labor evangélica, ministerios apostólicos de los obreros de la Compañía de Jesús*, ed. Pablo Pastells, vol. 3 (Barcelona: Imprenta y Litografía de Henrich y Compañía, 1900), 158–59; Hernando de los Ríos Coronel, "Reforms needed in Filipinas," in *Philippine Islands, 1493–1898*, ed. by Emma Helen Blair and James Alexander Robertson, vol. 18, *1617–1620* (Cleveland, OH: A. H. Clark Company, 1904), 309.

26. Horacio de la Costa, *The Jesuits in the Philippines, 1581–1768* (Cambridge, MA: Harvard University Press, 1961), 344.

27. de la Costa, *Jesuits in the Philippines*, 414.

28. Onofre D. Corpuz, *The Roots of the Filipino Nation* (Quezon City: University of the Philippines Press, 2005), 148; de la Costa, *Jesuits in the Philippines*, 141.

29. Corpuz, *Roots of the Filipino Nation*, 149; John L. Phelan, *The Hispanization of the Philippines: Spanish Aims and Filipino Responses 1565–1700* (Madison: The University of Wisconsin Press, 1959), 146.

30. Corpuz, *Roots of the Filipino Nation*, 619.

31. Antonio Morga, *Sucesos de las Islas Filipinas*, ed. J. S. Cummins (Cambridge: Cambridge University Press, 1971), 281.

32. William Henry Scott, *Cracks in the Parchment Curtain* (Quezon City: New Day, 1965), 46.

33. Morga, *Sucesos* (1971), 61.

34. Isacio Rodríguez Rodríguez, "El asentamiento: la fundación de Manila," in *España y el pacífico*, ed. Leoncio Cabrero Fernández, vol. 1 (Madrid: Sociedad Estatal de Conmemoraciones Culturales, 2004), 307–9.

35. Juan de Ronquillo, "The Pacification of Mindanao, 1597," in *Philippine Islands 1493–1898*, ed. Emma Helen Blair and James Alexander Robertson, vol. 9, *1593–1597* (Cleveland, OH: A. H. Clark Company, 1904), 290.

36. de la Costa, *Jesuits in the Philippines*, 300.

37. In Scott, *Cracks in the Parchment Curtain*, 72.

38. Ronquillo, "Pacification of Mindanao," 287.

39. de la Costa, *Jesuits in the Philippines*, 279.

40. de la Costa, *Jesuits in the Philippines*, 312.

41. Morga, *Sucesos* (1971), 263.

42. Jeronimo de Jesús (1595), in Juan Gil, *Hidalgos y samuráis: España y Japón en los siglos XVI y XVII* (Madrid: Alianza Editorial, 1991), 62.

43. Gil, *Hidalgos y samurais*, 106.

44. Charles R. Boxer, *The Christian Century in Japan, 1549–1650* (Berkeley: University of California Press, 1967), 158.

45. Michael Cooper, *Rodrigues the Interpreter and Early Jesuit in Japan and China* (New York: Weatherhill, 1974), 71.

46. Cooper, *Rodrigues the Interpreter*, 127.

47. Cooper, *Rodrigues the Interpreter*, 144.

48. Cooper, *Rodrigues the Interpreter*.

49. Cooper, *Rodrigues the Interpreter*, 161.

50. Gil, *Hidalgos y samurais*, 90–93, 95.

51. Boxer, *Christian Century*, 264.

52. Gil, *Hidalgos y samurais*, 63, 101.

53. Gil, *Hidalgos y samurais*, 120–21.

54. Gil, *Hidalgos y samurais*, 122–24.

55. Boxer, *Christian Century*, 302.

56. Gil, *Hidalgos y samurais*, 150–51.

57. Gil, *Hidalgos y samurais*, 178, 186–89.

58. Gil, *Hidalgos y samurais*, 231.

59. Morga, *Sucesos* (1971), 194.

60. Gil, *Hidalgos y samurais*, 269–70.

61. Boxer, *Christian Century*, 303.

62. Gil, *Hidalgos y samurais*, 400.

63. Cooper, *Rodrigues the Interpreter*, 140.

64. Boxer, *Christian Century*, 320, 368.

65. Gil, *Hidalgos y samurais*, 446, 447.

66. Gil, *Hidalgos y samurais*, 452.

67. James Murdoch and Isoh Yamagata, *A History of Japan* (London: K. Paul, Trench, Trubner, 1949), 624.

68. Morga, *Sucesos* (1971), 308–9.

69. Joseph de Navada Alvarado, "Discussion Regarding Portuguese Trade at Manila, 1632–36," in *Philippine Islands, 1493–1898*, ed. Emma Helen Blair and James Alexander Robertson, vol. 25, *1635–1636* (Cleveland, OH: A. H. Clark Company, 1905), 117, 119, 120.

70. Schurz, *Manila Galleon*, 133.

71. Vitorino Magalhães Godinho, *Os descobrimentos e a economia mundial*, vol. 1 (Lisbon: Editorial Presença, 1984), 133.

72. Han-sheng Chuan, "The Inflow of American Silver into China from the Late Ming to the Mid-Ch'ing Period," *Journal of the Institute of Chinese Studies of the Chinese University of Hong Kong* 2 (1969), 109.

73. M. N. Pearson, "Spain and Spanish Trade in Southeast Asia," *Journal of Asian History* 2, no. 2 (1968): 115.

74. Felipe Fernández-Armesto, *Pathfinders: A Global History of Exploration* (New York: W. W. Norton & Company, 2006), 212.

75. Israel, *Dutch Republic*, 319.

76. Joan de Ribera, "Filipinas Menaced by Dutch, 1618," in *Philippine Islands, 1493–1898*, ed. Emma Helen Blair and James Alexander Robertson, vol. 18, *1617–1620* (Cleveland, OH: A. H. Clark Company, 1904), 162.

77. Schurz, *Manila Galleon*, 142.

78. John Villiers, "Manila and Maluku: Trade and Warfare in the Eastern Archipelago 1580–1640," *Philippine Studies* 34 (1986): 155.

79. Sanjay Subrahmanyam, *The Portuguese Empire in Asia, 1500–1700: A Political and Economic History* (London: Longman, 1993), 214.

80. Holden Furber, *Rival Empires of Trade in the Orient 1600–1800* (Minneapolis: University of Minnesota Press, 1976), 271.

81. Vera Valdés Lakowsky, *De las minas al mar: Historía de la plata mexicana en Asia, 1565–1834* (México: Fondo de Cultura Económica, 1987), 148.

82. W. E. Cheong, "Changing the Rules of the Game (The India-Manila Trade 1785–1809)," *Journal of Southeast Asian Studies* 1, no. 2 (1970): 6.

83. Serafín D. Quiason, *English Country Trade with the Philippines, 1644–1765* (Quezon City: University of the Philippines Press, 1966), 93.

84. Subrahmanyam, *Portuguese Empire*, 117.

85. Jonathan I. Israel, *European Jewry in the Age of Mercantilism 1550–1750* (Portland: The Littman Library of Jewish Civilization, 1998), 92, 128.

86. Israel, *European Jewry*, 101, 102.

87. James C. Boyajian, *Portuguese Trade in Asia under the Habsburgs, 1580–1640* (Baltimore: The Johns Hopkins University Press, 1993), 76–81, 239–40.

88. Subrahmanyam, *Portuguese Empire*, 119; documents in José Toribio Medina, *Historia del tribunal de la Inquisición de Lima: 1569–1820*, vol. 2 (Santiago de Chile: Fondo Histórico y Bibliográfico José Toribio Medina, 1956), 45–71.

89. Pierre Chaunu, *Les Philippines et le Pacifique des Ibériques (XVI, XVII, XVIII siècles)* (Paris: S. E. V. P. E. N., 1960), 250.

90. Inmaculada Alva Rodríguez, *Vida municipal en Manila (Siglos XVI–XVII)* (Córdoba: Universidad de Córdoba, 1997), 366.

91. Schurz, *Manila Galleon*, 260.

92. Chaunu, *Les Philippines et le Pacifique*, 254–55.

Chapter 5. The Galleons

1. This chapter follows Shirley Fish, *The Manila-Acapulco Galleons: The Treasure Ships of the Pacific* (Central Milton Keynes, UK: AuthorHouseUK, 2011); Pablo E. Pérez-Mallaína, *Spain's Men of the Sea: Daily Life on the Indies Fleets in the Sixteenth Century* (Baltimore: The Johns Hopkins University Press, 1998); William L. Schurz, *The Manila Galleon* (New York: E. P. Dutton, 1959).

2. Gemelli G. Careri, *A Voyage to the Philippines: And an Appendix of the Chapters on the Philippines in the Travels of Fray Sebastián Manrique* (Manila: Filipiniana Book Guild, 1963), 131.

3. Charles R. Boxer, *The Tragic History of the Sea 1589–1622* (Cambridge: Cambridge University Press, 1959), 1.

4. Charles R. Boxer, *The Portuguese Seaborne Empire 1415–1825* (New York: Alfred A. Knopf, 1969), 205.

5. Carla Rahn Phillips, *The Short Life of an Unlucky Spanish Galleon: Los Tres Reyes 1628–1634* (Minneapolis: University of Minnesota Press, 1990), 26.

6. Hernando de los Ríos Coronel, "Reforms needed in Filipinas," in *Philippine Islands, 1493–1898*, ed. Emma Helen Blair and James Alexander Robertson, vol. 18, *1617–1620* (Cleveland, OH: A. H. Clark Company, 1904), 288.

7. Fish, *Manila-Acapulco Galleons*, 408–9.

8. Pérez-Mallaína, *Spain's Men of the Sea*, 140.

9. François Pyrard, *The Voyage of François Pyrard of Laval to the East Indies*, vol. 2 (London: Hakluyt Society, 1887–88), 196; Charles R. Boxer, *The Dutch Seaborne Empire: 1600–1800* (New York: Alfred A. Knopf, 1965), 76.

10. Fish, *Manila-Acapulco Galleons*, 409.

11. Pérez-Mallaína, *Spain's Men of the Sea*, 72.

12. Boxer, *Dutch Seaborne Empire*, 166.

13. Carlo M. Cipolla, *Guns, Sails and Empires: Technological Innovations and the Early Phases of European Expansion 1400–1700* (New York: Pantheon Books, 1965), 137.

14. Pérez-Mallaína, *Spain's Men of the Sea*, 63.

15. Schurz, *Manila Galleon*, Chapter 5.

16. Pérez-Mallaína, *Spain's Men of the Sea*, 66.

17. Boxer, *Portuguese Seaborne Empire*, 208; Kirti N. Chaudhuri, *The English East India Company: The Study of an Early Joint-Stock Company, 1600–1640* (London: F. Cass, 1965), 95.

18. David F. Marley, "The Great Galleon: The Santísima Trinidad (1750–1765)," *Philippine Studies* 41, no. 2 (1993): 180.

19. Oskar H. K. Spate, *The Spanish Lake* (Minneapolis: University of Minnesota, 1979), 20.

20. Fish, *Manila-Acapulco Galleons*, 162, 166.

21. Frederick L. Wernstedt and J. E. Spencer, *The Philippine Island World: A Physical, Cultural, and Regional Geography* (Berkeley: University of California Press, 1967), 87.

22. Domingo Navarrete, *The Travels and Controversies of Friar Domingo Navarrete 1618–1686*, vol. 1 (Cambridge: Cambridge University Press, 1962), 90–91.

23. Sebastián de Pineda, "Philippine Ships and Shipbuilding," in *Philippine Islands, 1493–1898*, ed. Emma Helen Blair and James Alexander Robertson, vol. 18, *1617–1620* (Cleveland, OH: A. H. Clark Company, 1904), 160–2.

24. Pineda, "Philippine Ships and Shipbuilding," 164.

25. Fish, *Manila-Acapulco Galleons*, 167.

26. Pineda, "Philippine Ships and Shipbuilding," 169.

27. Pineda, "Philippine Ships and Shipbuilding," 167.

28. Onofre D. Corpuz, *The Roots of the Filipino Nation* (Quezon City: University of the Philippines Press, 2005), 108.

29. Guillaume Le Gentil, *A Voyage to the Indian Seas* (Manila: Filipiniana Book Guild, 1964), 159, 167–71.

30. Le Gentil, *A Voyage to the Indian Seas*, 159.

31. Spate, *Spanish Lake*, 105.

32. Schurz, *Manila Galleon*, 221.

33. Le Gentil, *Voyage to the Indian Seas*, 163.

34. Joseph de Acosta, *The Natural and Moral History of the Indies*, vol. 1 (New York: Burt Franklin, 1970), 116.

35. Casimiro Díaz, "The Augustinians in the Philippines, 1670–1694," in *Philippine Islands 1493–1898*, ed. Emma Helen Blair and James Alexander Robertson, vol. 42, *1670–1700* (Cleveland, OH: A. H. Clark Company, 1906), 205.

36. "Glossary of Meteorology: Monsoon Trough," American Meteorological Society, last modified January 26, 2012, accessed February 1, 2013, http://glossary. ametsoc.org/wiki/Monsoon_trough.

37. Celia Martin-Puertas et al., "Regional Atmospheric Circulation Shifts Induced by a Grand Solar Minimum," *Nature Geoscience* 5 (2012): 397.

38. Miguel Selga, *Charts of Remarkable Typhoons in the Philippines, 1902–1934: Catalogue of Typhoons 1348–1934* (Manila: Bureau of Printing, 1935), 16, 28, 34.

39. Casimiro Díaz, *Conquistas de las Islas Filipinas: Parte Segunda* (Valladolid: De Gaviria, 1890), 38.

40. Pedro Cubero Sebastián, *Peregrinación del Mundo* (Madrid: Ediciones Polifemo, 1993), 340.

41. Boxer, *Dutch Seaborne Empire*, 244.

42. Boxer, *Tragic History of the Sea*, 24–29.

43. Schurz, *Manila Galleon*, 261.

44. Richard Walter, *A Voyage Round the World in the Years 1740, 41, 42, 42, 44* (London: n. p., 1818), 75.

45. Boxer, *Dutch Seaborne Empire*, 107.

46. Cubero Sebastián, *Peregrinación del Mundo*, 342.

47. Schurz, *Manila Galleon*, 266.

48. Pyrard, *The Voyage of François Pyrard of Laval*, vol. 2, 9, 11–12.

49. Boxer, *Dutch Seaborne Empire*, 243; Femme S. Gaastra, *The Dutch East India Company: Expansion and Decline* (Leiden: Walburg Press, 2003), 87.

50. Careri, *Voyage to the Philippines*, 127.

51. Careri, *Voyage to the Philippines*, 15.

52. Careri, *Voyage to the Philippines*, 156.

53. Careri, *Voyage to the Philippines*, 156.

54. Horacio de la Costa, *The Jesuits in the Philippines, 1581–1768* (Cambridge, MA: Harvard University Press, 1961), 229.

55. Careri, *A Voyage to the Philippines*, 229–30.

56. Fish, *Manila-Acapulco Galleons*, 415.

57. Careri, *A Voyage to the Philippines*, 230.

58. Pérez-Mallaína, *Spain's Men of the Sea*, 132.

59. de la Costa, *Jesuits in the Philippines*, 589–91.

60. de los Ríos Coronel, "Reforms needed in Filipinas," 288–89.

61. Boxer, *Tragic History of the Sea*, 20–21.

62. Francesco Carletti, *My Voyage Around the World* (New York: Pantheon Books, 1964).

63. Schurz, *Manila Galleon*, 272.

64. Navarrete, *Travels and Controversies*, vol. 1, 91; Pérez-Mallaína, *Spain's Men of the Sea*, 155.

65. Navarrete, *Travels and Controversies*, vol. 1, 46.

66. Fish, *Manila-Acapulco Galleons*, 463.

67. Schurz, *Manila Galleon*, 272.

68. Díaz, *Conquistas de las Islas Filipinas*, 200, 273.

69. Schurz, *Manila Galleon*, 282.

70. Navarrete, *Travels and Controversies*, vol. 2, 390.

71. de la Costa, *Jesuits in the Philippines*, 9.

72. Pérez-Mallaína, *Spain's Men of the Sea*, 76–77.

73. Schurz, *Manila Galleon*, 205.

74. John Hawkins, *Hawkins' Voyages* (London: The Hakluyt Society, 1878), 164–65.

75. Pyrard, *Voyage of François Pyrard of Laval*, vol. 2, 186.

76. Gaastra, *Dutch East India Company*, 91.

77. Boxer, *Dutch Seaborne Empire*, 70; Boxer, *Portuguese Seaborne Empire*, 213.

78. Fish, *Manila-Acapulco Galleons*, 310.

79. Fish, *Manila-Acapulco Galleons*, 318.

80. de los Ríos Coronel, "Reforms needed in the Philippines," 286–87.

81. Francisco Leandro de Viana,"Demonstración de misero deplorable estado de las Islad Philippinas, 1765," in *Philippine Islands, 1493–1898*, ed. Emma Helen Blair and James Alexander Robertson, vol. 48, *1751–1765* (Cleveland, OH: A. H. Clark Company, 1907), 301.

82. Gaastra, *Dutch East India Company*, 87.

83. Santiago de Vera, "Letter from Santiago de Vera to Philip II, 1589," in *Philippine Islands, 1493–1898*, ed. Emma Helen Blair and James Alexander Robertson, vol. 7, *1588–1591* (Cleveland, OH: A. H. Clark Company, 1903), 87.

84. Sebastián Hurtado de Corcuera, "Letters to Philip IV," in *Philippine Islands, 1493–1898*, ed. Emma Helen Blair and James Alexander Robertson, vol. 26, *1636* (Cleveland, OH: A. H. Clark Company, 1905), 194. One cavan was approximately 44 kgs; one cavan had 25 gantas; if rice had been husked, the cavan was equivalent to 56 kgs.

85. Charles Mann, *1493: Uncovering the New World Columbus Created* (New York: Random House, 2011), 323.

86. Gemelli G. Careri, *Viaje a la Nueva España: México a fines del siglo XVII*, vol. 1 (México: Ediciones Libro-Mex, 1955), 25, 31.

87. Careri, *Voyage to the Philippines*, 160.

88. Careri, *Voyage to the Philippines*, 169.

89. Careri, *Voyage to the Philippines*, 156, 172.

90. Navarrete, *Travels and Controversies*, 38–39, 43.

91. Fish, *Manila-Acapulco Galleons*, 433; Carletti, *My Voyage around the World*, 57.

92. Careri, *Viaje a la Nueva España*, vol. 1, 25–35.

93. Schurz, *Manila Galleon*, 364.

Chapter 6. The Economy of the Line

1. Frank Spooner, *The International Economy and Monetary Movements in France, 1493–1725* (Cambridge: Harvard University Press, 1972), 26, 45.

2. Juan Grau y Monfalcón, "Informatory Memorial Addressed to the King, Madrid, 1637," in *Philippine Islands 1493–1898*, ed. Emma Helen Blair and James Alexander Robertson, vol. 27, *1636–1637* (Cleveland, OH: A. H. Clark Company, 1905), 88.

3. Kirti N. Chaudhuri, *The English East India Company: The Study of an Early Joint-Stock Company, 1600–1640* (London: F. Cass, 1965), 135.

4. Han-sheng Chuan, "The Inflow of American Silver into China from the Late Ming to the Mid-Ch'ing Period," *Journal of the Institute of Chinese Studies of the Chinese University of Hong Kong* 2 (1969): 2.

5. Richard Von Glahn, *Fountain of Fortune: Money and Monetary Policy in China, 1000–1700* (Berkeley: University of California Press, 1996), 214.

6. Quoted in Charles R. Boxer, "Plata es Sangre: Sidelights on the Drain of Spanish-American Silver in the Far East, 1550–1700," *Philippine Studies* 18 (1970): 461.

7. Dennis Flynn and Arturo Giraldez, "Cycles of Silver: Globalization as Historical Process," *World Economics* 3, no. 2 (2002): 7.

8. Benito J. Legarda, *After the Galleons: Foreign Trade, Economic Change and Entrepreneurship in Nineteenth-Century Philippines* (Madison: Center for Asian Studies University of Wisconsin-Madison, 1999), 31.

9. Guillaume Raynal, "L'Histoire philosophique et politique des établissements et du commerce des Européens dans les deux Indes," in *Travel Accounts of the Islands (1513–1787)* (Manila: Filipiniana Book Guild, 1971), 205.

10. Raynal, "L'Histoire philosophique," 208.

11. William L. Schurz, *The Manila Galleon* (New York: E. P. Dutton, 1959), 33; Antonio Morga, *Sucesos de las Islas Filipinas*, ed. J. S. Cummins (Cambridge: Cambridge University Press, 1971), 2, 298.

12. Gregorio F. Zaide, *Philippine Political and Cultural History*, vol. 1 (Manila: Philippine Education Company, 1957), 490.

13. Hernando Riquel, "News from the Western Islands by Hernando Riquel and Others," in *Philippine Islands 1493–1803*, ed. Emma Helen Blair and James Alexander Robertson, vol. 3, *1569–1576* (Cleveland, OH: A. H. Clark Company, 1903), 247–49.

14. Benito J. Legarda, *After the Galleons: Foreign Trade, Economic Change and Entrepreneurship in Nineteenth-Century Philippines* (Madison: Center for Asian Studies University of Wisconsin-Madison, 1999), 43.

15. Casimiro Díaz, "The Augustinians in the Philippines, 1670–1694," in *Philippine Islands 1493–1898*, ed. Emma Helen Blair and James Alexander Robertson, vol. 42, *1670–1700* (Cleveland, OH: A. H. Clark Company, 1906), 206.

16. Vera Valdés Lakowsky, *De las minas al mar: Historia de la plata mexicana en Asia, 1565–1834* (México: Fondo de Cultura Económica, 1987), 94.

17. Morga, *Sucesos*, 136–41.

18. Schurz, *Manila Galleon*, 83.

19. Horacio de la Costa, *The Jesuits in the Philippines, 1581–1768* (Cambridge, MA: Harvard University Press, 1961), 132.

20. Legarda, *After the Galleons*, 43.

21. Schurz, *Manila Galleon*, 171.

22. Valdés Lakowsky, *De las minas al mar*, 84.

23. Díaz, "Augustinians in the Philippines," 203.

24. "Letter from the Manila Audiencia to Felipe II," in *Philippine Islands 1493–1898*, ed. Emma Helen Blair and James Alexander Robertson, vol. 6, *1583–1588* (Cleveland, OH: A. H. Clark Company, 1903), 311–12.

25. "Copy of Letter from London [1569]," in *Calendar of State Papers, Spain (Simancas)*, ed. Martin A. S. Hume, vol. 4, *1587–1603*. British History Online, 481. Accessed December 22, 2012. http://www.british-history.ac.uk/report.aspx?compid=87201

26. Chuan, "The Inflow of American Silver," 114.

27. Woodrow Borah, *Silk Raising in Colonial Mexico* (Berkeley: University of California Press, 1943), 97.

28. Woodrow Borah, *Early Colonial Trade and Navigation between Mexico and Peru* (Berkeley: University of California Press, 1954), 122.

29. Schurz, *Manila Galleon*, 366, 370.

30. Grau y Monfalcón, "Informatory Memorial," 88, 148–50.

31. Legarda, *After the Galleons*, 42.

32. Borah, *Early Colonial Trade*, 114.

33. Jonathan I. Israel, *Race, Class and Politics in Colonial Mexico 1610–1670* (Oxford: Oxford University Press, 1975), 192.

34. Borah, *Early Colonial Trade*, 123.

35. Israel, *Race, Class and Politics*, 101.

36. Schurz, *Manila Galleon*, 190.

37. Pierre Chaunu, *Les Philippines et le Pacifique des Ibériques (XVI, XVII, XVIII siècles)* (Paris: S. E. V. P. E. N., 1960), 269; Louisa S. Hoberman, "Merchants in Seventeenth-Century Mexico City: A Preliminary Portrait," *Hispanic American Historical Review* 57, no. 3 (1977): 493.

38. Chuan, "Inflow of American Silver"; Hoberman, "Merchants in Seventeenth-Century Mexico City," 219; Mariano Ardash Bonialian, *El Pacífico hispanoamericano: Política y comercio asiático en el Imperio Español (1680–1784), La centralidad de lo marginal* (México: El Colegio de México, 2012), 215.

39. Bonialian, *El Pacífico hispanoamericano*, 267, 279.

40. Kirti N. Chaudhuri, *The Trading World of Asia and the English East India Company, 1660–1760* (Cambridge: Cambridge University Press, 1978), 155.

41. Thomas Gage, *Travels in the New World* (Norman: University of Oklahoma Press, 1958), 77.

42. Gemelli G. Careri, *Viaje a la Nueva España: México a fines del siglo XVII*, vol. 1 (México: Ediciones Libro-Mex, 1955), 28.

43. Bonialian, *El Pacífico hispanoamericano*, 214; Guillermina Del Valle Pavón, "Los mercaderes de México y la transgresión de los límites al Comercio Pacífico en Nueva España," *Revista de historia económica*, Número Extraordinario. *La economía en tiempos de Don Quijote*, 2005: 236; Schurz, *Manila Galleon*, 188.

44. Schurz, *Manila Galleon*, 159.

45. Oskar H. K. Spate, *The Spanish Lake* (Minneapolis: University of Minnesota, 1979), 161.

46. Bonialian, *El Pacífico hispanoamericano*, 214.

47. Legarda, *After the Galleons*, 41; Schurz, *Manila Galleon*, 188.

48. Del Valle Pavón, "Los mercaderes de México," 236.

49. Charles R. Boxer, *The Portuguese Seaborne Empire 1415–1825* (New York: Alfred A. Knopf, 1969), 336.

50. Holden Furber, *Rival Empires of Trade in the Orient 1600–1800* (Minneapolis: University of Minnesota Press, 1976), 336.

51. William M. Mathers, "Nuestra Señora de la Concepción," *National Geographic* 178, no. 3 (1990): 40.

52. Israel, *Race, Class and Politics*, 45.

53. Israel, *Race, Class and Politics*, 180.

54. Israel, *Race, Class and Politics*, 185; José Carlos Chiaramonte, "En torno a la recuperación demográfica y la depresión económica novohispanas durante el siglo XVII," *Historia Mexicana* 30, no. 4 (1981): 593.

55. Israel, *Race, Class and Politics*, 192.

56. Israel, *Race, Class and Politics*, 193.

57. Schurz, *Manila Galleon*, 188.

58. José Montero y Vidal, *Historia general de Filipinas*, vol. 1 (Madrid: Est. Tip. Viuda e Hijos de Tello, 1887), 452.

59. Mathers, "Nuestra Señora de la Concepción," 40.

60. Timothy Brook, "Communications and Commerce," in *The Cambridge History of China*, vol. 8, bk. 2, *The Ming Dynasty, 1368–1644* (Cambridge: Cambridge University Press, 1998), 164.

61. Deng, *Chinese Maritime Activities*, 147–48.

62. In Zaide, *Philippine Political and Cultural History*, 270.

63. Gang Deng, *Chinese Maritime Activities and Socioeconomic Development c. 2100 B.C.–1900 A.D.* (Westport, CT: Greenwood Press, 1997), 110.

64. Brook, "Communications and Commerce," 698.

65. de la Costa, *Jesuits in the Philippines*, 206–7.

66. Onofre D. Corpuz, *The Roots of the Filipino Nation* (Quezon City: University of the Philippines Press, 2005), 305.

67. Schurz, *Manila Galleon*, 82.

68. Schurz, *Manila Galleon*, 71.

69. M. N. Pearson, "Spain and Spanish Trade in Southeast Asia," *Journal of Asian History* 2, no. 2 (1968): 114; Schurz, *Manila Galleon*, 71.

70. Hieronimo Bañuelos y Carrillo, "Relations of the Filipinas Islands (1638)," in *Philippine Islands 1493–1898*, vol. 29, ed. Emma Helen Blair and James Alexander Robertson, *1638–1640* (Cleveland, OH: A. H. Clark Company, 1905), 69–70.

71. Brook, "Communications and Commerce," 698.

72. Brook, "Communications and Commerce," 698.

73. de la Costa, *Jesuits in the Philippines*, 203–4.

74. Bartolomé Leonardo de Argensola, *The Discovery and Conquest of the Moluccas and Philippine Islands* (London: n. p., 1708), 219–26; de la Costa, *Jesuits in the Philippines*, 208.

75. de Argensola, *Discovery and Conquest*, 217.

76. Francisco Colín, *Labor evangélica, ministerios apostólicos de los obreros de la Compañía de Jesús*, ed. Leoncio Cabrero, vol. 2 (Barcelona: Imprenta y Litografía de Henrich y Compañía, 1900), 438.

77. de Argensola, *Discovery and Conquest*, 219–26.

78. Tellez de Almazán, "Relacion," in *Labor evangelica*, ed. Pablo Pastells (Barcelona: Imprenta y Litografia de Henrich y Compañía, 1902), 427.

79. de Argensola, *Discovery and Conquest*, 219–26; de la Costa, *Jesuits in the Philippines*, 219–26.

80. In Schurz, *Manila Galleon*, 91.

81. Berthold Laufer, "The Relations of the Chinese to the Philippine Islands," *Smithsonian Institution, Miscellaneous Collections* 50, no. 13 (1907): 272.

82. "Relation of the Insurrection of the Chinese," in *Philippine Islands 1493–1803*, vol. 29, ed. Emma Helen Blair and James Alexander Robertson (Cleveland, OH: A. H. Clark Company, 1909), 208n50.

83. Juan Lopez, "Events in the Filipinas Islands from August, 1639, to August, 1640," in *Philippine Islands 1493–1898*, ed. Emma Helen Blair and James Alexander Robertson, vol. 29, *1638–1640* (Cleveland, OH: A. H. Clark Company, 1905), 194–95.

84. Joseph de Navada Alvarado, "Discussion Regarding Portuguese Trade at Manila, 1632–36," in *Philippine Islands, 1493–1898*, ed. Emma Helen Blair and James Alexander Robertson, vol. 25, *1635–1636* (Cleveland, OH: A. H. Clark Company, 1905), 135.

85. George B. Souza, *The Survival of the Empire: Portuguese Trade and Society in China and the South China Sea, 1630–1754* (Cambridge: Cambridge University Press, 2004), 81.

86. "Relation of the Insurrection of the Chinese," 209.

87. Joaquín Martínez de Zúñiga and W. E. Retana, "Tomo Primero" and "Relación verdadera del levantamiento de los sangleys . . . el año pasado de 1640 y 1641," in *Estadismo de las Islas Filipinas ó Mis viajes por este país*, Apendix A (Madrid: Imprenta de la Viuda de M. Minuesa de los Rios, 1893), 50.

88. "Relation of the Insurrection of the Chinese," 202.

89. "Relation of the Insurrection of the Chinese," 249–50.

90. "Relation of the Insurrection of the Chinese," 250.

91. "Relation of the Insurrection of the Chinese," 222, 224, 226.

92. "Relation of the Insurrection of the Chinese," 222.

93. Joaquín Martínez de Zuñiga, *An Historical View of the Philippine Islands* (Manila: Filipiniana Book Guild, 1966), 50.

94. "Relation of the Insurrection of the Chinese," 253, 255.

95. Joaquín Martínez de Zuñiga, *An Historical View of the Philippine Islands* (Manila: Filipiniana Book Guild, 1966), 108.

96. de la Costa, Jesuits in the Philippines, 392; Zaide, Philippine Political and Cultural History, vol. 1, 281; Hubert S. C. Liao, *Chinese Participation in Philippine Culture and Economy* (Manila: Bookman, 1964), 26; Díaz, Conquistas de las Islas Filipinas, 287.

97. Zuñiga, *Historical View*, 54.

98. Deng, *Chinese Maritime Activities*, 148.

99. de la Costa, *Jesuits in the Philippines*, 392.

100. Inmaculada Alva Rodríguez, *Vida municipal en Manila (Siglos XVI–XVII)* (Córdoba: Universidad de Córdoba, 1997), 70–72.

101. Furber, *Rival Empires of Trade*, 142.

Chapter 7. The Eighteenth Century and the Galleon Line

1. Ping-ti Ho, *Studies on the Population of China, 1368–1953* (Cambridge: Harvard University Press, 1959), 193; Jonathan D. Spence, *The Search for Modern China* (New York: W. W. Norton & Company, 1990), 95.

2. Spence, *Chinese Roundabout*, 231, 233.

3. Ho, *Studies on the Population of China*, 2.

4. Sucheta Mazumdar, "The Impact of New World Food Crops on the Diet and Economy of China and India, 1600–1990," in *Food in Global History*, ed. Raymond Grew (Boulder: Westview Press, 1999), 62, 70.

5. John K. Fairbank, ed., *The Cambridge History of China*, vol. 10, part 1, *Late Ch'ing, 1800–1911* (Cambridge: Cambridge University Press, 1978), 35.

6. J. R. McNeill and William H. McNeill, *The Human Web: A Bird's-Eye View of World History* (New York: W. W. Norton & Company, 2003), 211.

7. McNeill and McNeill, *The Human Web*, 211.

8. F. W. Mote, *Imperial China 900–1800* (Cambridge: Harvard University Press, 1999), 941.

9. William H. McNeill, *The Pursuit of Power: Technology, Armed Force, and Society since A.D. 1000* (Chicago: The University of Chicago Press, 1982), 214–15.

10. Peter C. Perdue, *China Marches West: The Qing Conquest of Central Eurasia* (Cambridge, MA: Harvard University Press, 2005), 561.

11. John R. Fisher, "Mining and Imperial Trade in 18th-Century Spanish America," in *Monetary History in Global Perspective, 1500–1808: B6 Proceedings, Twelfth*

International Economic History Congress, ed. Clara Eugenia Núñez (Sevilla: Universidad de Sevilla, 1998).

12. Mark A. Burkholder and Lyman L. Johnson, *Colonial Latin America* (New York: Oxford University Press, 1988), 140.

13. John H. Coatsworth, "The Mexican Mining Industry in the Eighteenth Century," in *The Economies of Mexico and Peru During the Late Colonial Period, 1760–1810*, ed. Nils Jacobsen and Hans-Jurgen Puhle (Berlin: Colloquium Verlag, 1986), 26–27.

14. William A. Shaw, *Select Tracts and Documents Illustrative of English Monetary History 1626–1730* (London: Clement Wilson, 1896), 192, 295.

15. William L. Schurz, *The Manila Galleon* (New York: E. P. Dutton, 1959), 47.

16. Holden Furber, *Rival Empires of Trade in the Orient 1600–1800* (Minneapolis: University of Minnesota Press, 1976), 134, 232.

17. Kirti N. Chaudhuri, *The Trading World of Asia and the English East India Company, 1660–1760* (Cambridge: Cambridge University Press, 1978), 181–82.

18. Diego G. López Rosado, *Historia del peso mexicano* (México: Fondo de Cultura Económica, 1975), 27.

19. Rosado, *Historia del peso mexicano*, 32.

20. Richard Von Glahn, *Fountain of Fortune: Money and Monetary Policy in China, 1000–1700* (Berkeley: University of California Press, 1996), 57.

21. Dennis Flynn and Arturo Giraldez, "Cycles of Silver: Global Economic Unity through the Mid-Eighteenth Century," *Journal of World History* 13, no. 2 (2002): 410–11.

22. Flynn and Giraldez, "Cycles of Silver," 411.

23. Louis Dermigny, *La chine et l'occident: Le commerce á Canton au XVIIIe siècle, 1719–1833*, vol. 2 (Paris: SVEPN, 1964), 688–89; Louis Dermigny, *La chine et l'occident: Le commerce á Canton au XVIIIe siècle, 1719–1833*, vol. 1 (Paris: SVEPN, 1964), 432–33.

24. Furber, *Rival Empires of Trade*, 257.

25. K. Pomeranz and S. Topik, *The World That Trade Created* (Armonk, NY: M. E. Sharpe, 1999), 103.

26. Carl A. Trocki, *Opium, Empire and the Global Political Economy: A Study of the Asian Opium Trade, 1750–1950* (London: Routledge, 1999), 51, 54.

27. John Keay, *The Spice Route: A History* (Berkeley: University of California Press, 2006), 254–55.

28. Henry Kamen, *Spain 1469–1714: A Society in Conflict* (New York: Longman, 1983), 473.

29. Kamen, *Spain 1469–1714*, 474.

30. Stanley J. Stein and Barbara H. Stein, *Silver, Trade, and War: Spain and America in the Making of Early Modern Europe* (Baltimore: The Johns Hopkins University Press, 2000), 262, 265.

31. Kamen, *Spain 1469–1714*, 472.

32. Kamen, *Spain 1469–1714*, 475.

33. In Richard Walter, A Voyage Round the World in the Years 1740, 41, 42, 42, 44 (London: n. p., 1818), vi–vii.

34. Furber, Rival Empires of Trade, 160.

35. Benito J. Legarda, After the Galleons: Foreign Trade, Economic Change and Entrepreneurship in Nineteenth-Century Philippines (Madison: Center for Asian Studies University of Wisconsin-Madison, 1999), 48.

36. Mariano Ardash Bonialian, El Pacífico hispanoamericano: Política y comercio asiático en el Imperio Español (1680–1784). La centralidad de lo marginal (México: El Colegio de México, 2012), 164–65.

37. Furber, Rival Empires of Trade, 169.

38. Furber, Rival Empires of Trade, 272.

39. Chaudhuri, The Trading World of Asia, 180.

40. Furber, Rival Empires of Trade, 288.

41. Vera Valdés Lakowsky, De las minas al mar: Historía de la plata mexicana en Asia, 1565–1834 (México: Fondo de Cultura Económica, 1987), 148.

42. W. E. Cheong, "Changing the Rules of the Game (The India–Manila Trade 1785–1809)," Journal of Southeast Asian Studies 1, no. 2 (1970): 9.

43. Lakowsky, De las minas al mar, 189.

44. Guillaume Le Gentil, A Voyage to the Indian Seas (Manila: Filipiniana Book Guild, 1964) 182–83, 192.

45. José Montero y Vidal, Historia general de Filipinas, vol. 2 (Madrid: Est. Tip. Viuda e Hijos de Tello, 1894), 33.

46. Schurz, Manila Galleon, 341.

47. Joaquín Martínez de Zúñiga, An Historical View of the Philippine Islands, vol. 2 (London: J. Asperne, 1814), 208.

48. Nicholas P. Cushner, Documents Illustrating the British Conquest of Manila, 1762–1763 (London: Offices of the Royal Historical Society, 1971), 14–15.

49. Martínez de Zúñiga, Historical View, vol. 2, 208–9.

50. Martínez de Zúñiga, Historical View, vol. 2, 191.

51. Martínez de Zúñiga, Historical View, vol. 2, 211.

52. Montero y Vidal, Historia general de Filipinas, vol. 2, 82–83.

53. In Montero y Vidal, Historia general de Filipinas, vol. 2, 83.

54. Onofre D. Corpuz, The Roots of the Filipino Nation (Quezon City: University of the Philippines Press, 2005), 307.

55. Gregorio F. Zaide, Philippine Political and Cultural History (Manila: Philippine Education Company, 1957), 283.

56. Corpuz, Roots of the Filipino Nation, 381.

57. Zaide, Philippine Political and Cultural History, 283.

58. Martínez de Zúñiga, Historical View, vol. 2, 229.

59. Kamen, Spain 1469–1714, 484.

60. Ronald Findlay and Kevin H. O'Rourke, Power and Plenty: Trade, War, and the World Economy in the Second Millennium (Princeton, NJ: Princeton University Press, 2007), 247.

61. Felipe Fernández-Armesto, *The World: A History* (Upper Saddle River, NJ: Pearson, Prentice Hall, 2007), 705, 706.

62. Corpuz, *Roots of the Filipino Nation*, 305, 309.

63. Elliot C. Arensmeyer, "Foreign Accounts of the Chinese in the Philippines: 18th–19th Centuries," *Philippine Studies* 18 (1970): 91.

64. Edgar Wickberg, *The Chinese in Philippine Life* (New Haven: Yale University Press, 1965), 12.

65. José Vila, "Condition of the Islands, 1701," in *Philippine Islands 1493–1898*, ed. Emma Helen Blair and James Alexander Robertson, vol. 44, *1700–1736* (Cleveland, OH: A. H. Clark Company, 1906), 134, 137.

66. Edgar Wickberg, *The Chinese in Philippine Life* (New Haven: Yale University Press, 1965), 9–10.

67. Corpuz, *Roots of the Filipino Nation*, 306.

68. Martínez de Zúñiga, *Historical View*, vol. 2, 12–14.

69. Martínez de Zúñiga, *Historical View*, vol. 2, 89–90.

70. Arensmeyer, "Foreign Accounts of the Chinese," 89, 91.

71. Arensmeyer, "Foreign Accounts of the Chinese," 93.

72. Juan José Delgado, *Historia general sacro-profana, politica y natural de las islas del poniente llamadas Filipinas* (Manila: Imprenta del Eco de Filipinas, 1892), 52.

73. Martínez de Zúñiga, *Historical View*, vol. 2, 115.

74. Joaquín Martínez de Zúñiga, "Events in Filipinas, 1739–1762," in *Philippine Islands 1493–1898*, ed. Emma Helen Blair and James Alexander Robertson, vol. 48, *1751–1765* (Cleveland, OH: A. H. Clark Company, 1909), 183n104.

75. Corpuz, *Roots of the Filipino Nation*, 306.

76. Legarda, *After the Galleons*, 57.

77. Corpuz, *Roots of the Filipino Nation*, 307.

78. Wickberg, *The Chinese in Philippine Life*, 17.

79. Corpuz, *Roots of the Filipino Nation*, 307.

80. Victor Purcell, *The Chinese in Southeast Asia* (London: Oxford University Press, 1965), 529.

81. Cheong, "Changing the Rules," 147.

82. Wickberg, *The Chinese in Philippine Life*, 25, 31.

83. Miguel A. Bernard, "Father Ducos and the Muslim Wars: 1752–1759," *Philippine Studies* 16 (1968): 700.

84. Bernard, "Father Ducos and the Muslim Wars," 694, 696–97.

85. Bernard, "Father Ducos and the Muslim Wars," 702.

86. William Henry Scott, *Slavery in the Spanish Philippines*, 2nd ed. (Manila: De La Salle University Press, 1997), 56.

87. Linda A. Newson, *Conquest and Pestilence in the Early Spanish Philippines* (Honolulu: University of Hawaii Press, 2009), 33–34.

88. Carmen Yuste López, *El comercio de la Nueva España con Filipinas, 1570–1785* (México: Instituto Nacional de Antropología e Historia, 1987), 80.

89. Francisco Leandro de Viana, "Memorial of 1765," in *Philippine Islands 1493–1898*, ed. Emma Helen Blair and James Alexander Robertson, vol. 48, *1751–1765* (Cleveland, OH: A. H. Clark Company, 1907), 274–76.

90. Carmen Yuste López, "El eje comercial transpacífico en el siglo XVIII: la disolución imperial de una alternativa colonial," in *El comercio exterior de México 1713–1850: Entre la quiebra del sistema imperial y el surgimiento de una nación*, ed. Carmen Yuste López and Matilde Soto Mantecón (México: Instituto de Investigaciones Históricas Dr. José María Luis Mora, 2000), 26.

91. Viana, "Memorial of 1765," 315.

92. Viana, "Memorial of 1765," 334.

93. Legarda, *After the Galleons*, 53.

94. Yuste López, "El eje comercial transpacífico," 31.

95. Stein and Stein, *Silver, Trade, and War*, 231.

96. Luis Alonso Alvarez, *El costo del imperio Asiático: La formación colonial de las islas Filipinas bajo dominio español, 1565–1800* (La Coruña: Universidade da Coruña, 2009), 307.

97. Furber, *Rival Empires of Trade*, 225.

98. Legarda, *After the Galleons*, 60.

99. Bonialian, *El Pacífico hispanoamericano*, 407.

100. Hernández M. Sánchez-Barba, "Las Indias en el siglo XVIII," in *Historia de España y América social y económica*, vol. 4, *Los Borbones en el siglo XVIII en España y América*, ed. J. Vicens Vives (Barcelona: Vicens-Vives, 1972), 176–77.

101. J. H. Parry, *Trade and Dominion: The European Oversea Empires in the Eighteenth Century* (London: Phoenix Press, 2000), 279.

102. Legarda, *After the Galleons*, 61.

103. Legarda, *After the Galleons*, 77.

104. Cheong, "Changing the Rules," 147.

105. Legarda, *After the Galleons*, 80.

106. Carmen Yuste López, *El comercio de la Nueva España con Filipinas, 1570–1785* (México: Instituto Nacional de Antropología e Historia, 1987), 80.

107. Carmen Yuste López, *Emporios transpacíficos: Comerciantes mexicanos en Manila* (México: Universidad Nacional Autónoma de México, 2007), 11–12.

108. Bonialian, *El Pacífico hispanoamericano*, 195.

109. Yuste López, *El comercio de la Nueva España*, 81.

110. Lakowsky, *De las minas al mar*, 255.

111. W. E. Cheong, "Trade and Finance in China, 1784–1834," *Business History* 7, no. 1 (1965): 43, 45.

112. Legarda, *After the Galleons*, 44.

Bibliography

Aduarte, Diego. "Historia de la Provincia del Sancto Rosario de la Orden de Predicadores, Manila, 1640." In *Philippine Islands 1493–1898*. Vol. 32, *1640*, edited by Emma Helen Blair and James Alexander Robertson, 19–298. Cleveland, OH: A. H. Clark Company, 1905.

Alderly, Lord Stanley, ed. *The First Voyage Round. The World by Magellan Translated from Pigafetta and Other Contemporary Writers*. London: Hakluyt Society, 1874.

Almazán, Tellez de. "Relacion." In *Labor evangelica*, edited by Pablo Pastells. Barcelona: Imprenta y Litografia de Henrich y Compañía, 1902.

Alonso Alvarez, Luis. *El costo del imperio Asiático: La formación colonial de las islas Filipinas bajo dominio español, 1565–1800*. La Coruña: Universidade da Coruña, 2009.

Alva Rodríguez, Inmaculada. *Vida municipal en Manila (Siglos XVI–XVII)*. Córdoba: Universidad de Córdoba, 1997.

Alvarez de Toledo, Cayetana. "El 'caso Escalona,' 1640–1642." In *La Crisis de la Monarquía de Felipe IV*, edited by Geoffrey Parker, 255–86. Barcelona: Crítica, 2006.

Alzina, Francisco Ignacio. *Una etnografía de los indios bisayas del siglo XVII*. 2 vols. Edited by Victoria Yepes. Madrid: Consejo Superior de Investigaciones Científicas, 1996.

American Meteorological Society. "Glossary of Meteorology: Monsson Trough." Last modified January 26, 2012. Accessed February 1, 2013. http://glossary.ametsoc.org/wiki/Monsoon_trough

Arcilla, José S. *An Introduction to Philippine History*. Manila: Ateneo de Manila University Press, 1998.

———. *The Spanish Conquest: KASAYSAYAN. The Story of the Filipino People*, Vol. 3. Hong Kong: Asia Publishing Company, 1998.

Arensmeyer, Elliot C. "Foreign Accounts of the Chinese in the Philippines: 18th–19th Centuries." *Philippine Studies* 18 (1970): 82–102.

Artieda, Diego de. "Relation of the Western Islands Called Filipinas." In *Philippine Islands 1493–1803*. Vol. 3, *1569–1576*, edited by Emma Helen Blair and James Alexander Robertson, 190–208. Cleveland, OH: A. H. Clark Company, 1903.

Atwell, William S. "Ming China and the Emerging World Economy, c. 1470–1650." In *The Cambridge History of China*. Vol. 8, bk. 2, *The Ming Dynasty, 1368–1644*, 376–416. Cambridge: Cambridge University Press, 1998.

———. "Volcanism and Short-Term Climatic Change in East Asian and World History, c. 1200–1699." *Journal of World History* 12, no. 1 (2001): 29–98.

Bañuelos y Carrillo, Hieronimo. "Relations of the Filipinas Islands (1638)." In *Philippine Islands 1493–1898*. Vol. 29, *1638–1640*, edited by Emma Helen Blair and James Alexander Robertson, 66–85. Cleveland, OH: A. H. Clark Company, 1905.

Barret, Ward. "World Bullion Flows, 1450–1800." In *The Rise of Merchant Empires: Long-Distance Trade in the Early Modern World, 1350–1750*, edited by James D. Tracy, 224–54. Cambridge: Cambridge University Press, 1990.

Bauzon, Leslie. "Deficit Government: Mexico and the Philippine Situado (1606–1804)." Unpublished PhD diss., Duke University, 1970.

Bernard, Miguel A. "Father Ducos and the Muslim Wars: 1752–1759." *Philippine Studies* 16 (1968): 690–728.

Blair, Emma, and James A. Robertson, eds. *The Philippine Islands, 1493–1898*. 55 vols. Cleveland, OH: A. H. Clark Company, 1903–9.

Boomgaard, Peter. *Southeast Asia: An Environmental History*. Santa Barbara: ABC CLIO, 2007.

Bonialian, Mariano Ardash. *El Pacífico hispanoamericano: Política y comercio asiático en el Imperio Español (1680–1784). La centralidad de lo marginal*. México: El Colegio de México, 2012.

Borah, Woodrow. *Early Colonial Trade and Navigation between Mexico and Peru*. Berkeley: University of California Press, 1954.

———. *Silk Raising in Colonial Mexico*. Berkeley: University of California Press, 1943.

Borges Morán, Pedro. "Aspectos característicos de la evangelización en Filipinas (1521–1650)." In *España y el Pacífico: Legázpi*. Vol. 2, edited by Leoncio Cabrero, 285–318. Madrid: Sociedad Estatal de Conmemoraciones Culturales, 2004.

Boxer, Charles R. *The Christian Century in Japan, 1549–1650*. Berkeley: University of California Press, 1967.

———. *The Dutch Seaborne Empire: 1600–1800*. New York: Alfred A. Knopf, 1965.

———. "*Plata es sangre*: Sidelights on the Drain of Spanish-American Silver in the Far East, 1550–1700." *Philippine Studies* 18 (1970): 457–78.

———. *The Portuguese Seaborne Empire 1415–1825*. New York: Alfred A. Knopf, 1969.

———. *The Tragic History of the Sea 1589–1622*. Cambridge: Cambridge University Press, 1959.

Boyajian, James C. *Portuguese Trade in Asia under the Habsburgs, 1580–1640*. Baltimore: The Johns Hopkins University Press, 1993.

Braudel, Fernand. *The Mediterranean and the Mediterranean World in the Age of Philip II*. 2 vols. New York: Harper & Row, 1976.

——. *The Perspective of the World*, Vol. 3. Berkeley: University of California Press, 1993.

Bray, Francesca. *Science and Civilization in China*. Vol. 6, *Biology and Biological Technology Part II: Agriculture*, edited by Joseph Needham. Cambridge: Cambridge University Press, 1984.

Brook, Timothy. "Communications and Commerce." In *The Cambridge History of China*. Vol. 8, bk. 2, *The Ming Dynasty, 1368–1644*, 579–707. Cambridge: Cambridge University Press, 1998.

——. *Vermeer's Hat: The Seventeenth Century and the Dawn of the Global World*. New York: Bloomsbury Press, 2008.

Burkholder, Mark A., and Lyman L. Johnson. *Colonial Latin America*. New York: Oxford University Press, 1988.

Cabrero Fernández, Leoncio, ed. *España y el Pacífico: Legázpi*. 2 vols. Madrid: Sociedad Estatal de Conmemoraciones Culturales, 2004.

Campos y Férnandez Sevilla, Francisco Javier. "Las órdenes mendicantes en Filipinas: agustinos, franciscanos, dominicos y recoletos." In *España y el Pacífico: Legázpi*. Vol. 2, edited by Leoncio Cabrero, 251–84. Madrid: Sociedad Estatal de Conmemoraciones Culturales, 2004.

Carande, Ramón. *Carlos V y sus banqueros*. 3 vols. Barcelona: Crítica, 1990.

Careri, Gemelli G. *Viaje a la Nueva España: México a fines del siglo XVII*. 2 vols. México: Ediciones Libro-Mex, 1955.

——. *A Voyage to the Philippines: And an Appendix of the Chapters on the Philippines in the Travels of Fray Sebastián Manrique*. Manila: Filipiniana Book Guild, 1963.

Carletti, Francesco. *My Voyage Around the World*. New York: Pantheon Books, 1964.

Céspedes del Castillo, G. "Las indias durante los siglos XVI y XVII." In *Historia de España y América social y económica*. Vol. 3, *Los Austrias: El imperio español en América*, edited by J. Vicens-Vives, 321–536. Barcelona: Vicens-Vives, 1972.

Chaudhuri, Kirti N. *The English East India Company: The Study of an Early Joint-Stock Company, 1600–1640*. London: F. Cass, 1965.

——. *Trade and Civilization in the Indian Ocean: An Economic History from the Rise of Islam to 1750*. Cambridge: Cambridge University Press, 1985.

——. *The Trading World of Asia and the English East India Company, 1660–1760*. Cambridge: Cambridge University Press, 1978.

Chaunu, Pierre. *Les Philippines et le Pacifique des Ibériques (XVI, XVII, XVIII siècles)*. Paris: S. E. V. P. E. N., 1960.

Cheong, W. E. "Changing the Rules of the Game (The India-Manila Trade 1785–1809)." *Journal of Southeast Asian Studies* 1, no. 2 (1970): 1–19.

——. "The Decline of Manila as the Spanish Entrepot in the Far East, 1786–1826: Its Impact on the Pattern of Southeast Asian Trade." *Journal of Southeast Asian Studies* 2, no. 2 (1971): 142–58.

———. "Trade and Finance in China, 1784–1834." *Business History* 7, no. 1 (1965): 34–56.

Chiaramonte, José Carlos. "En torno a la recuperación demográfica y la depresión económica novohispanas durante el siglo XVII." *Historia Mexicana* 30, no. 4 (1981): 561–604.

Chirino, Pedro. "Relation of the Filipinas Islands and of What Has There Been Accomplished by the Fathers of the Society of Jesus." In *Philippine Islands, 1493–1898*. Vol. 12, *1601–1604*, edited by Emma Helen Blair and James Alexander Robertson, 169–322. Cleveland, OH: A. H. Clark Company, 1904.

Chuan, Han-sheng. "The Chinese Silk Trade with Spanish-America from the Late Ming to the Mid-Ch'ing Period," in Laurence G. Thompson (ed.), *Studia Asiatica. Essays in Asian Studies in Felicitation of the Seventy-Fifth Anniversary of Professor Ch'en Shou-yi*. San Francisco: Chinese Materials Center, 1975.

———. "The Inflow of American Silver into China from the Late Ming to the Mid-Ch'ing Period." *Journal of the Institute of Chinese Studies of the Chinese University of Hong Kong* 2 (1969): 61–75.

Cipolla, Carlo M. *Guns, Sails and Empires: Technological Innovations and the Early Phases of European Expansion 1400–1700*. New York: Pantheon Books, 1965.

Coatsworth, John H. "The Mexican Mining Industry in the Eighteenth Century." In *The Economies of Mexico and Peru During the Late Colonial Period, 1760–1810*, edited by Nils Jacobsen and Hans-Jurgen Puhle, 26–45. Berlin: Colloquium Verlag, 1986.

Colección de documentos inéditos para la historia de España, Vol. 3. Madrid: Academia de la Historia, 1886.

Colín, Francisco. *Labor evangélica, ministerios apostólicos de los obreros de la Compañía de Jesús*. 3 vols., edited by Pablo Pastells. Barcelona: Imprenta y Litografía de Henrich y Compañía, 1900.

Cooper, Michael. *Rodrigues the Interpreter and Early Jesuit in Japan and China*. New York: Weatherhill, 1974.

"Copy of a Letter Sent from Sevilla to Miguel Salvador of Valencia." In *Philippine Islands 1493–1803*. Vol. 2, *1521–1569*, edited by Emma Helen Blair and James Alexander Robertson, 220–31. Cleveland, OH: A. H. Clark Company, 1903.

"Copy of Letter from London [1569]." In *Calendar of State Papers, Spain (Simancas)*. Vol. 4, *1587–1603*, edited by Martin Hume, 474–92. British History Online. Accessed December 22, 2012. http://www.british-history.ac.uk/report. aspx?compid=87201

Corcuera, Sebastián Hurtado de. "Letters to Philip IV." In *Philippine Islands 1493–1898*. Vol. 26, *1636*, edited by Emma Helen Blair and James Alexander Robertson, 60–264. Cleveland, OH: A. H. Clark Company, 1905.

Corpuz, Onofre D. *The Roots of the Filipino Nation*. Quezon City: University of the Philippines Press, 2005.

Corrêa, Gaspar. *The Three Voyages of Vasco da Gama and His Viceroyalty*. London: Hakluyt, 1869.

Cortés, Hernan. "Letter from Hernan Cortés to the King of Cebú." In *Philippine Islands 1493–1803*. Vol. 2, *1521–1569*, edited by Emma Helen Blair and James Alexander Robertson, 39–41. Cleveland, OH: A. H. Clark Company, 1903.

Cross, Harry E. "South American Bullion Production and Export, 1550–1750." In *Precious Metals in the Later Medieval and Early Modern Worlds*, edited by J. F. Richards, 397–424. Durham, NC: Carolina Academic Press, 1983.

Cubero Sebastián, Pedro. *Peregrinación del Mundo*. Madrid: Ediciones Polifemo, 1993.

Cushner, Nicholas P. *Documents Illustrating the British Conquest of Manila, 1762–1763*. London: Offices of the Royal Historical Society, 1971.

———. "Legazpi, 1564–1572." *Philippine Studies* 13, no. 2 (1965): 163–202.

———. *Spain in the Philippines: From Conquest to Revolution*. Quezon City: Ateneo de Manila, 1971.

Dasmariñas, Gómez Pérez. "The Manners, Customs, and Beliefs of the Philippine Inhabitants of Long Ago, Being Chapters of a Late 16th Century Manila Manuscript." Translated by Carlos Quirino and Mauro Garcia. *Philippine Journal of Science* 87, no. 4 (1958): 389–445.

Dávalos, Melchor. "Letter to Felipe II." In *Philippine Islands, 1493–1898*. Vol. 6, *1583–1588*, edited by Emma Helen Blair and James Alexander Robertson, 54–65. Cleveland, OH: A. H. Clark Company, 1903.

de Acosta, Joseph. *The Natural and Moral History of the Indies*. 2 vols. New York: Burt Franklin, 1970.

de Argensola, Bartolomé Leonardo. *The Discovery and Conquest of the Moluccas and Philippine Islands*. London: n. p., 1708.

de Castro, Agustín M. *Misioneros Agustinos en el extremo oriente 1565–1780 (Osario Venerable)*. P.M. Merino Ed. Madrid: C. S. I. C., 1954.

de la Costa, Horacio. "The Development of the Native Clergy in the Philippines." In *Studies in Philippine Church History*, edited by Gerald Anderson, 65–104. Ithaca: Cornell University Press, 1969.

———. *The Jesuits in the Philippines, 1581–1768*. Cambridge, MA: Harvard University Press, 1961.

Delgado, Juan José. *Historia general sacro-profana, política y natural de las islas del poniente llamadas Filipinas*. Manila: Imprenta del Eco de Filipinas, 1892.

de los Ríos Coronel, Hernando. "Memorial on Navigation and Conquest." In *Philippine Islands, 1493–1898*. Vol. 9, *1593–1597*, edited by Emma Helen Blair and James Alexander Robertson, 299–314. Cleveland, OH: A. H. Clark Company, 1904.

———. "Reforms needed in Filipinas." In *Philippine Islands, 1493–1898*. Vol. 18, *1617–1620*, edited by Emma Helen Blair and James Alexander Robertson, 289–344. Cleveland, OH: A. H. Clark Company, 1904.

del Valle Pavón, Guillermina. "Los mercaderes de México y la transgresión de los límites al Comercio Pacífico en Nueva España." *Revista de historia económica*. Número Extraordinario. *La economía en tiempos de Don Quijote*, 2005: 213–40.

Deng, Gang. *Chinese Maritime Activities and Socioeconomic Development c. 2100 B.C.–1900 A.D.* Westport, CT: Greenwood Press, 1997.

Dermigny, Louis. *La chine et l'occident: Le commerce á Canton au XVIIIe siècle, 1719–1833*. 4 vols. Paris: SVEPN, 1964.

"Description of the Philippinas Islands." In *Philippine Islands, 1493–1898*. Vol. 18, *1617–1620*, edited by Emma Helen Blair and James Alexander Robertson, 93–106. Cleveland, OH: A. H. Clark Company, 1904.

de Vries, Jan. "Connecting Europe and Asia: A Quantitative Analysis of the Cape-route Trade, 1497–1795." In *Global Connections and Monetary History, 1470–1800*, edited by Flynn, Dennis, Arturo Giraldez, and Richard Von Glahn, 35–106. Aldershot, UK: Ashgate, 2003.

de Vries, Jan, and A. van der Woude. *The First Modern Economy: Success, Failure, and Perseverance of the Dutch Economy, 1500–1815*. Cambridge: Cambridge University Press, 1997.

Díaz, Casimiro. "The Augustinians in the Philippines, 1670–1694." In *Philippine Islands 1493–1898*. Vol. 42, *1670–1700*, edited by Emma Helen Blair and James Alexander Robertson, 117–312. Cleveland, OH: A. H. Clark Company, 1906.

———. *Conquistas de las Islas Filipinas: Parte Segunda*. Valladolid: De Gaviria, 1890.

Díaz-Trechuelo, María Lourdes. *Arquitectura española en Filipinas, 1565–1800*. Sevilla: Escuela de Estudios Hispano-Americanos (Consejo Superior de Investigaciones Científicas), 1959.

Domínguez Ortiz, Antonio. *The Golden Age of Spain, 1516–1659*. New York: Basic Books, 1971.

Elliott, J. H. *The Count-Duke of Olivares: The Statesman in an Age of Decline*. New Haven: Yale University Press, 1986.

———. "The Decline of Spain." *Past and Present* 20, no. 1 (1961): 52–75.

Elvin, Mark. *The Pattern of the Chinese Past*. Stanford: Stanford University Press, 1973.

"The Expedition of Ruy Lopez de Villalobos, 1541–46." In *Philippine Islands 1493–1803*. Vol. 2, *1521–1569*, edited by Emma Helen Blair and James Alexander Robertson, 47–73. Cleveland, OH: A. H. Clark Company, 1903.

Fagan, Brian. *Flood, Famines and Emperors*. New York: Basic Books, 1999.

———. *The Little Ice Age: How Climate Made History 1300–1850*. New York: Basic Books, 2000.

Fairbank, John K., ed. *The Cambridge History of China*. Vol. 10, *Late Ch'ing, 1800–1911*. Cambridge: Cambridge University Press, 1978.

Fernández-Armesto, Felipe. *Pathfinders: A Global History of Exploration*. New York: W. W. Norton & Company, 2006.

———. *The World: A History*. Upper Saddle River, NJ: Pearson, Prentice Hall, 2007.

Findlay, Ronald, and Kevin H. O'Rourke. *Power and Plenty: Trade, War, and the World Economy in the Second Millennium*. Princeton, NJ: Princeton University Press, 2007.

Fish, Shirley. *The Manila-Acapulco Galleons: The Treasure Ships of the Pacific*. Central Milton Keynes, UK: AuthorHouseUK, 2011.

Fisher, John R. "Mining and Imperial Trade in 18th-Century Spanish America." In *Monetary History in Global Perspective, 1500–1808: B6 Proceedings, Twelfth Interna-*

tional Economic History Congress, edited by Clara Eugenia Núñez, 109–19. Sevilla: Universidad de Sevilla, 1998.

Flynn, Dennis, and Arturo Giraldez. "Cycles of Silver: Global Economic Unity through the Mid-Eighteenth Century." In *China and the Birth of Globalization*, 391–427. Farham, UK: Ashgate, 2010.

———. "Cycles of Silver: Global Economic Unity through the Mid-Eighteenth Century." *Journal of World History* 13, no. 2 (2002): 391–427.

———. "Spanish Profitability in the Pacific: The Philippines in the Sixteenth and Seventeenth Centuries." In *Pacific Centuries: Pacific and Pacific Rim Histories Since the Sixteenth Century*, edited by Dennis Flynn, Lionel Frost, and A. J. H. Latham, 23–37. New York: Routledge Press, 1999.

Frank, Andre Gunder. *World Accumulation, 1492–1789*. New York: Monthly Review Press, 1978.

Furber, Holden. *Rival Empires of Trade in the Orient 1600–1800*. Minneapolis: University of Minnesota Press, 1976.

Gaastra, Femme S. *The Dutch East India Company: Expansion and Decline*. Leiden: Walburg Press, 2003.

Gage, Thomas. *Travels in the New World*. Norman: University of Oklahoma Press, 1958.

García-Abasolo, Antonio. "Llegada de los españoles al Extremo Oriente." In *Gran historia universal*. Vol. 27, *Descubrimiento y conquista de América*, 159–97. Madrid: Club Internacional del Libro, 1986.

———. "Relaciones entre españoles y chinos en Filipinas." In *España y el Pacífico: Legázpi*. Vol. 2, edited by Leoncio Cabrero, 231–50. Madrid: Sociedad Estatal de Conmemoraciones Culturales, 2004.

Geiss, J. P. "Peking under the Ming, 1368–1644." PhD diss., Princeton University, 1979.

Gil, Juan. *Hidalgos y samuráis: España y Japón en los siglos XVI y XVII*. Madrid: Alianza Editorial, 1991.

Grau y Monfalcón, Juan. "Informatory Memorial Addressed to the King, Madrid, 1637." In *Philippine Islands 1493–1898*. Vol. 27, *1636–1637*, edited by Emma Helen Blair and James Alexander Robertson, 55–214. Cleveland, OH: A. H. Clark Company, 1905.

Hamashita, Takeshi. "The Tribute System and Modern Asia." In *Memoirs of the Research Department of the Tokyo Bunko*. N. 46, Tokyo, 1988.

Hamilton, Earl J. *El Tesoro americano y la revolución de los precios en España, 1501–1650*. Barcelona: Ariel, 1975.

Hanke, Lewis. *Cuerpo de documentos del siglo XVI: Sobre los derechos de España en las Indias y las Filipinas*. México: Fondo de Cultura Económica, 1943.

———. *The Spanish Struggle for Justice in the Conquest of America*. Boston: Little, Brown and Co., 1965.

Haring, Clarence H. *Trade and Navigation between Spain and the Indies in the Time of the Hapsburgs*. Gloucester, MA: Peter Smith, 1964.

Hawkins, John. *Hawkins' Voyages*. London: The Hakluyt Society, 1878.

Headrick, Daniel R. *The Tools of Empire: Technology and European Imperialism in the Nineteenth Century*. New York: Oxford University Press, 1981.

Ho, Ping-ti. *Studies on the Population of China, 1368–1953*. Cambridge: Harvard University Press, 1959.

Hoberman, Louisa S. "Merchants in Seventeenth-Century Mexico City: A Preliminary Portrait." *Hispanic American Historical Review* 57, no. 3 (1977): 479–503.

———. *Mexico's Merchant Elite 1590–1660*. Durham, NC: Duke University Press, 1991.

Hurley, Vic. *Swish of the Kris*. Manila: Filipiniana Reprint Series, 1997.

Israel, Jonathan I., *The Dutch Republic and the Hispanic World 1606–1661*. Oxford: Oxford University Press, 1982.

———. *The Dutch Republic: Its Rise, Greatness, and Fall 1477–1806*. Oxford: Oxford University Press, 1998.

———. *European Jewry in the Age of Mercantilism 1550–1750*. Portland: The Littman Library of Jewish Civilization, 1998.

———. *Race, Class and Politics in Colonial Mexico 1610–1670*. Oxford: Oxford University Press, 1975.

Jara, Álvaro. "Las conexiones e intercambios americanos con el Oriente español bajo el marco imperial español." In *La comunidad del Pacifico en perspectiva*, Vol. 3, edited by Francisco Orrego Vicuña, 35–73. Santiago de Chile: Editorial Universitaria, 1979.

———. *Tres ensayos sobre economía minera hispanoamericana*. Santiago: Universidad de Chile, 1966.

Kamen, Henry. "The Decline of Spain: A Historical Myth?" *Past and Present* 81, no. 1 (1978): 24–50.

———. *Empire: How Spain Became a World Power, 1492–1763*. New York: Harper-Collins, 2003.

———. *Spain 1469–1714: A Society in Conflict*. New York: Longman, 1983.

Keay, John. *The Spice Route: A History*. Berkeley: University of California Press, 2006.

Keynes, John Maynard. *A Treatise on Money*. 2 vols. London: Macmillan, 1950.

Lach, Donald F.. *Asia in the Making of Europe*. Vol. 1, bk. 1. Chicago: Chicago University Press, 1965.

Laufer, Berthold. "The Relations of the Chinese to the Philippine Islands." *Smithsonian Institution, Miscellaneous Collections* 50, no. 13 (1907): 248–81.

Lavezaris, Guido de. "Slavery Among the Natives." In *Philippine Islands, 1493–1803*. Vol. 3, *1569–1576*, edited by Emma Helen Blair and James Alexander Robertson, 260–63. Cleveland, OH: A. H. Clark Company, 1903.

Legarda, Benito J. *After the Galleons: Foreign Trade, Economic Change and Entrepreneurship in Nineteenth-Century Philippines*. Madison: Center for Asian Studies, University of Wisconsin-Madison, 1999.

Legázpi, Miguel Lopez de. "Letters to Felipe II of Spain, 1567–68." In *Philippine Islands 1493–1803*. Vol. 2, *1521–1569*, edited by Emma Helen Blair and James Alexander Robertson, 232–43. Cleveland, OH: A. H. Clark Company, 1903.

———. "Relation of the Filipinas Islands and the Character and Condition of their Inhabitants." In *Philippine Islands, 1493–1803*. Vol. 3, *1569–1576*, edited by Emma Helen Blair and James Alexander Robertson, 40–47. Cleveland, OH: A. H. Clark Company, 1903.

———. "Relation of the Voyage to the Philippine Islands, 1565." In *Philippine Islands 1493–1803*. Vol. 2, *1521–1576*, edited by Emma Helen Blair and James Alexander Robertson, 196–216. Cleveland, OH: A. H. Clark Company, 1903.

Le Gentil, Guillaume. *A Voyage to the Indian Seas*. Manila: Filipiniana Book Guild, 1964.

Letona, Bartholomé de. "Description of Filipinas Islands, 1662." In *Philippine Islands, 1493–1898*. Vol. 36, *1649–1666*, edited by Emma Helen Blair and James Alexander Robertson, 189–217. Cleveland, OH: A. H. Clark Company, 1906.

"Letter from the Manila Audiencia to Felipe II." In *Philippine Islands 1493–1898*. Vol. 6, *1583–1588*, edited by Emma Helen Blair and James Alexander Robertson, 311–21. Cleveland, OH: A. H. Clark Company, 1903.

"A Letter from the Royal Officials of the Filipinas Accompanied by a Memorandum of the Necessary Things to be Sent to the Colony." In *Philippine Islands 1493–1803*. Vol. 2, *1521–1569*, edited by Emma Helen Blair and James Alexander Robertson, 183–95. Cleveland, OH: A. H. Clark Company, 1903.

Liao, Hubert S. C. *Chinese Participation in Philippine Culture and Economy*. Manila: Bookman, 1964.

Lieberman, Victor. *Strange Parallels: Southeast Asia in Global Context, c. 800–1830*. Vol. 1, *Integration on the Mainland*. Cambridge: Cambridge University Press, 2003.

———. *Strange Parallels: Southeast Asia in Global Context, c. 800–1830*. Vol. 2, *Mainland Mirrors: Europe, Japan, China, South Asia, and the Islands*. Cambridge: Cambridge University Press, 2009.

"Life and Voyages of Fernão de Magalhães." In *Philippine Islands 1493–1803*. Vol. 1, *1493–1529*, edited by Emma Helen Blair and James Alexander Robertson, 241–71. Cleveland, OH: A. H. Clark Company, 1903.

Lopez, Juan. "Events in the Filipinas Islands from August, 1639, to August, 1640." In *Philippine Islands 1493–1898*. Vol. 29, *1638–1640*, edited by Emma Helen Blair and James Alexander Robertson, 194–207. Cleveland, OH: A. H. Clark Company, 1905.

López Rosado, Diego G. *Historia del peso mexicano*. Mexico: Fondo de Cultura Económica, 1975.

Lynch, John. *Spain under the Habsburgs*. Vol. 2, *Spain and America 1598–1700*. New York: Oxford University Press, 1969.

Magalhães Godinho, Vitorino. *Mito e mercadoria, utopía e prática de navegar, séculos XIII–XVIII*. Lisboa: Difusao Editorial, 1990.

———. *Os descobrimentos e a economia mundial*. 2nd ed. 4 vols. Lisbon: Editorial Presença, 1984.

Mann, Charles. *1491: Una nueva historía de las Américas antes de Colón / A New History of the Americas before Columbus*. Madrid: Taurus Ediciones, 2007.

———. *1493: Uncovering the New World Columbus Created*. New York: Random House, 2011.

Marley, David F. "The Great Galleon: The Santísima Trinidad (1750–1765)." *Philippine Studies* 41, no. 2 (1993): 167–81.

Martin-Puertas, Celia, Katja Matthes, Achim Brauer, Raimund Muscheler, Felicitas Hansen, Christof Petrick, Ala Aldahan, Göran Possnert, and Bas van Geel. "Regional Atmospheric Circulation Shifts Induced by a Grand Solar Minimum." *Nature Geoscience* 5 (2012): 397–401.

Martínez de Zúñiga, Joaquín. "Events in Filipinas, 1739–1762." In *Philippine Islands 1493–1898*. Vol. 48, *1751–1765*, edited by Emma Helen Blair and James Alexander Robertson, 137–96. Cleveland, OH: A. H. Clark Company, 1907.

———. *An Historical View of the Philippine Islands*. Manila: Filipiniana Book Guild, 1966.

———. *An Historical View of the Philippine Islands*. Vol. 2. London: J. Asperne, 1814.

Martínez de Zúñiga, Joaquín, and W. E. Retana. "Tomo Primero" and "Relación verdadera del levantamiento de los sangleys . . . el año pasado de 1640 y 1641." In *Estadismo de las Islas Filipinas ó Mis viajes por este país*, Apendix A. Madrid: Imprenta de la Viuda de M. Minuesa de los Rios, 1893.

Mathers, William M. "Nuestra Señora de la Concepción." *National Geographic* 178, no. 3 (1990): 39–53.

Matsuda, Matt K. *Pacific Worlds: A History of Seas, Peoples, and Cultures*. New York: Cambridge University Press, 2012.

Mazumdar, Sucheta. "The Impact of New World Food Crops on the Diet and Economy of China and India, 1600–1990." In *Food in Global History*, edited by Raymond Grew, 58–78. Boulder: Westview Press, 1999.

McCarthy, Edward. *Spanish Beginnings in the Philippines, 1564–1572*. Washington: The Catholic University of America Press, 1943.

McCulloch, J. R., ed. *A Select Collection of Scarce and Valuable Tracts on Money 1856*. New York: Kelley, 1966.

McNeill, J. R. "From Magellan to MITI: Pacific Rim Economies and Pacific Islands Ecologies Since 1521." In *Studies in the Economic History of the Pacific Rim*, edited by Sally M. Miller, A. J. H. Latham, and Dennis O. Flynn, 72–93. London: Routledge, 1998.

McNeill, J. R., and William H. McNeill. *The Human Web: A Bird's-Eye View of World History*. New York: W. W. Norton & Company, 2003.

McNeill, William H. *Keeping Together in Time: Dance and Drill in Human History*. Cambridge, MA: Harvard University Press, 1995.

———. *The Pursuit of Power: Technology, Armed Force, and Society Since A.D. 1000*. Chicago: The University of Chicago Press, 1982.

Medina, José Toribio. *Historia del tribunal de la Inquisición de Lima: 1569–1820*. Tomo 2. Santiago de Chile: Fondo Histórico y Bibliográfico José Toribio Medina, 1956.

Meilink-Roelofsz, M. A. P. *Asian Trade and European Influence in the Indonesian Archipelago between 1500 and about 1630*. The Hague: Martinus Nijhoff, 1962.

Mendes Pinto, Fernão. *The Travels of Mendes Pinto.* Edited by Rebecca D. Catz. Chicago: University of Chicago Press, 1989.

Mitchell, Mairin. *Friar Andres de Urdaneta, O.S.A.* London: MacDonald and Evans, 1964.

Montero y Vidal, José. *El archipélago filipino y las islas Marianas, Carolinas y Palaos: Su historia, geografía y estadística.* Madrid: Imprenta de Manuel Tello, 1886.

———. *Historia general de Filipinas.* Tomo 1. Madrid: Imprenta y Fundición de Manuel Tello, 1887.

———. *Historia general de Filipinas.* Tomo 2. Madrid: Est. Tip. Viuda e Hijos de Tello, 1894.

Morga, Antonio. *Sucesos de las Islas Filipinas.* Edited by J. S. Cummins. Cambridge: Cambridge University Press, 1971.

———. *Sucesos de las Islas Filipinas.* Madrid: Ediciones Polifemo, 1997.

Morison, Samuel Eliot. *The European Discovery of America: The Southern Voyages. A.D. 1492–1616.* New York: Oxford University Press, 1974.

Mote, F. W. *Imperial China 900–1800.* Cambridge: Harvard University Press, 1999.

Mun, John. "England's Treasure by Forraign Trade: or, The Ballance of our Forraign Trade is the Rule of our Treasure." In *A Select Collection of Early English Tracts on Commerce, from the Originals of Mun, Roberts, North, and Others,* edited by John Ramsay McCulloch, 115–210. London: Political Economy Club, 1856.

Murdoch, James, and Isoh Yamagata. *A History of Japan.* 2 vols. London: K. Paul, Trench, Trubner, 1949.

Navada Alvarado, Joseph de. "Discussion Regarding Portuguese Trade at Manila, 1632–36." In *Philippine Islands, 1493–1898.* Vol. 25, *1635–1636,* edited by Emma Helen Blair and James Alexander Robertson, 111–44. Cleveland, OH: A. H. Clark Company, 1905.

Navarrete, Domingo. *The Travels and Controversies of Friar Domingo Navarrete 1618–1686.* 2 vols. Cambridge: Cambridge University Press, 1962.

Newson, Linda A. *Conquest and Pestilence in the Early Spanish Philippines.* Honolulu: University of Hawaii Press, 2009.

Ollé, Manel. *La empresa de China: De la armada invencible al galeón de Manila.* Barcelona: El Acantilado, 2002.

Pacheco Maldonado, Juan. "Letter to Felipe II." In *Philippine Islands, 1493–1803.* Vol. 3, *1569–1576,* edited by Emma Helen Blair and James Alexander Robertson, 295–303. Cleveland, OH: A. H. Clark Company, 1903.

Palanco, Fernando. "Resistencia y rebelión indígena durante los primeros cien años de soberanía española." In *España y el Pacífico: Legázpi.* Vol. 2, edited by Leoncio Cabrero, 71–98, Madrid: Sociedad Estatal de Conmemoraciones Culturales, 2004.

Panikkar, K. M. *Asia and Western Dominance.* New York: Collier Books, 1969.

Parker, Geoffrey. "El desarrollo de la crisis." In *La crisis de la Monarquía de Felipe IV,* edited by Geoffrey Parker, 19–169. Barcelona: Crítica, 2006.

———. *Europa en crisis: 1598–1648.* Madrid: Siglo XXI, 3 a. ed, 1986.

———. *Europe in Crisis: 1598–1648.* Oxford: Wiley-Blackwell, 1979.

————. *The Military Revolution: Military Innovation and the Rise of the West, 1500–1800*. Cambridge: Cambridge University Press, 1988.

Parker, Geoffrey, ed. *La crisis de la monarquía de Felipe IV*. Barcelona: Crítica, 2006.

Parry, J. H. *Trade and Dominion: The European Oversea Empires in the Eighteenth Century*. London: Phoenix Press, 2000.

Pearson, M. N. "Spain and Spanish Trade in Southeast Asia." *Journal of Asian History* 2, no. 2 (1968): 109–29.

Perdue, Peter C. *China Marches West: The Qing Conquest of Central Eurasia*. Cambridge, MA: Harvard University Press, 2005.

Pérez-Mallaína, Pablo E. *Spain's Men of the Sea: Daily Life on the Indies Fleets in the Sixteenth Century*. Baltimore: The Johns Hopkins University Press, 1998.

Perrin, Noel. *Giving Up the Gun: Japan's Reversion to the Sword, 1543–1879*. Boston: D. R. Godine, 1979.

Phelan, John L. *The Hispanization of the Philippines: Spanish Aims and Filipino Responses 1565–1700*. Madison: The University of Wisconsin Press, 1959.

————. *The Kingdom of Quito in the Seventeenth Century: Bureaucratic Politics in the Spanish Empire*. Madison: The University of Wisconsin Press, 1967.

Pigafetta, Antonio. "Account of Magellan's Voyage." In *The First Voyage Round: The World by Magellan Translated from Pigafetta and Other Contemporary Writers*, edited by Lord Stanley Alderly, 35–163. London: Hakluyt Society, 1874.

Pineda, Sebastián de. "Philippine Ships and Shipbuilding." In *Philippine Islands, 1493–1898*. Vol. 18, *1617–1620*, edited by Emma Helen Blair and James Alexander Robertson, 169–88. Cleveland, OH: A. H. Clark Company, 1904.

Plasencia, Juan de. "Customs of the Tagalogs." In *Philippine Islands, 1493–1898*. Vol. 7, *1588–1591*, edited by Emma Helen Blair and James Alexander Robertson, 173–98. Cleveland, OH: A. H. Clark Company, 1903.

Pomeranz, K., and S. Topik. *The World That Trade Created*. Armonk, NY: M. E. Sharpe, 1999.

Prieto Lucena, Ana M. *El contacto hispano-indígena en Filipinas según la historiografía de los siglos XVI y XVII*. Córdoba: Servicio de Publicaciones Universidad de Cordoba, 1993.

Purcell, Victor. *The Chinese in Southeast Asia*. London: Oxford University Press, 1965.

Pyrard, François. *The Voyage of François Pyrard of Laval to the East Indies*. 2 vols. London: Hakluyt Society, 1887–1888.

Quiason, Serafín D. *English Country Trade with the Philippines, 1644–1765*. Quezon City: University of the Philippines Press, 1966.

Rafael, Vicente L. *Contracting Colonialism: Translation and Christian Conversion in Tagalog Society under Early Spanish Rule*. Durham: Duke University Press, 1993.

Rahn Phillips, Carla. *The Short Life of an Unlucky Spanish Galleon: Los Tres Reyes 1628–1634*. Minneapolis: University of Minnesota Press, 1990.

Raynal, Guillaume. *Historie philosophique et politique des establissements et du commerce des Europeens dans les deux Indes*. In *Travel Accounts of the Islands (1513–1787)*. Manila: Filipiniana Book Guild, 1971.

Reed, Robert R. "The Colonial Origins of Manila and Batavia: Desultory Notes on Nascent Metropolitan Primacy and Urban Systems in Southeast Asia." *Asian Studies* 5, no. 3 (1967): 543–62.

Reid, Anthony. "Economic and Social Change, c. 1400–1800." In *The Cambridge History of Southeast Asia*, Vol. 1, *From Early Times to c. 1800*, edited by Nicholas Tarling, 460–507. Singapore: Cambridge University Press, 1992.

———. "The Seventeenth-Century Crisis in Southeast Asia." *Modern Asian Studies* 24, no. 4 (1990): 639–59.

———. *Southeast Asia in the Age of Commerce 1450–1680*. Vol. 1, *The Lands below the Winds*. New Haven: Yale University Press, 1988.

———. *Southeast Asia in the Age of Commerce 1450–1680*. Vol. 2, *Expansion and Crisis*. New Haven: Yale University Press, 1993.

"Relation of the Insurrection of the Chinese (1640)." In *Philippine Islands 1493–1898*. Vol. 29, *1638–1640*, edited by Emma Helen Blair and James Alexander Robertson, 208–58. Cleveland, OH: A. H. Clark Company, 1905.

"Resume of Contemporaneous Documents, 1559–68." In *Philippine Islands 1493–1803*. Vol. 2, *1521–1569*, edited by Emma Helen Blair and James Alexander Robertson, 77–160. Cleveland, OH: A. H. Clark Company, 1903.

Retana, W. E. *Relación de la conquista de la Isla de Luzón*. Madrid: Viuda de M. Minuesa de los Ríos, 1898.

Ribera, Joan de. "Filipinas Menaced by Dutch, 1618." In *Philippine Islands 1493–1898*. Vol. 18, *1617–1620*, edited by Emma Helen Blair and James Alexander Robertson, 161–68. Cleveland, OH: A. H. Clark Company, 1904.

Riquel, Hernando. "News from the Western Islands by Hernando Riquel and Others." In *Philippine Islands 1493–1803*. Vol. 3, *1569–1576*, edited by Emma Helen Blair and James Alexander Robertson, 230–49. Cleveland, OH: A. H. Clark Company, 1903.

Rodríguez Rodríguez, Isacio. "El asentamiento: la fundación de Manila." In *España y el pacífico*, Vol. 1, edited by Leoncio Cabrero, 291–318. Madrid: Sociedad Estatal de Conmemoraciones Culturales, 2004.

Ronquillo, Juan de. "The Pacification of Mindanao, 1597." In *Philippine Islands 1493–1898*. Vol. 9, *1593–1597*, edited by Emma Helen Blair and James Alexander Robertson, 281–99. Cleveland, OH: A. H. Clark Company, 1904.

Sánchez-Barba, Hernández M. "Las Indias en el siglo XVIII." In *Historia de España y América social y económica*. Vol. 4, *Los Borbones en el siglo XVIII en España y América*, edited by J. Vicens Vives, 261–460. Barcelona: Vicens-Vives, 1972.

Sánchez Gómez, Luis Angel. "Las élites nativas y la construcción colonial de Filipinas (1565–1789)." In *España y el pacífico: Legázpi*. Vol. 2, edited by Leoncio Cabrero, 37–70. Madrid: Sociedad Estatal de Conmemoraciones Culturales, 2004.

Schurz, William L. *The Manila Galleon*. New York: E. P. Dutton, 1959.

Scott, William Henry. *Barangay: Sixteenth-Century Philippine Culture and Society*. Quezon City: Ateneo de Manila University Press, 1994.

———. "Boat-Building and Seamanship in Classic Philippine Society." *Philippine Studies* 30, no. 3 (1982): 335–76.

——. *Cracks in the Parchment Curtain and Other Essays in Philippine History*. Quezon City: New Day, 1985.

——. *The Discovery of the Igorots: Spanish Contacts with the Pagans of Northern Luzon*. Quezon City: New Day Publishers, 1974.

——. *Looking for the Prehispanic Filipino and Other Essays in Philippine History*. Quezon City: New Day Publishers, 1992.

——. *Slavery in the Spanish Philippines*. 2nd ed. Manila: De La Salle University Press, 1997.

Selga, Miguel. *Charts of Remarkable Typhoons in the Philippines, 1902–1934: Catalogue of Typhoons 1348–1934*. Manila: Bureau of Printing, 1935.

Shaw, William A. *Select Tracts and Documents Illustrative of English Monetary History 1626–1730*. London: Clement Wilson, 1896.

Smith, Adam. *An Inquiry into the Nature and Causes of the Wealth of Nations*. New York: Random House, 1937.

Souza, George B. *The Survival of the Empire: Portuguese Trade and Society in China and the South China Sea, 1630–1754*. Cambridge: Cambridge University Press, 2004.

Spate, Oskar H. K. *The Spanish Lake*. Minneapolis: University of Minnesota, 1979.

Spence, Jonathan D. *Chinese Roundabout: Essays in History and Culture*. New York: W. W. Norton & Company, 1992.

——. *The Search for Modern China*. New York: W. W. Norton & Company, 1990.

Stein, Stanley J., and Barbara H. Stein. *Silver, Trade, and War: Spain and America in the Making of Early Modern Europe*. Baltimore: The Johns Hopkins University Press, 2000.

Subrahmanyam, Sanjay. *The Portuguese Empire in Asia, 1500–1700: A Political and Economic History*. London: Longman, 1993.

Trivellato, Francesca. *The Familiarity of Strangers: The Sephardic Diaspora, Livorno, and Cross-Cultural Trade in the Early Modern Period*. New Haven: Yale University Press, 2009.

Trocki, Carl A. *Opium, Empire and the Global Political Economy: A Study of the Asian Opium Trade, 1750–1950*. London: Routledge, 1999.

Valdés Lakowsky, Vera. *De las minas al mar: Historía de la plata mexicana en Asia, 1565–1834*. México: Fondo de Cultura Económica, 1987.

Vera, Santiago de. "Letter from Santiago de Vera to Philip II, 1589." In *Philippine Islands 1493–1898*. Vol. 7, *1588–1591*, edited by Emma Helen Blair and James Alexander Robertson, 83–94. Cleveland, OH: A. H. Clark Company, 1903.

Viana, Francisco Leandro de. "Memorial of 1765." In *Philippine Islands 1493–1898*. Vol. 48, *1751–1765*, edited by Emma Helen Blair and James Alexander Robertson, 197–338. Cleveland, OH: A. H. Clark Company, 1907.

Vila, José. "Condition of the Islands, 1701." In *Philippine Islands 1493–1898*. Vol. 44, *1700–1736*, edited by Emma Helen Blair and James Alexander Robertson, 120–41. Cleveland, OH: A. H. Clark Company, 1906.

Villiers, John. "Manila and Maluku: Trade and Warfare in the Eastern Archipelago 1580–1640." *Philippine Studies* 34 (1986): 146–61.

Von Glahn, Richard. *Fountain of Fortune: Money and Monetary Policy in China, 1000–1700*. Berkeley: University of California Press, 1996.

Walter, Richard. *A Voyage Round the World in the Years 1740, 41, 42, 42, 44*. London: n. p., 1818.

Warren, James Francis. "Weather, History and Empire: The Typhoon Factor and the Manila Galleon Trade, 1565–1815." In *Anthony Reid and The Study of the Southeast Asian Past*, edited by Geoff Wade and Li Tana, 221–40. Singapore: Institute of Southeast Asian Studies, 2012.

Watts, Sheldon. *Epidemics and History. Disease, Power and Imperialism*. New Haven: Yale University Press, 1997.

Wernstedt, Frederick L., and J. E. Spencer. *The Philippine Island World: A Physical, Cultural, and Regional Geography*. Berkeley: University of California Press, 1967.

Wickberg, Edgar. *The Chinese in Philippine Life*. New Haven: Yale University Press, 1965.

Williams, Glyn. *The Prize of All the Oceans: The Triumph and Tragedy of Anson's Voyage Round the World*. London: Harper Collins, 1999.

Williams, Neville. *The Sea Dogs: Privateers, Plunder and Piracy in the Elizabethan Age*. New York: Macmillan Publishing Co., 1975.

Yuste López, Carmen. *El comercio de la Nueva España con Filipinas, 1570–1785*. México: Instituto Nacional de Antropología e Historia, 1987.

———. "El eje comercial transpacífico en el siglo XVIII: la disolución imperial de una alternativa colonial." In *El comercio exterior de México 1713–1850: Entre la quiebra del sistema imperial y el surgimiento de una nación*, edited by Carmen Yuste López and Matilde Soto Mantecón, 21–41. México: Instituto de Investigaciones Históricas Dr. José María Luis Mora, 2000.

———. *Emporios transpacíficos: Comerciantes mexicanos en Manila*. México: Universidad Nacional Autónoma de México, 2007.

Zaide, Gregorio F. *Philippine Political and Cultural History*. Vol. 1. Manila: Philippine Education Company, 1972.

Zhang, David D., Jane Zhang, Harry F. Lee, and Yuan-qing He. "Climate Change and War Frequency in Eastern China over the Last Millennium." *Human Ecology* 35, no. 4 (2007): 403–14.

Index

~

About the Author

Arturo Giraldez is professor of modern languages and literature at the University of the Pacific. He received his doctorate in history from the University of Amsterdam. He has published widely on early globalization and the role of precious metals in the world economy in the modern era in collaboration with Dennis O. Flynn.